LOIS HOLE'S Favorite Trees & Shrubs

LOIS HOLE'S Favorite Trees & Shrubs

by Lois Hole

WITH JILL FALLIS

PHOTOGRAPHY BY
AKEMI MATSUBUCHI

First printed in 1997 10 9 8 7 6 5

Printed in Canada

The Publisher: Lone Pine Publishing

206, 10426–81 Ave.	202A, 1110 Seymour St.	1901 Raymond Ave. SW, Suite C
Edmonton, AB	Vancouver, BC	Renton, WA
Canada T6E 1X5	Canada V6B 3N3	USA 98055

Canadian Cataloguing in Publication Data
Hole, Lois, 1933–
Lois Hole's favorite trees & shrubs
Includes bibliographical references and index.
ISBN 1-55105-081-1

1. Ornamental trees—Canada 2. Ornamental shrubs—Canada I. Fallis, Jill, 1960– II. Matsubuchi, Akemi, 1967– III. Title. IV. Title: Favorite trees & shrubs.
SB435.6.C3H64 1997 635.9'76'0971 C96-910897-4

Senior Editor: Nancy Foulds
Project Editor: Lee Craig
Editorial: Roland Lines, Nancy Foulds, Lee Craig
Design and Layout: Carol S. Dragich
Production Management: David Dodge, Carol S. Dragich
Cover Design: Carol S. Dragich
Technical Review: Jim Hole, Shane Neufeld
Printing: Quality Color Press, Edmonton, AB
Prepress: Elite Lithographers Co. Ltd., Edmonton, AB
Principal Photography: Akemi Matsubuchi

Additional Photography: Marilyn Wood, Photo/Nats, Inc., p. 76; Steven Nikkila, pp. 79 (top right), 201 (top left), 311 (bottom); Monrovia Nursery Co., pp. 89, 179 (top), 212 (bottom), 249 (middle); Derek Fell, pp. 121 (top), 243, 261, 339 (top); Bob Lyons, p. 99 (top); Bailey Nurseries, Inc., pp. 129 (bottom), 183 (bottom), 235 (left); Richard Shiell, pp. 151 (top left), 274, 276, 311 (top); Alan Craig/Iseli Inc., pp. 171 (top), 209 (top), 270 (bottom), 271 (top right), 326 (bottom); Photos Horticultural Library, pp. 175 (top right), 265 (top right); Sonja Bullaty & Angelo Lomeo, p. 182, (top); Jean Baxter, Photo/Nats, Inc., p. 183 (bottom); Garden Picture Library/Didier Willery, p. 189 (right); Gary E. Leyrer, pp. 194, 269 (bottom); Henry Kock, The Arboretum, University of Guelph, p. 234; Brian Davis, p. 237 (bottom); Jill Fallis, p. 275; Carol S. Dragich, p. 5.

The recipe for highbush cranberry jelly (p. 142) was supplied by Blue Flame Kitchen, Northwestern Utilities.

NORTHWESTERN UTILITIES LIMITED An ATCO Company • blue flame kitchen

We have made every effort to correctly identify and credit the sources of all photographs, illustrations and information used in this book. Lone Pine Publishing appreciates any further information or corrections; acknowledgement will be given in subsequent editions.

The publisher gratefully acknowledges the support of Alberta Community Development and the Department of Canadian Heritage.

Acknowledgements

A warm thank you to all the wonderful people who made this book possible. In particular, I would like to thank Joan Green for her skill in gathering information, and the following people for sharing their knowledge of trees and shrubs: Brendan Casement, from Alberta Agriculture, Food & Rural Development; Campbell Davidson, from Agriculture and Agri-Food Canada's Morden Research Centre; and Barry Greig, from the University of Alberta's Devonian Botanic Garden. Finally, I give a special thank you to all of the people who welcomed us into their yards and gardens to take photographs.

Contents

Favourite Trees & Shrubs

Introduction

'I think that I shall never see
a poem as lovely as a tree ...'

—Joyce Kilmer (1886–1918)

My husband Ted and I bought our farm almost 50 years ago. From the moment we first saw it, we knew that it was where we wanted to live. One of the things that attracted us most was the three long rows of Manitoba maples lining the oval lane near the farmhouse.

Those trees look even more magnificent today, and first-time visitors to our home never fail to remark on their beauty. Over the years Ted has planted hundreds more trees and shrubs around our property—windbreaks around the fields and vegetable garden, an apple orchard, a test garden for new varieties, various shrub beds and a large stand of spruce trees next to the house. Ted's passion for planting and growing trees resulted in our family opening our own tree nursery.

In the early 1970s, we began to sell small trees and shrubs. We soon discovered that our customers' enthusiasm for new types was almost limitless, so today we offer several hundred varieties, and the list just keeps growing.

I give many talks to lots of gardeners, and I am often asked, 'What are your favourite trees and shrubs?' My answer is always the same: 'I have so many favourites that it would take an entire book to describe them all.' Here, for every gardener who loves trees, is that book.

TREES & SHRUBS IN MY GARDEN

The nearby town has grown into a city around us, so our farm is no longer out in the country. Neither do we sell plants or vegetables from outside the barn anymore. We do, however, still have a very large yard where we grow all kinds of plants. I love to walk down the path that leads from our greenhouses to my home and to my garden, where the gentle rustling of the leaves and constant songs of the birds gives a sense of peace.

As well as providing privacy and beauty, our trees and shrubs add to my family's enjoyment of life. We hang wind-chimes and baskets of flowers from the trees' branches, string them with lights, make jam and jelly from their fruit, and snip off flowering stems for bouquets. My grandchildren love to climb the inviting branches of the Manitoba maples, and happily play for hours in their tree-house in the woods.

Our garden is not only for pleasure; it also serves as a 'trial garden' where we test the hardiness and quality of different plants. The beds are filled with many new, unique trees and shrubs—the number of new varieties never ceases to amaze me.

Nursery managers John Hettle (left) and Shane Neufeld (right) discuss the finer points of sandcherries.

Among our greenhouse staff, we are fortunate to have many knowledgeable people, and they have contributed greatly to this book. Shane Neufeld is our nursery manager, in charge of trees, shrubs and roses. Based on Shane's knowledge, experience and instincts, the number of woody plants that we grow has increased immensely, and we have discovered some very intriguing new varieties.

Phil Croteau is our consulting horticulturist. He is a professional agrologist with the Alberta Institute of Agrologists and a certified arborist with the International Society of Arboriculture. Chris Hamilton, our landscape planner, consultant and pruning expert, is also a certified arborist.

You can choose from hundreds of different trees and shrubs. They will thrive in areas with extreme weather conditions, and are tough, beautiful and undemanding. Combined, trees and shrubs provide a wide range of sizes, colours, flowers, fruit and beauty for all seasons. There is a tree or shrub for every corner of the garden.

Trees & Shrubs in the Garden

By strict definition, a tree is a tall woody plant, usually with a single trunk supporting a leafy crown of leaves, and a shrub is a woody plant, usually smaller, that naturally has branches at ground level. Trees are usually longer lived than most shrubs.

In reality, however, a tree can have more than one main trunk, and a shrub can be grafted onto a single trunk or be trained by pruning to look more like a tree. (For instructions, see *How to Train Shrubs to 'Tree' Form* on page 64.) In the garden, it doesn't really matter whether a plant is truly a tree or a shrub; it matters only that you like the way it looks.

Generally, trees and shrubs fall into two basic categories: *evergreen*, those that have green foliage throughout the year, and *deciduous*, those that lose their leaves in fall. These and other terms are commonly used to describe trees and shrubs, and it is helpful if gardeners understand them.

THE DIFFERENCES BETWEEN TREES & SHRUBS

'He that plants trees loves others beside himself.'

—*Thomas Fuller (1608–61)*

Normally, shrubby plants like Nanking cherry can be trained to 'tree' form.

Evergreen. *Evergreen* trees and shrubs keep their foliage year-round. Most evergreens have needles, like pines, spruces and firs. However, there are also evergreens with broad leaves, such as rhododendrons and azaleas, and evergreens with scale-like leaves, such as cedars and junipers.

Deciduous. Trees and shrubs that shed all of their foliage during fall to prepare for dormancy during winter are *deciduous*. These trees and shrubs are the source of glorious fall colour; many have leaves that turn splendid shades of orange, red and yellow before falling from the branches. Not all deciduous trees have leaves—the larch sheds its soft needles in fall, after a display of brilliant yellow foliage.

Coniferous. Trees and shrubs, such as pine, spruce and cedar, that produce their seeds within cones are called *conifers*. Male cones produce pollen, which blows on the wind to female cones. Once the pollen is shed, the male cone falls. Seeds develop within the female cone, which can remain on the tree for three years or longer.

There are three types of evergreen leaves: needles (left), broad leaves (centre) and scales (right).

Shade Tree. Obviously all trees provide shade, but when you are shopping for trees, you will often hear a certain type described as a *shade tree*. This common term refers to a large deciduous tree.

Dwarf. Although the term *dwarf* is generally considered to indicate small, slow-growing trees or shrubs—those that may be only a few feet tall—keep in mind the true meaning of this word. 'Dwarf' actually means 'smaller than the usual size for that species.'

A tree variety that grows to 10 feet (3 m) tall may be considered a dwarf if the usual height of that tree species is 100 feet (30 m). Dwarf Alberta spruce, for example, which eventually becomes 15 feet (4.6 m) tall, is a dwarf variety of white spruce (100 feet/30 m), but it takes about 60 to 70 years to reach that size. Dwarf varieties are always slow growing and gain only a few inches in size each year.

TOP: Maples are deciduous trees that range in colour from yellow to brilliant red in fall.
BOTTOM: Dwarf Korean lilac (above) grows to 3 1/2–6 feet (1.1–1.8 m) tall, while French hybrid lilac, a regular-sized lilac, can reach a height of 8–12 feet (2.4–3.7 m).

TOP: With its short lifespan, a tower poplar will live less than 50 years. BOTTOM: Although bur oak is a slow-growing tree, it is long lived.

Growth Rate

Trees and shrubs vary tremendously in their growth rates. A tower poplar may reach its full size within 10 to 12 years of planting, but a bur oak could take 60 years. Most often the growth rate refers to height, but with groundcover shrubs, the rate refers to width.

- A *fast-growing* tree or shrub grows 2 feet (61 cm) or more per year.
- A *slow-growing* tree or shrub grows less than 1 foot (30 cm) each year.
- A tree or shrub with a *medium* rate of growth falls somewhere in between.

Lifespan

How long a tree or shrub lives depends on many factors, including its planting site and how well it is maintained. Based on average performance, you can get a pretty good idea of how many years a tree or shrub will last. Usually, fast-growing trees are shorter lived than slow-growing trees, but even the shortest-lived trees last a few decades.

- A tree or shrub with a *short* lifespan lives less than 50 years.
- A tree or shrub with an *average* lifespan lives 50 to 100 years.
- A tree or shrub with a *long* lifespan lives 100 years or longer. Oaks are among the longest-lived trees, with a potential lifespan of more than 500 years.

A 4700-year-old bristlecone pine in California is the world's oldest-known living tree, according to *The Guinness Book of Records.*

Hardiness Ratings

The accepted standard of determining the hardiness of a particular plant is its zone rating. Canadian zone maps, which divide the country into areas, are based primarily on the minimum winter temperatures but also take into account other factors such as the length of the growing season, soil conditions and fluctuating winter temperatures.

Many 'out of zone' plants are worth trying in your yard. This zone 4 boxwood performs extremely well in zone 3.

Canadian plant hardiness zones run from 0, which is the coldest zone, to 9, which is the warmest zone. Generally speaking, the higher the zone number, the greater the number of plant species that can be grown in that zone. The U.S. plant hardiness zone system is similar to Canada's, and each country's zones can, by and large, be treated the same.

In the Edmonton, Alberta, area where I live, there is, on average, a 140-day frost-free growing season. This zone is classified as 3A: in theory, a plant that is capable of surviving temperatures as low as -35° F (-37° C) will die at lower temperatures. In reality, however, we can successfully grow many 'out-of-zone' plants—those that are rated as zone 4, 5 or even occasionally as high as zone 6.

Experience has taught me that zone ratings should be used as a general guide rather than an absolute rule. For example, there is some disagreement on the hardiness of daphne, a low-growing, flowering evergreen shrub. I have seen daphnes listed as hardy to zones 5 or 6, but daphnes are common in gardens throughout my zone 3 region and they have flourished for years.

It's true that there are only so many species of plants that can be grown in any zone. The problem is that there is no guaranteed way of determining precisely which ones will survive in your garden, and which ones will not. Zone ratings may not accurately reflect the conditions specific to your backyard.

Star magnolia is one of the earliest spring-blooming shrubs.

In the show garden at our greenhouses, we grow many plants that are 'not hardy' and they thrive anyhow, regardless of their official zone ratings. The trick to the survival of small shrubs is to provide a nice deep covering of snow, which acts like an insulating blanket throughout winter, protecting them from extreme cold. The tremendous insulation value of snow can allow a zone 5 or 6 plant to grow in zone 3 or 4, as long as it can be completely covered by snow during the deepest cold. For taller trees and shrubs that can't be covered, the zone ratings are harder to disregard. And furthermore, in some cases, even if the parent stock is fully hardy to a zone, the cultivars that are developed from it may not be.

Three years ago we planted a small star magnolia tree in a sheltered corner of a shrub bed alongside my son Bill and daughter-in-law Valerie's house. The tree itself appears to be fully hardy, but its flowerbuds are not; often the branches that were beneath the snowline are the only ones that bloom in spring. Since the mature height of a star magnolia is about 18 feet (5.5 m), it is unlikely that our magnolia tree will ever bloom as profusely as it would in a milder climate, such as Vancouver's or Seattle's.

And so, although I don't bother with zone ratings in my other books, I do provide them for the trees and shrubs. Zones vary across the country. You can find out what zone you live in by calling a local garden centre, or talking to experienced gardeners or a district agriculturist in your county.

If you live in zone 3 and a tree or shrub is rated for zone 4, by all means, give the zone 4 plant a try. Remember that zone ratings are good guidelines but they are not absolutes. Each year I gamble by planting several different plants that are 'not hardy for zone 3,' and I win more often than I lose. The magnolia is one of my favourite plants, and although it may suffer through a severe winter, it has not yet failed to produce some flowers each spring.

An 'out-of-zone' tree will likely grow more slowly, and may never attain its full potential size. In warmer parts of eastern Canada, such as southern Ontario, huge Crimson King maple trees are a common sight. In my area, Crimson King grows nowhere near that size, although in sheltered sites, I have seen quite a few Crimson King maples that have become reasonably large trees. My Crimson King dies back after a severe winter, so Ted simply cuts back the tree, and it now grows as a large, very attractive shrub.

Here are some tips to increase chances of success when experimenting in your own garden with 'out-of-zone' plants:

- Choose a protected area of the garden, such as a flowerbed on the south or west side of the house, that is sheltered from wind.
- Consider mulching the plant in late fall, at least for the first winter. Use peat moss, dry grass clippings, dry fallen tree leaves or other 'clean' available organic matter. Cover plants with a hill of mulch about 10–12 inches (25–30 cm) high, or use a special insulating fabric available from garden centres.
- Water the plant well in late fall, shortly before the ground freezes.
- Ensure that the plant has a good snowcover throughout winter. Throw loose, salt-free fresh snow overtop whenever you shovel the walks and driveway.

For more details, see *Where to Plant Tender Trees & Shrubs* on page 30.

EXPERIMENTING WITH NEW VARIETIES

Although Crimson King maple suffers some dieback in zone 3, there are still some excellent specimens to be found.

Planning & Designing

'The best time to plant
a tree was 20 years ago.
The second best time is now.'

—Anonymous

Designing an entire yard can be an overwhelming project—there are so many things to consider! It takes a lot of time, effort and knowledge to do it right, so whenever gardeners ask me, 'What's the secret to designing a beautiful garden?' I tell them, 'Get a professional to help you with it.'

Now if you simply want to add a couple of shrubs here and there, a design is not essential. What is essential is to understand the characteristics and needs of the shrubs. Once you know that, then by all means, proceed. But if you want to redesign your whole yard, or are starting from scratch, the best choice is to hire a professional landscape designer. Remember that you are working *with* the designer. Explain what you like and don't like. Jot down some ideas and think carefully about what you want most, and then let the landscape designer pull it all together.

Before you hire a landscape designer, consider the following points.

- **Theme**. Have you always longed for a certain type of garden—Victorian, English or some other particular theme? Is there a favourite colour or a certain plant that you absolutely *must* have? Keep a list of plants that you have seen, heard about or would like to try.
- **Maintenance**. How much time do you want to spend looking after the garden? Reducing the lawn area—perhaps replacing much of it with some groundcover shrubs—is just one way to save the time spent on maintenance.

When planning a yard, consider whether you want a low-maintenance garden, such as the one above—a shrub bed with drought-tolerant junipers and potentillas—or a high maintenance garden, such as the yard on the opposite page.

Cotoneaster can be planted as a hedge to provide privacy or as a screen to hide unsightly power boxes.

As a general rule, install plants from largest to smallest. If you have a new yard, install decks, large rocks, patios and retaining walls before anything else. With plants, large trees go in first, then smaller trees and shrubs, perennials, bedding plants and lawns last. It's easier, and avoids plants being trampled or damaged by heavy equipment.

- **Purpose**. What are you going to do in your yard? If privacy is important, then perhaps plant a hedge or a screen of columnar shrubs. Do you want a lot of beautiful flowers for cutting, fragrant blossoms or just a colourful display around the deck?
- **Site**. Are there large steep slopes or drainage problems? What type of soil do you have? In certain situations, choosing plants that will thrive in the existing site is easier and cheaper than renovating the planting area.
- **Continuity**. Consider your surroundings and the style of the neighbourhood, so that your newly landscaped yard will not look out of place. Walk around the block and look at what other people have done with their yards. Take note of which trees, shrubs or design ideas you like or dislike.

TREES & SHRUBS FOR FOUNDATION PLANTINGS

Foundation plantings are the shrub borders or flowerbeds that line your house, creating a transitional border of plants between the building and the landscape. Because they grow so close to the house, only certain shrubs are suitable. They must be low enough not to block views from windows, compact enough that they won't sprawl over walkways after a few years and have non-invasive roots that won't interfere with the house foundation.

Burning Bush
Cedar
Cranberry
Dogwood
Double-flowering Plum
Groundcover Juniper
Lilac
  Dwarf Korean
Mockorange
Ninebark
Pine
Russian Almond
Sandcherry
Spirea
Willow
  Dwarf Arctic
  'Blue Fox'
  Hakura Nishiki

A good mixture of 'foundation friendly' shrubs blends the structure with the landscape.

LOW-MAINTENANCE TREES & SHRUBS

Low-maintenance trees and shrubs are adaptable, durable, drought tolerant and rarely bothered by disease or insects. They don't spread excessively or produce suckers, and they need very little pruning. Since these trees and shrubs do not drop messy seeds or fruit, they are particularly well suited for planting by patios or swimming pools, near decks and close to driveways or sidewalks.

Arrowwood
Ash (seedless)
Bog Rosemary
Boxwood
Caragana
  Globe
  Pygmy
  Walker's Weeping
  Weeping
Cedar
  'Wareana'
Cork Tree
  (male trees only)
Cranberry
Currant
  Golden Flowering
Dogwood
  Grey
  Pagoda
Double-flowering Plum
Fir
  Blue
Genista
Hackberry
Juniper
Larch
  'Newport Beauty'
Linden
Nannyberry
Ninebark
Oak
Pine
Potentilla
Russian Almond
Sea Buckthorn
Snowball
Spruce
Wayfaring Tree

Properly designed yards enhance the entire property and increase the real estate value of your home. Landscape designers can create plans for yards with low maintenance as a priority.

WINDBREAKS

Windbreaks reduce wind, noise and soil erosion, and they help to retain moisture by collecting snow and by creating a milder microclimate for nearby plants. Before planting a windbreak, study your land carefully to determine where the windbreak should be planted. This work beforehand will ensure the greatest amount of protection to both plants and buildings. Consider the direction of prevailing winds. Don't plant a windbreak too close to the garden, because the trees and shrubs will rob the soil of valuable moisture and nutrients.

Farmers often plant windbreaks around their fields. If your yard is large enough, you can also use a windbreak to advantage around your home. Properly designed windbreaks reduce the amount of wind hitting your house, and may, as a result, help to reduce your heating costs by 10 to 30 percent.

A windbreak can provide protection as far downwind as 15 times its height! A 10-foot (3 m) windbreak would give you protection up to 150 feet (46 m) downwind.

Many types of poplar are appropriate for a windbreak.

Trees & Shrubs for Windbreaks

The following trees and shrubs are hardy, low-maintenance, consistently uniform in their height and generally readily available.

Ash
- 'Fallgold'
- 'Patmore Green'

Aspen

Buffaloberry

Caragana
- 'Sutherland'

Crabapple
- Siberian

Elm
- Siberian

Lilac
- except Dwarf Korean Japanese tree lilac and 'Miss Kim'

Maple
- 'Baron Manitoba'

Poplar
- Griffin
- Northwest
- Tower

Sea Buckthorn

Spruce
- 'Fat Albert'
- 'Hoopsii'

Willow
- Laurel Leaf
- Silver

HEDGES

Hedges can be used to replace fences, to divide a property, line a driveway, create a windbreak or provide summer privacy. Plant a hedge to hide a plain concrete wall or compost area, or use the hedge as an ornamental feature in front of a fence. Taller hedges help to create microclimates in your yard, enabling you to successfully grow tender plants nearby.

Trees & Shrubs for Formal Hedges

Choose from the following trees and shrubs to create a superb formal hedge.

Boxwood
Burning Bush
  Compact
Caragana
  Globe
  Pygmy
Cedar
  'Danica'
  'Golden Champion'
  'Little Giant'
  'Wareana'
  'Woodwardii'
Cherry Prinsepia
Cotoneaster
  Peking
Cranberry
  Dwarf European
Currant
  'Schmidt'

A fence provides instant privacy while a hedge may take several years to reach mature size. Hedges, however, usually cost less than half of the cost of a fence.

Where to Plant

The planting sites for trees and shrubs are best considered as permanent. Unlike perennials, most of which can be easily split and divided and rearranged in the garden, trees and shrubs do not take well to being moved.

It is important to take some time to think about where you are going to plant a tree. Although it may be hard to imagine when looking at a thin walnut sapling at the nursery or garden centre, trust that the tree will eventually become 50 feet (15 m) tall and almost as wide. Allow sufficient space to accommodate mature size. If you don't have sufficient space, choose a smaller tree.

Every tree or shrub has its ideal spot in the yard. Trees and shrubs will be healthiest and look most attractive when provided with their preferred growing conditions. For example, a flowering shrub that grows in a shady area tends to produce few flowers and to 'stretch'—become taller and less bushy. Even the time of day that the sun shines makes a difference; afternoon sun is hotter than morning sun.

Within every yard there are microclimates: spots that may be either warmer or colder than other parts of the garden. On a fall morning after a freezing night, you will sometimes notice that frost has hit only certain spots in your yard—usually exposed, low-lying areas. Trees help create microclimates; the warmest parts of your garden will be areas near tall trees or large shrubs, hedges, fences and walls. These 'obstructions' trap heat and provide shelter from the wind. Choose protected spots for the more tender varieties, and reserve exposed areas for hardier ones.

'He plants trees to benefit another generation.'

—*Caecilius Statius (220–168 BC)*

THE IDEAL SITE FOR EVERGREENS

Because evergreens have year-round foliage, they should be planted in a site that puts the least stress on them during winter. Ideally, evergreens should be planted in a site that is sunny in summer and shaded during winter. This isn't as impossible as it at first sounds; a site on the north side of a fence, for example, can meet those qualifications because during winter months the sun shines from a lower point in the sky.

The purpose of this site is to prevent evergreen needles from browning. Needles have a waxy coating that prevents 'desiccation'—drying-out of foliage—which results in browning. Sun and wind, especially during winter, take moisture from needles, and too much of either puts a strain on the tree. Remember, too, that the healthiest evergreens are least likely to have browned foliage, because the needles contain more moisture and the protective waxy coating on their needles is thicker.

Sheared 'Brandon' cedar

WHERE TO PLANT TENDER EVERGREENS

Tender evergreens, such as rhododendrons, cedars and yews, are more susceptible to foliage damage. Avoid planting tender evergreens in very hot sites or near reflective walls. In these situations, leaves can become 'sun-burned,' turning brown or reddish and remaining that way for several years. Newly planted and young spruces are particularly susceptible to this type of damage.

WHERE TO PLANT TENDER TREES & SHRUBS

If you want to experiment by growing tender or 'out-of-zone' shrubs or smaller trees, plant them in a sheltered site where they will be protected from wind and have good snowcover throughout winter. Snowcover is particularly important for tender evergreen shrubs such as holly. A protected site against the house is even better, because the shrub will receive some warming in winter from the house.

TREES & SHRUBS FOR SHADY SPOTS

Certain trees and shrubs thrive, even in sites that receive less than three hours of full sun per day. The trees and shrubs marked with an asterisk (*) will tolerate full shade.

Bog Rosemary	Hazelnut
Boxwood	Hemlock
Coralberry*	Hydrangea
Cranberry	Ninebark
Dwarf European*	'Tilden Parks'
Dogwood	Rhododendron
Euonymus	Russian Cypress*
'Gold Prince'	Snowberry
Fir	Sumac
Dwarf Balsam*	'Gro-low'
Flowering Raspberry*	Yew*

Dwarf European cranberry

TREES & SHRUBS FOR WET SPOTS

Low-lying, wet areas are often the most frustrating parts of the garden. In these areas, only a limited number of trees and shrubs will flourish. The ones listed below thrive in sites where water pools periodically, in heavy clay soil with poor drainage, and even in sites where soil rarely dries out.

Alder	Larch
Ash	Maple
Birch	Silver
Bog Rosemary	Red
Chokecherry	Oak
'Autumn Magic'	Pin
Dogwood	Poplar
Elm	Willow
Holly	

American Elm

TREES & SHRUBS FOR HOT, DRY SPOTS

Potentilla

In sun-baked sites with no supplemental watering, not many trees or shrubs thrive. Choose heat-loving, drought-tolerant trees and shrubs for these areas of the garden. Remember, though, that even drought-tolerant plants need to be watered well when young—at least once a week throughout the first growing season after planting, until their root systems develop to the point where they can sustain the plants through periods of drought.

Amur Maackia
Ash
Buffaloberry
Caragana
Cherry Prinsepia
Currant
  Golden Flowering
Genista
Hackberry
Honeysuckle
Juniper
Pincherry
Pine
Potentilla
Russian Olive
Salt Bush
Sea Buckthorn
Spruce
Sumac

TREES & SHRUBS FOR SHADY, DRY SPOTS

Snowball

Dry, shaded spots, such as areas beneath large trees, areas with little sunlight, or areas where rain has trouble penetrating, can be difficult for plants. Only a few trees or shrubs can thrive in those conditions.

Boxwood
Cranberry
  Dwarf European
Ninebark
  'Tilden Parks'
Snowball
Snowberry
Sumac

SOIL pH

The ability of plants to absorb nutrients depends, to a large extent, on the soil pH. This pH is measured on a scale from 1 to 14. Low numbers indicate acidity, and high numbers indicate alkalinity; 7.0 is considered neutral. Most trees and shrubs grow best in soils with a pH between 6.5 and 7.5, and garden soils generally fall into that range. Soil tests are useful if you have difficulty growing plants, because they may indicate an imbalance. Minor pH imbalances can be corrected rather easily, but with major pH imbalances, the best solution is to grow plants that are suited to either acidic or alkaline soils.

Larch

Trees & Shrubs for Acidic Soil

In extremely acidic soil, few plants grow well. Exceptions include the following trees and shrubs, which are suited to soils with a pH less than 6.0.

Alder
Arrowwood
Azalea
Birch
Bog Rosemary
Cedar
Daphne
Falsecypress
Fir
Hemlock
Holly
Juniper
Larch
Pine
  Eastern White
Rhododendron
Russian Cypress
Serviceberry
Spruce

Trees & Shrubs for Alkaline Soil

In alkaline soil, choose trees and shrubs that easily tolerate or even prefer that condition. The following plants are also salt tolerant.

Buffaloberry
Caragana
Hackberry
Maple
  Manitoba
Potentilla
Russian Olive
Salt Bush
Sea Buckthorn
Tamarisk

Silver buffaloberry

Buying Trees & Shrubs

Once you have decided where and what to plant, you are ready to select your plants at the garden centre. Usually, you will find the best selection early in the season.

Choose only the healthiest trees and shrubs; a diseased, spindly or damaged plant is never a good deal, no matter how low the sale price. Make sure roots are well wrapped in burlap or in a pot. When choosing shrubs, look for bushy ones that branch out near to the ground. Avoid any plants with large gashes in the bark. Look closely at leafbuds and flowerbuds; if they are dry, brittle and fall off easily, it is a sign that the tree has been allowed to dry out.

Avoid larger trees with trunks so scrawny that they must be supported by a tall stake. Keep in mind, though, that young trees are often sold staked so their trunks stay straight. That stake can be left in place after planting, and removed after one or two growing seasons. Other exceptions include grafted trees or shrubs and 'trained' evergreens, such as juniper or weeping Norway spruce, which, without the stake, would naturally grow flat along the ground.

If your nice-looking, new balled-and-burlapped pine or spruce tree turns brown shortly after planting, it is most likely because many of its roots were damaged when you bought it—it takes a little longer for the damage to show on the foliage. You can avoid this scenario by closely inspecting the tree first, before you make a purchase. Problem signs include drooping or browned 'candles'—the lighter-coloured, softer new growth on the branch ends—and dry needles that drop readily. Touch the root-ball with your hand. It should feel soft and moist; if it's dry, don't buy it.

'Men seldom plant trees until they begin to be wise.'

—John Evelyn (1620–1706)

Don't worry about leaves that are browned on the edges by an early spring frost—this minor damage is temporary. Do worry, however, if leaves are completely brown and the branch tips also look dead; that's a sign of more serious damage.

Evergreen trees naturally shed needles in fall; with natural 'needle drop,' the needles on inside branches turn yellow and fall off. Brown or grey needles that shed from all over the branches are a sign of other problems—most often a severe lack of water.

Shopping for trees and shrubs late in the season often results in great savings on good-quality plants, although your selection of varieties may be more limited. Some of these plants are, however, 'root-bound,' because they've been growing in pots all season long, with nowhere for their roots to go but around and around the inside of the pot. Before planting root-bound trees or shrubs, cut off any big roots that are encircling the main root-ball. Left intact, that root can choke off or 'girdle' the other roots or trunk, resulting in the tree's death. Once that root is cut off, however, the tree will do just fine.

THREE WAYS TO BUY TREES & SHRUBS

A container-grown globe spruce.

Container-grown

Container-grown plants are in a pot filled with soil and have an established root system, which makes them easier to transplant.

Container-grown nursery stock is more expensive, because the plants have been actively growing and nurtured for months.

This type of nursery stock becomes established more quickly after planting in your garden.

Balled-and-burlapped

Young trees are sometimes sold with their roots surrounded with a ball of soil and wrapped in burlap. Often, even large evergreens, such as spruce and pine, are sold in this manner.

It is essential that the root-ball be kept consistently moist. Balled-and-burlapped trees are often displayed at garden centres or tree nurseries in a large wooden box filled with wood chips. The tree's root-ball should feel moist; don't buy a tree that has been allowed to dry out.

This type of nursery stock is usually less expensive—except if the tree is very large. The soil and root-ball are likely too heavy for you to lift. Remember to consider the additional expense of delivery and mechanical planting.

Bare-root

'Bare-root' means just what it sounds like: the roots are not covered by soil or a container.

Bare-root shrubs—especially roses—are what you usually get from a mail-order supplier. They come in plastic bags filled with moist sawdust or peat moss.

It is very important that the roots be kept consistently moist and cool prior to planting. Bare-root trees or shrubs should be planted as soon as possible in spring.

Bare-root trees or shrubs must not be subjected to freezing temperatures during shipping. Plants that have been frozen often produce shoots after transplanting, but die rather quickly. Unfortunately, it is difficult to tell whether a plant has been frozen before it is planted.

This route is the least expensive.

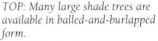

TOP: Many large shade trees are available in balled-and-burlapped form.
BOTTOM: A well-rooted black ash is ready for planting.

SIZING UP YOUR PURCHASE

Deciduous trees are most often sold by caliper size, while evergreen trees tend to be sold by height.

With the exception of the forest industry, trees are rarely grown from seed, simply because they take so long to reach mature size. Occasionally, however, a gardener wants tree seeds; if you do, be careful what you order: 2.2 lbs (1 kg) gives you about 11 million birch seeds, 165,000 pine seeds, 155,000 lilac seeds, or 90,000 larch seeds!

Trees and shrubs are sold with various size descriptions, which initially can seem rather mystifying. A '5-foot blue spruce,' for example, is taller than 5 feet (1.5 m). There are set standards for measuring nursery stock, and once you understand them, it's easier to 'size-up' the value of your purchase.

- **Caliper**. This term refers to the diameter of a tree's trunk, usually expressed in millimetres and always measured at a standard distance—6–12 inches (15–30 cm) from the ground.

  For example, a 50-millimetre caliper shade tree will have a trunk about 6 inches (15 cm) around, measured 6 inches (15 cm) from the ground, and will be about 10 feet (3 m) tall with at least eight strong branches.
- **Height**. If you are 6 feet (1.8 m) tall, you may be wondering why that 6-foot spruce tree you're considering buying is towering over you. It's because tree height is measured from the top rim of the pot—the level where the tree will sit once it is planted rather than from where the pot now sits—up to the top lateral branches. The tree's 'leader'—the central branch or growing tip—may extend another foot or two higher.
- **Pot size**. Nursery stock is often sold by pot size: 1-gallon, 2-gallon, 5-gallon, 10-gallon, 15-gallon, 25-gallon pots.
- **Whips**. 'Whips' are saplings—usually fast-growing trees such as poplar and willow. Although they obviously take longer to mature, whips are a good choice when you need large quantities of trees—perhaps for a shelterbelt—because they are cheaper to buy, and faster and easier to plant.

The tradition of planting trees on Arbor Day started over 100 years ago in Nebraska, U.S. More than one million trees were planted in Nebraska on the first Arbor Day in 1882, and in celebration of this holiday, millions more trees have been planted since then. 'Arbor' is the Latin word for 'tree.'

Tree 'plugs' are an inexpensive way to start a windbreak, but the trade-off is time. It would take five to six years for a spruce tree to reach 5–6 feet (1.5–1.8 m) and a cedar to reach 3–4 feet (91–120 cm).

- **Plugs**. Most people are familiar with tree 'plugs' from the little seedlings given away to children on Earth Day or Arbor Day. Occasionally, entire trays or flats of plugs are available through tree nurseries, but the selection and availability is rather limited.
- **Field-grown**. When buying a balled-and-burlapped tree, a field-grown tree is your best bet. This term indicates that the tree was raised on a 'tree farm,' in a field where it was well watered and had adequate room to bush out evenly on all sides. Nursery-grown trees tend to be thicker, more compact and have a stronger, more vigorous root system than a tree dug out of the wild.

Another consideration is that, with a field-grown tree, you know exactly what you are getting. A field-grown spruce, for example, will be identified as a specific species or variety. A tree dug out of the bush, on the other hand, could be any old spruce and is often of poor ornamental quality.

Gardeners sometimes ask whether a tree that is not locally grown will be hardy. The answer is that, by and large, it doesn't matter whether the tree was raised in California or two miles from your hometown—its hardiness depends more on its genetic make-up.

Planting Trees & Shrubs

WHEN TO PLANT

Generally, you can plant trees and shrubs at any time from spring to fall. Start planting in early spring as soon as the ground has thawed enough for you to put your shovel into it, and stop planting in late fall, a few weeks before the ground freezes again. Trees and shrubs are hardy plants and can withstand frosts.

It is, however, only the container-grown and dormant balled-and-burlapped (see page 36) trees and shrubs that can be planted at anytime during the growing season. Allow at least two to three weeks before the ground freezes in fall—enough time for newly planted roots to become sufficiently established to enable the trees or shrubs to survive the coming winter.

Bare-root trees and shrubs are exceptions and should be planted in spring or early summer. They need a longer growing period to establish their root systems. Plants with well-established, healthy root systems are better able to withstand stressful conditions, and to make it through that first winter.

Evergreens are another exception and must be allowed to get a good head start before the arrival of winter. Evergreens such as cedar, juniper, pine and spruce should be planted at least six weeks before the ground freezes—about the same time that you would plant your spring-flowering bulbs (tulips, daffodils, etc.). Broad-leaved evergreens such as rhododendrons and daphne are best planted in spring.

Don't plant trees and shrubs when the ground is frozen. Deb Wiebe knows the general rule: 'if you can push the shovel in the ground, you can plant.'

BEFORE YOU PLANT

The term 'well-drained soil' is often used to describe optimum conditions for plants, but what does it actually mean? Well-drained soil is neither too wet nor too dry; water percolates through very easily. Most trees and shrubs are happiest in well-drained soil.

If you are not sure about the drainage of your soil, try this simple test. Dig a hole, about as wide and deep as your spade, and fill the hole with water. Note the time then, and note it again once the water has completely drained away. If less than half an inch (1.3 cm) of water drains per hour, your soil drainage is poor. In poorly drained or wet soil, only a few types of trees and shrubs thrive (for a specific list, see *Trees & Shrubs for Wet Spots* on page 31).

Avoid planting during the heat of the day—mornings, evenings or cool cloudy days are easier on plants.

Generally, heavy clay soil drains poorly and very sandy soil drains fast—too fast for most plants. Because tree roots spread over a wide area, it's difficult to amend the soil enough to make much difference. In sandy soil, you'd be best off to choose drought-tolerant trees and shrubs (see *Trees & Shrubs for Hot, Dry Spots* and *Trees & Shrubs for Shady, Dry Spots* on page 32).

Before planting anything in the garden, however, there are still a couple of things that you can do to greatly improve results—regardless of what type of soil you have. Remember that a newly planted tree or shrub has a small root system, and to help the tree or shrub get off to the best start, it is terribly important to do what you can to make it easiest for new roots to grow and spread. Roots are the basis for a tree's health; if the root system is strong and healthy, it can sustain the tree through all sorts of stresses.

The first step is to ensure that there is enough good topsoil. I always recommend about 8–12 inches (20–30 cm) of topsoil.

The second step is to add lots of organic matter—peat moss, compost or well-rotted manure. Organic matter improves the ability of soil to retain water and nutrients, resulting in impressive plant growth and vigour. It also loosens clay soil, making it easier for roots to penetrate, and binds sandy soil so that it dries out less quickly.

The third step is to give roots a 'boost' when the tree or shrub is planted. Add some bonemeal—a phosphorous-rich, slow-release, organic fertilizer—or a granular fertilizer with a high middle number, such as 10-52-10. Phosphorous (indicated by the middle number in fertilizer formulations) helps roots become established more quickly.

If you are planting into poorly drained soil, raise the planting depth so that the tree or shrub will sit slightly—about an inch (2.5 cm)—above the soil level. This small adjustment makes enough of a difference that it will prevent roots from rotting in excess moisture. Even a moisture-loving tree or shrub can suffer in wet soil until its roots become established.

Bare soil or mulched borders around the base of trees or shrubs prevent damage from lawnmowers and grass-trimmers and reduce competition between lawn and tree roots for moisture and nutrients. These borders are especially beneficial during the first few years of plant establishment. The objective is to give as much competitive advantage to the young tree or shrub as possible.

On April 13, 1964, Alice Mitchell bought a 'Toba' hawthorn tree for $5. Over 30 years later, the hawthorn has grown into a splendid tree that blooms wonderfully each spring. (Mrs. Mitchell is proud of her tree and still owns the original receipt.)

HOW TO PLANT TREES & SHRUBS

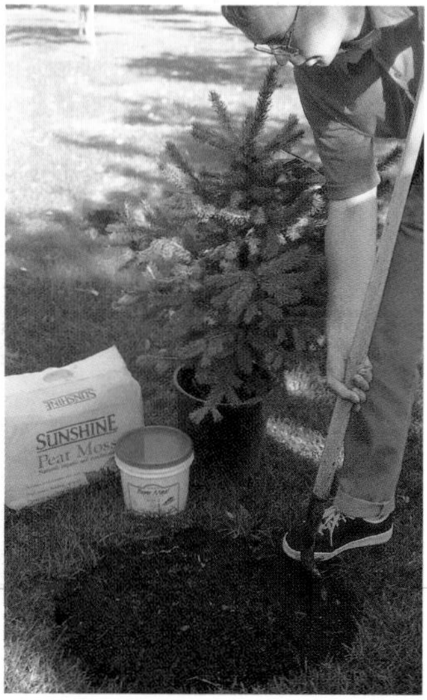

1.

2.

3.

Remember the slogan: 'Dial before you dig.' Be sure to contact your municipal office or local utility board to have all underground utilities marked off before your shovel hits the soil.

1. *As a general rule, prepare the soil in an area three times greater than the diameter of the nursery pot or root-ball of the new tree, and slightly deeper than the depth of the nursery pot or root-ball. This encourages roots to spread outward.*
2. *Dig your planting hole. Add lots of organic matter—about 20 percent—to the soil. Stir in a few handfuls of bonemeal to aid root development.*
3. *Mix well, and add water if the mixture seems dry.*
4. *Remove the tree or shrub from its pot. Gently untangle the root-ball to enable the roots to spread into the soil as the plant grows. Remove any 'girdling' roots—ones that encircle the root-ball and could choke the tree.*

4.

5.

6.

5. *Set the tree or shrub into the planting hole to check its planting depth. Remove the tree, and add or remove soil mixture so that the tree or shrub will be sitting at soil level, with its trunk vertical to the ground.*
   Do not compact soil around the root-ball by tamping or stepping on the soil. Let the soil settle naturally by watering the area, and then 'top up' with more soil, if required. Ensure there is drainage away from the base of the plant. This will prevent root/crown rot and encourage root growth into the prepared soil site.
6. *Water until the soil is evenly wet. Newly planted trees and shrubs should be watered regularly and thoroughly once a week during the first growing season after planting. Fertilize once a month with 20-20-20 until the first of August.*

How much bonemeal? As a rule of thumb, I just add one handful for each foot of height or spread (whichever is greater) at the time of planting.

PLANTING LARGER TREES

1.

2.

3.

4.

1. *When a tree requires mechanical planting, a large mechanical tree spade first removes a soil core from the ground to create a planting hole.*
2. *A balled-and-burlapped tree over 10 feet (3 m) in height or with a root-ball over 3 feet (91 cm) in diameter usually requires mechanical planting.*
3. *If your tree is in a wire basket, before planting it, cut off as much of the wire as possible around the top and sides.*
4. *Never completely remove burlap from balled-and-burlapped trees, but do remove the string tying the ball together. Cut the sides of the root-ball to promote root growth. Place the tree in the planting hole, open up the burlap and lay it along the sides of the planting hole. Cut off any exposed burlap.*

GENERAL PLANTING RULES

- Planting shrubs in small containers (1–5 gallons/4.5–22.7 l) is very similar to planting perennials and should be treated as such.
- Planting young trees in mid-sized containers (5–15 gallons/22.7–68 l) is quite easy and can be done by one person.
- You may require additional help when planting large caliper trees (opposite page).
- If the tree is container-grown, try to preserve the root-ball intact. If the roots have grown in a circle, try prying loose a few of them so they may grow outwards. If you can't pry them out, use pruning shears to cut through a few of the roots to encourage lateral root development.
- If your tree is purchased in a 'peat pot,' it is not necessary to remove the pot before planting. You must, however, first slash the sides of the pot and remove the top lip that protrudes above the soil line.
- If your tree or shrub is 'bare-root,' be sure to dig the planting hole large enough to enable the roots to spread fully. Make a mound of soil at the bottom of the planting hole and sit the tree or shrub on top, with its roots spread out over the mound, like a little octopus. Otherwise, follow the general planting steps, but also fertilize with 10-52-10 once a week for the first three weeks after planting, to help roots become established.

STAKING TREES

Newly transplanted trees that are taller than 5–6 feet (1.5–1.8 m) should be staked for support against wind. The purpose of a stake is to steady the tree until its roots become well established—not to provide a crutch for a weak, spindly trunk.

If you are thinking of pruning your shrub to 'tree' form (see page 64), or have planted many young whips, keep in mind that one way to avoid excessive bending from wind on young trees is to leave one-half of the foliage on the lower two-thirds of the tree. Since the wind is interrupted all along the trunk, it bends much less than it would if the tree top were full of leaves and the trunk were bare.

There are two ways to stake a tree: a two-stake system and a three-stake or tripod system. Tripod systems are great for large spruce, pine or fir, and also for any large tree planted where wind is very strong or shifts frequently. With either method, use rigid metal or wooden stakes for support and a flexible, non-abrasive material for tying.

Two-stake Method

- After planting, place one stake on the windward side of the tree and one stake on the opposite side. Drive each stake 18–24 inches (46–61 cm) deep into undisturbed soil along the outside edge of the prepared planting area—not right next to the tree.
- Tie strings or cables to each stake and then loosely secure them to the tree's trunk, about 3–4 feet (91–120 cm) from ground level. The tie should allow some freedom of movement and it must be covered in soft material where it contacts the trunk.
- Be sure that the tie is not secured so tightly that it completely restricts movement of the tree in a moderate wind. Moderate trunk movement increases the tree's strength.

Tripod Staking System

- Space the three stakes about 120 degrees from each other, encircling the tree. Drive each stake 18–24 inches (46–61 cm) deep into undisturbed soil.
- Secure strings using soft, padded ties or a nylon trunk harness, attached approximately 3 feet (91 cm) above ground level. Tie strings to the stakes.
- Allow only a slight amount of tension on the strings to permit some movement of the tree.

Only soft, padded material should contact the tree to avoid abrasions to the trunk.

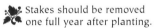

Stakes should be removed one full year after planting.

WINDBREAKS

Windbreaks are grown for a variety of reasons: prevention of soil erosion, privacy, reduction of wind and noise. Ensure that where you grow your windbreak has been well thought out in advance. For example, you don't want to plant a windbreak too close to your garden—trees and shrubs will rob the garden of needed moisture. See *Windbreaks* on page 25 (under *Planning & Designing*) for more advice on growing this popular feature.

Thousands of windbreaks are grown on the Prairies to reduce soil erosion.

Growing

- For the most efficient windbreak, grow a variety of trees and shrubs planted perpendicular to the prevailing wind. More protection will be provided by this arrangement than by a single row of trees of the same height.
- To reduce wind-speed at a particular site, plant the windbreak at a distance no greater than five times the windbreak's height. For example, 'Sutherland' caragana grows to 15 feet (4.6 m), so the windbreak should be planted within 75 feet (22 m) of the building being protected.
- Water and fertilize regularly for the first three years after planting to help the trees or shrubs become well established, and to promote deep roots.

HEDGES

Hedges can be grown in two ways: formal—clipped and sheared into a continuous, perfectly shaped row—or informal—with the shrubs allowed to retain their natural form. Almost any bushy shrub can be used to create an informal hedge, but only certain shrubs are suitable for shearing.

Informal hedges are generally wider than formal hedges—keep potential width in mind when planning. 'Woodwardii' cedar, for example, grows up to 8 feet (2.4 m) wide.

Growing

- If you are planting an entire hedge at once, the best way to do it is to dig a trench. A trench is easier to dig than individual planting holes, and a trench also results in roots becoming established more quickly and growing more vigorously.
- Make the trench about 18 inches (45 cm) wide and 15 inches (38 cm) deep. Refer to *How to Plant Trees & Shrubs* on page 44.
- Space shrubs more closely together than you normally would. As a general rule, allow 2–4 feet (61–120 cm) between the shrubs.
- Fertilize and water hedges as you would any other shrub. See pages 53-58.

How to Care for Trees & Shrubs with a Minimum of Effort

'Woodman, spare that tree!
Touch not a single bough!
In youth it sheltered me,
And I'll protect it now.'

—George Pope Morris (1802–64)

Overall, trees and shrubs are quite undemanding—especially once the crucial first year or two has passed. Planting the trees and shrubs in areas that best suit them is half the battle. If you have a hot, dry, sun-baked area of your yard, choose a drought-tolerant shrub for that spot, rather than constantly battling to provide a moisture-loving shrub with sufficient water. Refer to the listings on pages 23-33, and to individual plant listings, to find what suits your garden.

WATERING

There are no concrete rules for watering, but over many years of growing trees, we have developed a rule of thumb that works extremely well.

As a general rule, provide 1 gallon (4.5 l) of water per foot of height or spread (whichever is greater), once a week. Both a 5-foot-tall (1.5 m) spruce tree and a 5-foot-wide (1.5 m) juniper need 5 gallons (22.7 l) of water, per week. To give yourself an idea of how much water this is, time how long it takes to fill up a 5-gallon bucket. If it takes two minutes, then you know that, if you turn on your hose for the same amount of time, you will have provided sufficient water for a 5-foot (1.5 m) shrub.

In early summer when a large, mature tree is in full leaf, it may lift a ton of water each day from the soil and carry it up its trunk to the leaves.

This, of course, is only a general rule; in periods of hot, dry weather, you may need to water two to three times a week, and during rainy spells, you may need to water only once every two to three weeks. But remember, if the amount of precipitation from a rain-shower is 1/4 inch (0.5 cm) or less, that isn't enough water to satisfy your plants. Water the same as you would if it had not rained at all.

Flood nozzles create large water droplets that reduce water loss through evaporation.

Trees and shrubs most often need watering

- immediately after being transplanted
- throughout their first two to three years in the garden (even drought-tolerant trees and shrubs need regular watering during this stage of life, to allow their root systems to become established)
- if they are growing on slopes or in very sandy soil
- during extended periods with no rain
- when blooming and while fruit is forming
- in late fall, just before freeze-up.

Allow water to soak deep into the soil, to encourage roots to grow deeper. Soil always dries at the surface first, so trees with deep roots need watering less often, and shrubs with shallow, fibrous roots need watering more often.

Remember that a tree's roots can spread considerably wider than the tree is tall. Rather than watering around the trunk, always water at or slightly beyond the tree's *drip-line*—the imaginary line that dripping raindrops would follow from the outermost branch tips straight down to the ground. That is where most of the tree's *feeder roots* are—small, fine roots that more easily absorb water.

Once trees become large, their wide-spreading roots can draw moisture from a wide area. Generally, shrubs don't need watering once they have reached mature size, and trees don't need watering after they have grown to 22–32 feet (7–10 m) tall—except during periods of drought or if they are growing in dry locations.

Roses and other small shrubs are exceptions: they need more moisture than most plants and should continue to be watered regularly, every single year, no matter how old they are.

For the first two to three years after planting, water all trees and shrubs once a week throughout spring and summer. During early fall, allow the soil to become slightly drier in order to slow down plant growth in preparation for winter. Ensure, however, that trees and shrubs are well watered in late fall, a few weeks before the ground freezes. Late fall watering is an important step in ensuring that plants have the best chance for winter survival. Plants that enter winter with their roots in dry soil are likely to suffer.

Easy Ways to Reduce Your Water Bill

Most gardeners spend about half their total water bill to water lawns and gardens. A great deal of that water is wasted through evaporation and inefficient watering techniques. Making a few simple changes to your garden and the way that you water can immediately reduce your water bill.

- In dry areas, plant drought-tolerant trees and shrubs.
- Use lots of organic matter, such as compost, peat moss and well-rotted manure, to help retain water. Add organic matter to soil before planting, and supplement shrub beds each spring and fall. Organic matter acts like a sponge: peat moss, for example, holds several times its weight in water.
- An organic mulch helps soil to retain moisture and also chokes out moisture-robbing weeds.
- Whenever possible, water in the morning or evening to reduce moisture loss through evaporation.
- Collect rainwater in barrels to use in the garden.

When choosing a planting site, keep in mind how much water a mature tree can use. Ted and I planted a large row of poplars as a windbreak at the edge of the field where we have our vegetable garden. The trees provide a microclimate, enabling the vegetables to grow faster, but they also use up a lot of moisture. The first year, we didn't take that into consideration, and were constantly battling to provide the vegetables with enough water. In following years, we planted the vegetables further away.

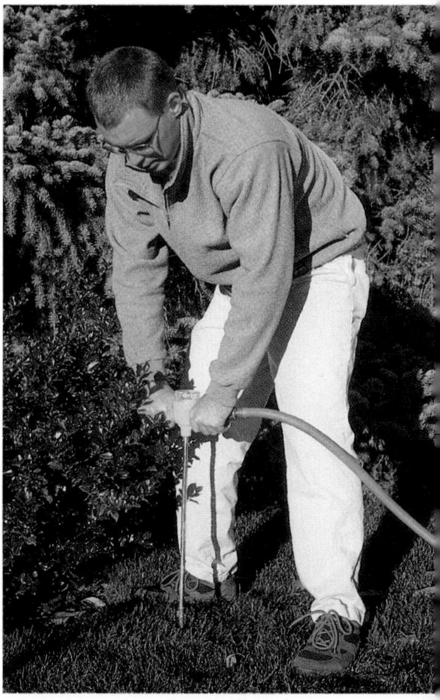

A 'root feeder' is the most efficient method of watering trees and shrubs. Use a zig-zag pattern around the drip-line.

FERTILIZING

Fertilizer can be injected into the soil by professionals. Here, a Green Drop representative makes a spring application of fertilizer.

Most garden soils contain all of the nutrients essential for plant growth, but sometimes the quantities are insufficient to suit the plants' needs. Regularly adding lots of organic matter, such as compost or peat moss, helps tremendously. Usually, though, I find the healthiest plants are the ones that are also fertilized on a regular basis.

The numbers on fertilizer containers indicate the major plant nutrients by weight. An evergreen fertilizer 30-10-10, for example, contains 30 percent nitrogen, 10 percent phosphate and 10 percent potash.

There are fertilizers designed specifically for trees and shrubs, but you can also use a general, all-purpose fertilizer such as 20-20-20. For best results, consider the primary feature of your tree or shrub. When choosing a fertilizer, keep in mind

- the first number (N=nitrogen) results in lush growth
- the middle number (P=phosphorous) helps with root development and flower formation
- the third number (K=potassium) helps improve fruit quality and disease resistance.

Evergreens—needled ones, such as pine and spruce, as well as broad-leaved ones, such as rhododendron and daphne—have specialized needs. Use an acidic fertilizer formulated specifically for evergreens, such as 30-10-10, and for other shrubs, such as azaleas, that prefer acidic soil.

Certain trees and shrubs, such as Russian olive and caragana, have the ability to 'fix' their own nitrogen. They need less fertilizer than other trees and shrubs.

Although you cannot change a normally green spruce to blue, you can enhance the existing blue colour of spruce needles by using a fertilizer that contains chelated iron.

There are two basic types of fertilizer: those you add directly to soil and those you mix with water first. Granular fertilizers, the first type, are usually slow releasing; they feed plants slowly, over a long period of time. Water-soluble fertilizers, the second type, produce quick results by rapidly releasing all of their nutrients. Either type is fine; it's a matter of personal preference. Some gardeners prefer an annual application of granular fertilizer; others like fertilizing as they water. I sometimes use a combination of both methods.

How Often to Fertilize?

- If you are using *water-soluble* fertilizer, fertilize *once a month* from spring to early August; stop fertilizing after that point to allow growth to slow down in preparation for winter.
- If you are using *granular* fertilizer, fertilize *once a year* in very late fall, which in my area means the end of October. Because granular fertilizers are slow release, they won't stimulate growth before spring. Fall is one of the best times to fertilize, because roots start to grow quickly in spring, before the tree leafs out.

Large, well-established trees and shrubs have extensive, spreading roots that are capable of drawing nutrients from a large area and therefore require less fertilizing. In my experience, trees and shrubs that are watered and fertilized on a regular basis are the healthiest.

If a mature tree is subjected to severe stress, it's a very good idea to give it some fertilizer to help it survive. When my son Bill and daughter-in-law Valerie built their house, the driveway was laid very close to a huge elm—a tree that is treasured by our entire family. The weight of the concrete and the soil compaction by the construction vehicles caused some unavoidable root damage. We helped the elm tree overcome this stress by watering and fertilizing, and today the tree is fine.

TOP: A fertilizer dispenser that attaches to your hose makes applying water-soluble fertilizers much easier.
BOTTOM: Fertilizer spikes are cheap, effective and easy to use. Simply pound the spikes in a band around the tree's drip-line, and the tree will use the fertilizer as it needs it. Avoid direct contact with tree roots.

Give the dog a bone … some bonemeal. Dogs love this stuff, so don't leave an open container lying around.

Special Fertilizers to Use When Planting

Bonemeal is a slow-release, organic fertilizer (4-14-0) that is rich in phosphorous. We use it when we plant trees and shrubs, because phosphorous—indicated by the middle number—encourages root development.

Bare-root trees and shrubs have few roots, unlike container-grown nursery stock, so they can use a stronger boost to help them get going. Fertilize these shrubs or trees with 10-52-10, a plant starter fertilizer that releases its nutrients more quickly than bonemeal. Use 10-52-10 immediately after transplanting and once a week for the next three weeks afterward.

PRUNING

Pruning trees and shrubs can be simple, or it can be very complicated. It's somewhat like looking after a lawn: some people want a carefully trimmed, perfect lawn that could match the greens of any golf course, and others just want grass. How much time and effort you are willing to spend is a matter of choice.

When you hire someone to prune your trees, choose an International Society of Arboriculture (ISA) certified arborist. To earn certification, an arborist must have at least three years of practical work experience or equivalent education, and pass the certification exam. ISA certification guarantees that you will be hiring someone who knows what to do to keep your tree in the best possible health.

When it comes to pruning, remember the three Ds: always remove damaged, diseased or dead branches.

There are other good reasons to prune, but they are not essential to your tree or shrub's survival. You can choose to prune if you want

- more flowers and fruit
- a tidier, more shapely shrub
- a shaped, formal hedge
- controlled growth of certain branches or overall size.

Some trees and shrubs require more pruning, and others need very little. Initially, pruning can seem intimidating—where do you make that first cut, and how do you do it without harming the tree?

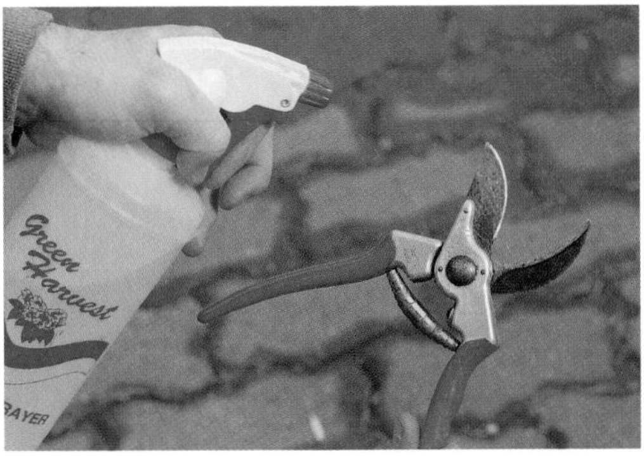

If you have just moved into a new house with a yard full of overgrown, unruly trees and shrubs, the easiest solution is to hire a professional pruner who is a certified arborist. Eventually, you may choose to do the pruning yourself, but at least then you'll be able to more easily tell what guidelines to follow. Removal of large branches or pruning of tall trees should be done by a certified arborist. I, for one, am not eager to clamber up a ladder with a large saw and take responsibility for where that big cut branch may fall.

Pruning is both an art and a science, and it requires a fair bit of knowledge and talent to do it properly. The adverse effects of improper pruning can be as simple as delayed flowering to as drastic as large trees being uprooted during a storm. Knowing when, how and where to cut a branch of a specific tree or shrub species demands that you understand a fair bit about tree physiology in general.

If the branch has been cut incorrectly, it becomes more susceptible to disease and insect pests. It is therefore important to know how, and where, to make a pruning cut that allows the tree to protect itself from further damage.

LEFT: Always ensure that pruning tools are clean and sharp. Dull tools cause 'rough' cuts that are more susceptible to disease. It's a good idea to clean tools between each use with a mild (10 percent) solution of bleach and water. RIGHT: Certified arborists have specialized equipment that enables them to easily reach high branches.

When cut, pines ooze a sticky sap called 'pitch,' which seals pruning wounds. Pitch is loaded with antiseptic chemicals that prevent bacteria from invading the tree. Native Peoples of North America used pitch to treat wounds. Today many household disinfectants contain pine oil.

Excessive pruning or tree injury can cause a number of sprouts to emerge on the trunk base or around pruning cuts. Sprouts should be removed.

As well as having a good general understanding of tree physiology, anyone intending to prune should know the specific needs of each tree or shrub. For example, while most shade trees can be pruned in late winter to early spring, birch and maple trees are exceptions. Because these two species have a tremendous sap flow, they will 'bleed' excessively if pruned too early. It is best to wait until early summer to prune them, after they have fully leafed out.

Ideally, trees and shrubs should be pruned annually—or at least inspected regularly so that you will notice any signs of potential problems.

Mature shrubs benefit from an annual *thinning* and *heading-back*.

- To *thin* a shrub, remove a few of the oldest stems as near to the base as possible. The result is fresh new growth, a better display of flowers and fruit, and improved air circulation within the shrub, which helps to prevent disease.
- To *head-back* a shrub, cut shoots back to a bud or lateral branch. Such a cut promotes more branching from longer, vigorous shoots, resulting in a bushier shrub. Heading-back can also be done to keep a shrub at a fixed size.

Basic Pruning Tools

The basic equipment needed by gardeners to do three-quarters of the pruning in an average yard is good quality secateurs, lopping shears and a pruning saw.

Secateurs (or hand shears) are used to cut branches less than ¾ inch (1.9 cm) in diameter. Always use by-pass or scissor-type secateurs.

Good quality lopping shears (or long-handled shears) are used to cut branches from ¾–1½ inches (1.9–3.8 cm) in diameter. They are very useful for removing old stems from older shrubs.

A proper pruning saw will cut live wood much more efficiently and quickly than a carpenter's saw. A small pruning saw, with a 10-inch (25 cm) blade, can be used to remove branches from 1½–6 inches (3.8–15 cm) in diameter. Pruning saws are a much better and safer tool than chainsaws.

If you have a formal hedge, hedge shears are useful for shearing and shaping. Whenever you are pruning, it's always a good idea to wear protective eye-wear, gloves and a long-sleeved shirt or jacket.

TOP LEFT: Hedge clippers, like Tammy Belley uses, are excellent for shearing and shaping.
TOP RIGHT: Secateurs are excellent for clean, smooth cuts on branches ¾ inch or less in diameter.
MIDDLE: Lopping shears have greater leverage than secateurs, which makes cutting much easier.
BOTTOM: Pruning saws have teeth especially designed for cutting live wood.

Spruce (top) and fir (middle) can be pruned to promote density by removing about a third of the 'candle' in early spring. BOTTOM: Junipers and cedars can be 'headed-back' in spring to maintain size and density.

When to Prune

Pruning at the right time produces the best show of flowers and the healthiest trees and shrubs.

- Prune *spring-flowering* trees and shrubs shortly after they finish blooming and after newly emerged leaves have fully opened.
- Prune *summer-flowering* trees and shrubs in late winter to early spring, before the leaves appear.
- Prune *evergreens* while they are actively growing in late spring.
- Prune *birch* and *maple* trees when they are in full leaf—ideally, these trees should be pruned in July.
- Prune *all other* trees and shrubs while they are dormant in late winter to early spring, before leaves open.

Pruning Evergreens

Most evergreens—those with needles, such as pine, spruce and fir, and those with scale-like leaves, such as cedar and juniper—generally need little pruning.

Broad-leaved evergreens, such as rhododendrons and daphne, can be treated the same way as other flowering shrubs.

Dwarf, mounding and columnar evergreen varieties can be lightly sheared with a clean, sharp set of secateurs or hedge shears to accentuate their shape. For a bushier shrub, clip off one-third of the new growth or *cap* as it is **maturing**—in my area, about mid-June. This will allow new buds to form after shearing and ensure that there is an even flush next year.

Cedars, junipers, hemlock and falsecypress can be cut back by one-quarter to one-third of the new growth after it has emerged in spring but before it has started to harden and mature in mid- to late summer.

1.

2.

3.

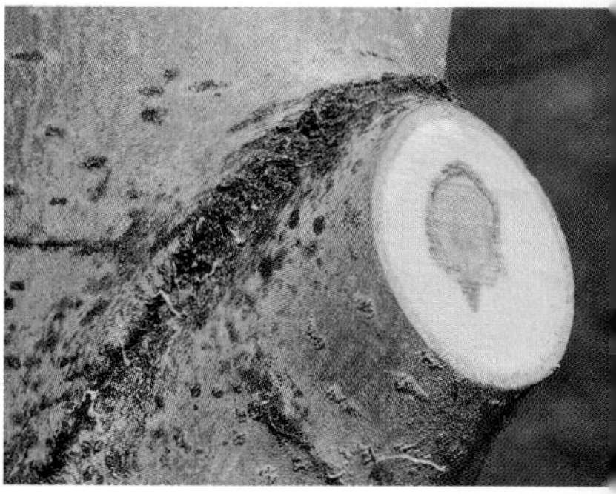

4.

How to Prune a Large Branch

The best time to remove large branches from most shade trees is late winter to early spring, before the leaves obscure the branches. (Remember that birch and maple are exceptions.)

Clear an area beneath the branch to reduce the chance of damage to structures or other plants.

The first step is to make a 'pre-cut' about 18–24 inches (46–61 cm) up the branch from the 'crotch'—where the branch joins the trunk. This 'pre-cut' effectively removes the weight of the branch so that while the final cut is being made, the weight won't carry the branch down and tear the bark. If the branch falls off before you finish cutting it, there is a risk that bark will tear, resulting in a large wound that won't easily heal.

1. *Make a cut on the underside of the branch approximately one-quarter to one-third of the way through the branch.*
2. *Make the top cut slightly ahead—towards the branch end—of the bottom cut. Continue cutting until you are through the branch.*
3. *After the 'pre-cut,' you have a short stub that is easier to remove.*
4. *The final cut should be clean and straight.*

You should call for certified arborist services when

- the branch is too large to support and lower safely
- a limb greater than 6 inches (15 cm) wide needs to be removed
- the tree that needs pruning is near overhead utility lines, or the branches are higher than 10 feet (3 m)
- branches have been damaged by snow, wind or lightning.

Myth: **Pruning paint promotes healing of pruning wounds.**

Fact: Pruning paint can actually promote decay and disease. Wounds on trees don't 'heal'—they may close over but essentially the wounded area is 'walled-off' by the trees' chemical and physical barriers.

Myth: **Before planting a new tree or shrub, you should prune living branches to balance the roots.**

Fact: Removing living branches takes energy from the young plant. Only remove dead branches if dieback occurs after planting.

Myth: **Do not prune trees that 'bleed' in spring.**

Fact: Sap flow is a defence mechanism. If proper tools and methods are used, the amount of injury is reduced. Sap flow may, however, discolour light-coloured bark, causing it to look unsightly. To avoid or minimize excessive sap flow, prune birch and maple when they are in full leaf—any time in July is best in my area.

HOW TO TRAIN SHRUBS TO 'TREE' FORM

- Wait until your shrub is at least two to three years old. Best results are from healthy shrubs.
- Select one strong, vertical stem and prune off all the other basal growth—bottom stems—so that you are left with a single 'trunk.'
- Over the course of the next few seasons, prune the selected stem to encourage vigorous, upright top growth and strong branching, while continuing to remove basal growth and any growth along the 'trunk' area up to a selected branching height.

Mugo pine can be pruned to an attractive bonsai-like tree.

- The height of the canopy is set by removing any new growth between the base of the trunk and a preferred branching height. Above that level, prune to maintain a proper 'tree' form. Remove any crossing branches or weakly attached, diseased or dead branches.
- Depending on the species selected, the 'tree' should be pruned on an annual basis or, at least, inspected annually.

Shrubs commonly trained to 'tree' form include Amur maple, serviceberry, Japanese tree lilac, American highbush cranberry, pincherry, dogwood, alder and Nanking cherry.

Many of the above shrubs can be purchased either in 'tree' form or as a shrub. The benefit of a 'tree' form shrub is that it creates a unique feature for a small garden, or can be used as a small tree or focal point in a large shrub bed.

'Woodwardii' cedar makes an excellent informal hedge.

Pruning Hedges

- Formal hedges should be pruned at least twice each growing season.
- Shear all sides of your hedge. Pruning only along the top reduces the number of new twigs sprouting at the base.
- Make your hedge slightly narrower at the top than at the bottom, to allow light to penetrate to lower branches and encourage bushy lower growth.
- For directions on how to prune in order to fix an old hedge that is not performing well, see *Pruning to Rejuvenate Hedges*. This type of pruning can greatly extend a hedge's life.

Pruning to Rejuvenate Hedges

- If you've inherited an old, established hedge when you moved into an older neighbourhood, or your hedge has lots of dieback, then 'rejuvenation' is a good idea. The purpose of this type of pruning is to
    - remove dead, diseased or insect-infested branches
    - stimulate new growth and vigorous upright stems
    - 're-train' the hedge—to either shorten or narrow the hedge entirely.

- The best time to prune for rejuvenation is late winter to early spring before leaves appear.
- For best results, use long-handled lopping shears or a pruning saw. Do not use a chain-saw; cutting at ground level is awkward at best and can be dangerous with power equipment. Chain-saws aren't suited to cutting numerous, small, densely clustered branches, and the resulting cuts are not 'clean'—they may decrease vigour and eventually cause dieback or death.
- Cut back all stems as low to the ground as possible. Do not cut below ground level, since it can promote sprouts from below a graft if the plants were initially grafted.
- Fertilize every three to four weeks from spring to mid-summer.
- Allow new stems to develop for one full growing season before doing any further pruning.
- If new stems are very densely clustered, prune again the next year, in late winter to early spring while the shrubs are still dormant. Thin out excess stems to promote thick yet not congested growth.
- Maintain your hedge's form, height, width and density by setting up and following a regular annual pruning schedule. Combine both heading-back and thinning techniques for best results.

SEASONAL CARE FOR TREES & SHRUBS

One of the most important steps in pest prevention is to clean up the garden every fall. Pick up and dispose of any fallen leaves, which may harbour over-wintering insect and disease pests.

Fall

- Clean up fallen leaves. Remove and destroy any diseased or insect-infested plant material to ensure a healthy start next spring. Never add diseased material to your compost bin.
- Water heavily a few weeks prior to freeze-up, which in my area occurs about late October. 'Watering-in,' as it is called, is important because it prevents roots from being damaged in cold, dry soil.
- Use tree guards or wraps to protect tree trunks from sun scald and trunk injury (splitting and blistering of trunks from repeated heating and freezing).

Additional Care Required for Tender Evergreens

- Protect susceptible evergreens from winter damage and browning of foliage by erecting a screen. You'll need a few 2x2 inch (5x5 cm) stakes from 4–8 feet (1.2–2.4 m) tall, some burlap and a few staples.
- In late fall, before the ground freezes, drive the stakes into the ground around the windward and southern perimeter of the plant. Allow about 4–8 inches (10–20 cm) between the stakes and the outermost edge of the plant.
- Just after the ground freezes, staple the burlap to the outside of the framework to create a semi-circular screen.

Burlap attached to a wooden frame provides a cheap and effective screen that helps reduce winter injury to sensitive evergreens.

Winter

- Remember that snow provides moisture and acts as insulation to prevent plant damage caused by freezing and thawing during and after winter warm spells.
- Whenever possible during winter, cover tender or evergreen shrubs with fresh snow to prevent repeated thawing and freezing. Do not use hard snow or snow that contains de-icing salt. Try to add more snow whenever shovelling walks; often only the branches exposed above the snowline die.
- If there is a wet, heavy snowfall, remove snow from branches as much as possible, to prevent them from breaking.

Spring

- In late winter to early spring, prune most types of trees and shrubs. See page 62 for details.
- Throw snow overtop of shrubs in dry, sheltered beds underneath house overhangs.
- Make a habit of annual spring maintenance: remove all dead, damaged or diseased branches.
- As soon as the garden is dry enough to walk on, clear away any debris left from fall. Once leafbuds break open and you can see what survived the winter, cut off the dead parts of branches.

Additional Care Required for Tender Evergreens

- As soon as the ground thaws, remove protective screens from evergreens.

Ensure that evergreens are well watered in late fall to minimize winter browning.

Trees can be used as 'indicator plants.' As soon as the leafbuds of native trees start to swell, the area is pretty much safe from hard frosts until fall, and protective mulch coverings can be removed from any tender roses and perennials in your garden.

Common Problems with Trees & Shrubs

'If a tree dies, plant another in its place.'

—Linnaeus (Carl von Linné), (1707–78)

Although trees and shrubs can be attacked by a multitude of different insects and diseases, surprisingly few cause any long-term damage. Often it's only the unhealthiest trees and shrubs that succumb to pests. Frequently, insects are blamed for most problems when the real cause of a tree's decline could be poor soil or a severe lack of water. The insects are really just indicators of a much greater problem.

Before any insect or disease becomes a pest, three conditions must exist: first and foremost, you must have the pest; secondly, you must have a susceptible host—a plant that the pest is capable of attacking; thirdly, you must have the right environment.

The first two conditions, pest and host, seem rather obvious. If you have the right insect on a tree that it likes to eat, the insect is going to want to eat the tree. The third condition, the environment, is less obvious. If you have the pest and the host but the environment is not right—the tree is very healthy and able to resist the pest's attack—then very little damage will be done to the tree.

The damage to spruce trees caused by spider mites is an example of this triangle. Spruce spider mites are very tiny insects that feed on sap from spruce needles, causing needles to become greyish and speckled, and the spruce tree to lose a tremendous amount of vigor.

Fall needle drop is natural for most spruce, pine and fir species.

Out of the hundreds of spider mite–damaged spruce boughs that customers have brought in to show me over the years, not one bough was from a healthy tree. You can distinguish a healthy bough from an unhealthy bough by looking at the needles. When spruce trees grow in hot, dry areas with insufficient moisture, their needles are smaller and have a very thin protective wax coating. Without that wax coating, the environment is just right for the spider mites, and they are able to cause severe damage.

Identification of every insect or disease is less important than is a gardener's understanding of the most common problems—which arise for reasons other than insects or disease. Below are some of the questions that I hear most often at our garden centre.

Why do the leaves on my newly planted tree wilt and turn brown, and what can I do about it?

Infrequent or inadequate watering is the likely cause, particularly on newly planted trees. See page 53 for details on proper watering. Remember that trees need watering more often during heat waves. If the tree was not grown in a container before transplanting, water several times a week.

My shrub was growing fine when I initially planted it two years ago, but now the leaves are sparse and weak looking. Why? What can be done?

Light is critical for proper plant growth. If a sun-loving shrub receives too little light, it tends to drop leaves and the remaining leaves are soft and weak. For shady areas, choose shrubs that thrive with less light. See page 32 for a list.

Why do the leaves on my shrub look 'bleached'? Can you help me solve this problem?

Excessive sunlight can scorch leaves on plants that enjoy shade. Scorching can also occur on sun-loving plants that were grown in partial shade, and then suddenly exposed to strong sunlight. Again, choose the right plants for the right location and don't prune excessively, particularly during hot, sunny weather.

My shade tree was growing fine during spring but in July the leaves developed a scorched appearance around the edges. What can I do about it?

Scorched leaves can often occur when hot, dry winds are prevalent during summer. The tree's root system is simply incapable of replacing the amount of moisture lost through the leaves, and scorching results. Trees that have damaged root systems or a restricted root zone suffer the greatest. This problem is all too common on street trees growing near or in sidewalks. Leaf scorch can be substantially reduced by ensuring that the trees are consistently and thoroughly watered during hot weather, and the roots have lots of room to grow.

My shrubs grew wonderfully during the summer but died back severely the following spring. Why? What can be done?

Winter damage is the likely cause. The severity of damage depends on several factors: how suitable the shrub is for a particular climate; how well it was prepared for winter; and the degree of winter and spring temperature fluctuations. I find that the better my plants are prepared for winter and into spring, the fewer problems I encounter. See *Seasonal Care for Trees & Shrubs* on page 68.

Why does my young shade tree have a big dead patch on the trunk? What can be done about this problem?

If the dead patch occurs near ground level, it could be caused by 'mechanical damage'—from lawn mowers, weed whippers, dog chains, etc. This type of damage is extremely serious and can easily kill a tree. The best solution is prevention. Never tie anything around a tree trunk, and if possible, leave a turf-free area around the tree to keep mowers and trimmers away.

If the dead patch is higher on the trunk, it may still be the result of some type of mechanical damage. More likely, however, the cause is freezing and thawing of bark. In my region, this type of damage occurs primarily on the side of the trunk that faces south or southwest. Typically during winter, and particularly in early spring, the sun heats those sides of the tree, causing the trunk to thaw. When temperatures drop below freezing at night, the trunk tissue freezes and becomes damaged. Any screening material that keeps direct sunlight off the trunk helps considerably (see page 68).

I sprayed my trees to kill the bugs, and now the trees are not growing properly. Why? What can be done?

Pest control products used incorrectly can cause severe injury to plants. I find that most problems related to pest control products arise from either the wrong product being used on the pest, or the pest being incorrectly identified. Before you spray any pesticide, ask yourself if the insect is actually a pest or if it is harmless? Many insects are harmless; some even help fight off other pests.

If the insect is actually a pest, is its population large enough to cause damage? If control is warranted, can the pest be eliminated by other means—pruning, or hand-picking it off the tree? If a chemical treatment is required, be sure to choose and use the product correctly.

Whenever you run into a severe pest problem, try to obtain a 'sample' of the infested area from the shrub or tree. Take the leaves or other plant parts, inside a plastic bag, to a reputable garden centre with staff trained in pest identification and control. Let staff identify the problem and recommend the best and safest method of treatment.

My soil is very poor and few shrubs grow well. How do I correct this situation?

Most of the soils that cause problems share one trait: they are low in organic matter. Organic matter is the component of soil that gives it a nice 'rich' feel. Compost, peat moss and well-rotted manure are good sources of organic matter, and they should be added regularly to improve the soil.

Work with care around your plants. Tree stakes pounded too close to the tree will damage the roots, too many attacks by weed-eaters or lawn mowers can eventually kill a tree, and tight support wires or ties can choke a plant or tree and kill it.

Tree collars provide excellent protection against lawn mowers and rodents.

My shrub looks 'okay' but it's not really vigorous or lush. Why? Is there something I can do to help the situation?

Again, it could be a problem with not enough organic matter, but if your soil looks quite rich, the problem may simply be a nutrient deficiency. Having your soil tested is an excellent way of determining not only if the soil is lacking particular nutrients, but also if its pH balance is correct.

A simpler approach, although not the most scientific, is to just give the shrub a shot of fertilizer on a regular basis. I like to use a complete fertilizer: one that contains nitrogen, phosphorous and potassium. Fertilize more frequently as the shrub ages. Older trees and shrubs have a more extensive root system and are thus better able to draw up plant nutrients from a greater area. Just be careful not to over-fertilize. Too much fertilizer can cause excessively lush, weak growth or even burn roots. I prefer to use less fertilizer more often, rather than giving my trees and shrubs a lot all at once.

The leaves on my tree look 'veiny.' What's the problem, and is there a solution?

Iron deficiency causes leaves to become 'veiny.' In alkaline soil, it's difficult for roots to absorb iron. Adding chelated iron (a form of iron easily absorbed by plants) to the soil will alleviate this problem.

Alder

Alnus tenuifolia
Mountain Alder
River Alder
Speckled Alder
Thin-leaf Alder

Height • 30–35 feet (9.1–11 m)

Spread • 20–25 feet (6.1–7.6 m)

Flowers • greenish-yellow catkins in early spring

Fruit • cone-like seeds (winged nutlet)

Growth Rate • slow to medium

Lifespan • short to average

Zone Rating • 2

Alder is related to birch, and like birch, it loves moist soil. In the wild, alder grows along the banks of rivers and lakes; in the garden, it's a good choice for low-lying, wet areas where water pools periodically. Alder is a large shrub or small tree that bears catkins and seed-cones similar to those of birch. The bark is a lovely greenish bronze. The leaves are a glossy dark green on top with pale, ribbed, sticky undersides; they are larger than birch leaves. Alder is not the showiest shrub, but it provides a solution for difficult areas of the yard where few other plants grow well.

GROWING

Sun; best in moist to wet soil.

As a large, informal screen; for naturalizing.

Alder wood has a remarkable resistance to wet rot, making it a prime choice for bridge posts and pilings, including those that support bridges in cities like Amsterdam and Venice. Dutch wooden shoes are made of alder.

LEFT: Alder is a nice, small tree that tolerates poorly drained soil extremely well.
RIGHT: Alder has beautiful, shiny bark.

RECOMMENDED SPECIES OR VARIETIES

Mountain Alder

Also called river alder, speckled alder and thin-leaf alder.

TIPS

Prune alder when it is in full leaf. If it is pruned in spring while sap is running, it will 'bleed' excessively. You will be left with an unsightly tree for the rest of the season, but pruning won't actually harm it. Sometimes the sweet sap also attracts insects.

If you prefer, you can safely prune alder at the same time as most other shrubs: in late winter or early spring, before the leaves open. This shrub can be grown as a small tree. See *How to Train Shrubs to 'Tree' Form* on page 64.

You can use alder wood for smoking fish and meat. It is also popular for bridge foundations, because of its durability underwater. The charcoal in gunpowder comes from alder wood, and the bark has been used to make throat medicine, dyes and tannin.

Alder is particularly attractive in winter, when the long, slender branches are often decorated with hoarfrost.

Arrowwood

Viburnum dentatum
Arrowwood

Height • 10–20 feet (3–6.1 m)

Spread • 7–15 feet (2.1–4.6 m)

Flowers • large clusters of white flowers in late spring

Fruit • large clusters of blue-black berries in fall

Growth Rate • medium

Lifespan • short

Zone Rating • 2

Arrowwood is a large, dense, rounded shrub that blooms in late spring with clusters of creamy white flowers. Its foliage is lustrous and dark green. Depending on the weather, fruit colour can vary from year to year. Arrowwood is an adaptable and durable shrub, growing well in sun or partial shade and in heavy or sandy soil. It is rarely bothered by insects or disease. Fall colour varies from yellow to red to reddish purple, depending, apparently to an equal degree, on weather and genetics.

GROWING

Sun to partial shade; best in moist, well-drained soil.

Feature shrub, in mass plantings, as a screen or hedge.

Stop fertilizing by about the beginning of August.

Arrowwood's strong, straight branches are said to have been popular with Native Peoples for making arrows, hence the name.

RECOMMENDED SPECIES OR VARIETIES

Arrowwood

TIPS

Arrowwood has the greatest berry production when other arrowwoods are planted nearby for cross pollination. The shiny berries attract many birds.

Arrowwood tends to spread readily, which is great if you are growing it as a hedge or screen. If you want to control spreading, prune the basal growth.

When planting arrowwood as a formal hedge (one which you would clip to shape), space the shrubs 2–3 feet (61–91 cm) apart. If you want an informal hedge (one in which the shrubs are allowed to retain their natural shape), space 10–12 feet (3–3.7 m) apart.

Arrowwood requires general pruning; prune while it is dormant, in late winter to early spring, before leaves appear.

TOP LEFT: Arrowwood has been cultivated since 1736.
TOP RIGHT: Arrowwood blooms for about two weeks in late spring, with showy, 2–4-inch (5.1–10 cm) wide flower clusters.
BOTTOM: The species name dentatum *means 'toothed,' referring to the jagged edges of the leaves.*

Ash

Fraxinus nigra
Black Ash
Swamp Ash

Fraxinus pennsylvanica
Green Ash
Red Ash

Fraxinus mandshurica
Manchurian Ash

Height • 40–50 feet (12–15 m)

Spread • 30–45 feet (9.1–14 m)

Flowers • not showy

Fruit • winged seeds only on female trees

Growth Rate • medium

Lifespan • long

Zone Rating
Black: 3
Green: 2
Manchurian: 3

As well as supposedly bringing luck, ashes are remarkable trees with a long list of virtues. They are tough, hardy, disease resistant and drought tolerant; they thrive in a wide range of conditions and need little pruning. Many varieties are seedless, making them tidy trees for growing near decks or patios. In fall, ashes are among the first trees to change colour. Black ash is an elegant tree that grows well in wet to dry sites. It makes an attractive addition to yards, parks or commercial sites. Green ash is a common shade tree in yards and boulevards. It is less tolerant of moist soil than other types. Manchurian ash is a very attractive, wide-headed tree with dense foliage that turns bright yellow in fall.

GROWING

Sun; average to moist soil.

Shade tree; good boulevard tree. Black ash or Manchurian ash as feature tree. Green ash as windbreak.

RECOMMENDED SPECIES OR VARIETIES

Black Ash

'Fallgold': 40–50 feet (12–15 m) tall and 30–35 feet (9.1–11 m) wide; foliage looks different from most ashes because the leaves have no stalks; turns vibrant yellow in fall; holds leaves longer than most ashes; a seedless variety from Manitoba.

Green Ash

'Patmore Green': 45–50 feet (14–15 m) tall and 35–40 feet (11–12 m) wide; an extremely hardy, seedless variety selected from native trees growing near Edmonton, Alberta.

TOP: The variety 'Patmore Green' leafs out earlier in spring and keeps its leaves longer in fall than most other green ashes.
BOTTOM: 'Fallgold' is a black ash variety noted for its outstanding, long-lasting (when compared to other ashes) fall foliage.

'Even ash, I do thee pluck,
hoping thus to meet good luck,
If no good luck I get from thee,
I'll wish I'd left thee on the tree.'

—*old English rhyme*

LEFT & RIGHT: Manchurian ash has a dense, compact growth habit and attractive lance-shaped leaves.

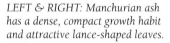

An ash leaf with an equal number of divisions on each side is supposed to bring good luck. If you find one, pick the leaf and recite this rhyme:

'An even-leaved ash,
and a four-leaved clover
You'll see your love,
'fore the day is over.'

Manchurian Ash

'**Mancana**': 40–50 feet (12–15 m) tall and wide; a more compact, seedless variety from Morden, Manitoba.

TIPS

To avoid excessive bleeding of sap, prune ashes while they are in full leaf during summer. The loss of sap through bleeding does not harm the tree but sap deposition on the trunk can be unsightly. You can, if you like, prune while the tree is dormant in late winter to early spring, before leaves appear.

Ash trees turn colour about two weeks earlier in fall than most other trees.

One disadvantage of ashes is that they are one of the last trees to leaf out in spring and one of the first to lose their leaves in fall. You can take advantage of this feature, however, by planting an ash near a flowerbed, because perennials growing underneath the tree receive more sunlight, giving them a headstart in spring.

Manchurian ash and black ash thrive even in low-lying, wet areas.

The winged seeds of ash trees are called 'samaras.' Female ash trees can produce large amounts of seed, which hang on bare branches and look rather messy in winter. Seedlings sprout up everywhere, even in eavestroughs. Seedless varieties—male trees—are preferable for growing in yards.

In Norse mythology, a mighty ash tree called Yggdrasil linked the earth with heaven and hell. Yggdrasil was the tree of life; all ashes are now considered to have this symbolic meaning.

Aspen

Populus tremula
Swedish Aspen
European Aspen

Populus tremuloides
Trembling Aspen
Quaking Aspen

Height • 40–60 feet (12–18 m)

Spread • 5–30 feet (1.5–9.1 m)

Flowers • long catkins in spring

Fruit • capsules

Growth Rate • fast

Lifespan • average

Zone Rating
Swedish: 2
Trembling: 1

The most distinctive feature of aspen is its leaves, which tremble and shiver in the slightest breeze. Even a light wind causes a very soothing, soft, rustling sound. Native Peoples called aspen 'the noisy leaf tree.' The Columnar variety of Swedish aspen is quite a narrow, tall tree, growing about six times taller than wide. It looks dramatic in groups or in front of a house, and it provides an effective solution for limited spaces. Trembling aspen is a tough, adaptable shade tree, and one of the best sources of yellow fall foliage.

GROWING
Sun; prefers moist, well-drained soil.

Windbreak. Trembling aspen for large, open areas. Swedish Columnar aspen as a feature tree, beside decks and pathways, in 'tight' spaces; good for smaller yards.

LEFT: Swedish Columnar aspen is one of the nicest feature trees for smaller yards. It can be planted next to the house, as its smaller, shallow roots are not invasive. RIGHT: Although trembling aspens are not suitable as feature trees, they are rather attractive in groups with their white bark and leaves.

RECOMMENDED SPECIES OR VARIETIES

Swedish Aspen

Swedish Columnar (*P. tremula* 'Erecta'): 30–45 feet (9.1–14 m) tall and 5–8 feet (1.5–2.4 m) wide; a nice columnar tree with a dense canopy; dark green leaves with wavy edges; excellent screen or windbreak; all trees sold are males, which do not produce fluff.

Trembling Aspen

30–50 feet (9.1–15 m) tall and 30 feet (9.1 m) wide; an upright, oval-headed tree; rounded, bright green leaves; smooth, nearly white bark that darkens and roughens with age.

Aspens spread by suckers, and a large stand of aspen in a forest may originate from a single tree. In fact, the most massive organism in the world is said to be a network of trembling aspen trees growing in the Wasatch Mountains, Utah, covering 106 acres (43 ha) and weighing an estimated 6600 tons (6000 tonnes)! These trees have a single root system and are 'clones'—they are genetically uniform, changing colour and shedding leaves in unison.

If you ever get lost in the woods, an aspen tree could help you by letting you know what direction you are facing. The chalky-white material that is found on its bark is usually thickest on the south side of the tree.

TIPS

Generally, little pruning is needed, but when necessary, prune in late winter to early spring, before the leaves appear.

Aspens are small members of the poplar family. Like all poplars, aspens produce fluffy seeds in spring, but to a far lesser degree than other poplars.

Both male and female aspens produce flowers in long catkins that appear about a month before the leaves open in spring. Only female trees produce the fluffy seed, however, so nurseries quite often sell only male trees.

Trembling aspen is usually available in a wide range of sizes, from tiny rooted cuttings to huge, 4-inch (10 cm) caliper trees that need to be mechanically planted with a tree spade. See *Buying Trees & Shrubs* on page 35.

Aspen tree, aspen tree, shake and shiver, instead of me. It was once believed that by cutting off a lock of your hair, tying it to an aspen tree and reciting this line, you would be cured of fever and chills.

Aspens are adaptable trees that grow well in clay, sandy or shallow soil.

To reduce suckering, plant aspens in an area where their roots will not be disturbed by activities such as digging.

Swedish Columnar aspens do not produce suckers or basal shoots unless under stress. These narrow, upright trees are excellent for windbreaks, defining boundaries, or creating a screen around small properties. To create a solid 'wall,' space the trees 4 feet (1.2 m) apart.

As well as providing a lovely sound, the nearly constant motion of the aspen's leaves helps deter insects from feeding or laying eggs on them.

Although aspens are generally considered to be rather short-lived trees (with an average lifespan of about 50 years), in an ideal environment they can live much longer. There is an immense trembling aspen in the Swan Hills area of Alberta that is estimated to be more than 125 years old. It is about 95 feet (29 m) tall and 25 feet (7.6 m) wide—the largest aspen on record in Alberta.

Aspen is one of the best trees for fall colour. Its leaves turn a warm, bright yellow. In fall, the aspens of Jasper National Park set the mountainsides aglow, with the yellow leaves highlighted amidst the dark foliage of evergreens.

Aspen is the most widespread tree in North America. It grows from the tree-line in Alaska and Canada all the way to northern Mexico.

Azalea

Rhododendron x 'Cannon's Double'
Cannon's Double Azalea

Rhododendron x 'Northern Lights'
Northern Lights Azalea

Height • 2½–5 feet (76–150 cm)

Spread • 2½–5 feet (76–150 cm)

Flowers • large, pink, purple, orange or white flower clusters in spring

Fruit • capsules

Growth Rate • slow

Lifespan • short to medium

Zone Rating
Cannon's Double: 5 [3]
Northern Lights: 3

Azaleas are one of the most spectacular spring-blooming shrubs. They are often confused with rhododendrons, which is not surprising. Since 1834, azaleas have been botanically classified as rhododendrons. Gardeners, however, still consider the two to be distinctly different shrubs. The easiest way to distinguish between the two is to see them in bloom: most azaleas, hardy to northern gardens, bloom on bare branches before the leaves appear; rhododendrons bloom while in full leaf since most of them are evergreen. Most azaleas are deciduous—they lose their leaves in fall. Although the flower clusters look similar, under close examination you'll notice that azalea flowers are trumpet-shaped while rhododendron flowers are bell-shaped. Both shrubs make magnificent additions to the garden. Planted in a perennial bed, azaleas often provide the first colour, as they bloom earlier than most perennials. As well as providing a splendid show of flowers in spring, azaleas look dramatic in fall when their foliage turns wine-red.

Azaleas are one of the showiest spring-flowering shrubs.

Cannon's Double is an unusual azalea. Few others have double flowers, and it is rare for a hardy azalea to have two-toned petals.

GROWING

Sun to partial shade; rich, moist, acidic soil.

Accent in flowerbed or with other shrubs, in rock gardens, as a foundation plant.

Use an acidic fertilizer, such as 30-10-10, monthly, three to four times each year. Stop fertilizing at the end of July.

Azaleas usually need very little pruning. Prune only after flowering, to allow flowerbuds to form for next spring's bloom.

RECOMMENDED SPECIES OR VARIETIES

Cannon's Double

3–4 feet (91–120 cm) tall and wide; deep pink flowers with orange shading; dark green leaves; a beautiful addition to any garden; flowerbuds hardy to -26° F (-32° C).

'Azalea' is Latin for 'dry plant.' Originally it was thought that azaleas would thrive only in arid conditions, but in reality, these plants do best in moist soil.

LEFT: 'Orchid Lights' is a compact azalea that is extremely showy in bloom. It is the hardiest variety in the Northern Lights series.
RIGHT: Azalea flowers usually have five protruding stamens, whereas rhododendron flowers have 10 stamens. 'Golden Lights' is also fragrant.
BOTTOM: You can't miss an azalea in full bloom! The dramatic display of flowers lasts anywhere from 10 to 20 days. 'Pink Lights' has deep pink flowerbuds that open to light pink flowers.

Northern Lights Series

This extremely hardy group of azaleas was developed in Minnesota by crossing hardy native azaleas with large-flowered garden azaleas. The series includes the following varieties:

'**Golden Lights**': 2½–3½ feet (76–110 cm) tall and wide; fragrant, deep yellow-orange flowers; flowerbuds hardy to -31° F (-35° C).

'**Hi-Lights**': 3–4 feet (91–120 cm) tall and wide; fragrant, creamy white flowers; flowerbuds hardy to -40° F (-40° C).

'**Orchid Lights**': 2½ feet (76 cm) tall and wide; pale purple flowers; flowerbuds hardy to -45° F (-43° C).

'**Pink Lights**': 3½–4 feet (1.1–1.2 m) tall and wide; light pink flowers; flowerbuds hardy to -35° F (-37° C).

'**Rosy Lights**': 4–5 feet (1.2–1.5 m) tall and 5–6 feet (1.5–1.8 m) wide; deep pink flowers; flowerbuds hardy to -45° F (-43° C).

'**Spicy Lights**': 3–3½ feet (91–110 cm) tall and wide; fragrant, dark apricot-orange flowers; flowerbuds hardy to -29° F (-34° C).

'**White Lights**': 3½–4 feet (1.1–1.2 m) tall and wide; pink flowerbuds open to fragrant, white flowers with pink high-lights; flowerbuds hardy to -35° F (-37° C).

TIPS

Only a few azalea varieties are cold-hardy, so be sure to choose a recommended variety.

Although its official hardiness rating is for zone 5, we have successfully grown Cannon's Double in zone 3 for years.

In my region, even the hardiest azaleas do best in a protected site. Ideally, find a spot in your garden that is sunny in summer but shaded in winter, and protected from wind. Good snowcover throughout winter helps; if possible, cover the plants with light, fresh snow.

These shrubs are prone to powdery mildew. To help prevent this fungal disease, plant azaleas in a sunny site with good air circulation: don't crowd the plants. Water at the base of the shrub rather than from overhead.

Azaleas thrive when soil is mulched. A mulch helps to keep the soil cool and improves moisture retention. Use composted spruce or pine needles, or shredded fir bark, because these mulches also help to increase soil acidity, which azaleas like.

LEFT: Azalea's tubular, 1-inch (2.5 cm) flowers attract hummingbirds. 'Spicy Lights' is a fragrant variety.
BOTTOM: The purple-red fall foliage of 'Rosy Lights' is an added bonus long after the shrub's pink flowers fade.

Birch

Betula nana
Dwarf Birch

Betula papyrifera
Paper Birch
Canoe Birch
White Birch

Betula pendula
Weeping Birch
European Silver Birch
European White Birch

Height • 2–70 feet (61 cm–21 m)

Spread • 2–50 feet (61 cm–15 m)

Flowers • long catkins in spring

Fruit • cone-like seedheads
shed in fall (winged nutlets)

Growth Rate
dwarf varieties: slow
most varieties: medium to fast

Lifespan
dwarf varieties: short
most varieties: average

Zone Rating • 2 [1]

With their bright white bark and rich yellow fall leaves, birches are among my favourite trees. In Sweden, where my mother was born, bundles of birch branches are sold in outdoor markets about the time that Lent begins. The branches are a foot or two long and have colourful dyed feathers wired onto the ends. If you put these branches into a vase with water, the leaves emerge in a couple of weeks—a welcome sign of spring for city apartment dwellers. The best-known birch is the paper birch, with its wonderful, thin bark that peels away from the trunk. Weeping birches have long, graceful, drooping branches. Most people think of birches as huge, towering trees, but there are also dwarf varieties that remain as short as 2 feet (61 cm)! Even in a small garden, you can grow a birch tree.

Birches are splendid, moisture-loving trees with attractive bark and bright fall foliage.

Dwarf birch is a native birch that is extremely tough. The leaves of dwarf birch are small—just ¼–½ inch (0.6–1.3 cm) across.

GROWING

Sun; rich, moist, acidic soil is best.

Feature tree, shade tree. Dwarf birches in rock gardens, flowerbeds or shrub beds, on decks and patios, as a screen.

Keep birches well watered; these trees do not do as well in dry soil.

RECOMMENDED SPECIES OR VARIETIES

Dwarf Birch

2–4 feet (61–120 cm) tall and wide; a very fine-textured, dwarf tree with small, rounded leaves; excellent for rock gardens or small shrub beds; does well in wet soil.

TOP LEFT & RIGHT: The species name papyrifera *means 'paper-like bark.' The smooth, chalky-white, papery bark of the paper birch peels in layers, and it is often used for crafts. Native Peoples made their famous birch-bark canoes from this tree, hence its other common name: canoe birch. BOTTOM LEFT: The young leaves of 'Purple Rain' are bright purple. They turn dark purple in summer and remain that colour until the tree drops its leaves.*

Paper Birch

Paper: 50–70 feet (15–21 m) tall and 35–45 feet (11–14 m) wide; an extremely handsome tree, especially against an evergreen background; excellent for large area plantings; papery white bark; cultivated since 1750.

'**Purple Rain**': 40–50 feet (12–15 m) tall and 20–30 feet (6.1–9.1 m) wide; a very graceful, oval tree; unique purple foliage is striking against papery white bark; an uncommon variety.

Birches were once considered to be holy trees.

Weeping Birch

Cutleaf (*B. pendula* 'Lacinata'): 45–50 feet (14–15 m) tall and 20–30 feet (6.1–9.1 m) wide; a very attractive, fine-textured tree with weeping branches and dark green, lacy leaves.

LEFT: Cutleaf weeping birch is a slightly smaller tree than paper birch (opposite page). Both have the characteristic beautiful, papery white bark, but it's harder to see the bark of Cutleaf weeping birch under its weeping branches. This variety is an excellent choice for a small area.
RIGHT: Cutleaf weeping birch has vibrant fall colour.

Birch trees can be 'tapped,' like maples, for their sweet sap during a five- to six-week period from the end of March to May. Collected sap is boiled down to make birch syrup, which has a light 'honey' flavour but is not as sweet as maple syrup. One gallon (4.5 l) of birch sap makes 3 ounces (85 ml) of birch syrup. North American settlers used birch syrup as a substitute for treacle. In Europe today, mineral-rich 'birch water'—syrup mixed with apple juice—is popular as a health tonic.

'Trost Dwarf' looks quite different from most birches, and, like all dwarf trees, it is slow growing—the tree shown above was planted in 1971. 'Trost Dwarf' has thin, thread-like leaves; contrast its fine-textured foliage by growing it with coarse-textured evergreens, such as pine or spruce.

The seeds of birches provide a plentiful food source in fall and early winter for many birds, including goldfinches, chickadees, blue jays, waxwings, pine siskins, common redpolls and grosbeaks.

'Trost Dwarf': 3–5 feet (91–150 cm) tall and wide; thread-like leaves; a very compact, shrubby variety; slow growing, takes 8 to 10 years to reach mature size; an interesting addition to any garden.

Young's (*B. pendula* 'Youngii'): the most pendulous birch; white bark; an excellent specimen tree; height can be set by pruning or training; can be trained to grow in all sorts of directions; also available in 'twisted stem' form; fits into almost any landscape.

TIPS

Birch trees are sometimes sold in 'clump' form—as a multi-stemmed tree as opposed to a tree with a single main trunk. 'Clump' birches are very attractive.

Although paper birch's official hardiness rating is zone 2, we have seen large paper birches growing in zone 1.

Trees growing in lawns often lack water because the grass absorbs most of the moisture before it gets to the tree roots. Birches are moisture loving, and, unless they are planted in a naturally moist area, even mature trees should be watered regularly, especially during summer heat waves.

The roots of birch trees are sensitive to high soil temperatures, which can occur in summer if the lawn is closely clipped, or if low-growing plants that had offered shade are removed. If the soil becomes too warm, a birch's leaves will eventually turn yellow and drop, especially from the top of the tree and from some side branches. Any remaining foliage will be sparse and yellow. Frequently, in successive years, the tops of these trees will die and the lower branches will have only sparse foliage. Prevent such dieback by keeping the base of birch trees moist and cool.

Birch is the provincial tree of Saskatchewan.

Young's birch can be topped at the final desired height and trained to flow in any direction.

It is commonly advised not to prune birch trees before they are in full leaf. The timing is more for aesthetics than health. The sap of birches runs in spring, and if a tree is pruned while sap is running, it will 'bleed' excessively, leaving an unsightly tree. The sweet sap also attracts insects. Therefore, it is best to wait until early summer to prune birch. Ideally, July is the best time. Remember, though, that pruning while the sap is running does not harm the trees.

If a old birch tree dies, take advantage of it—birch is good firewood, and the papery bark is great for starting fires.

It was once customary for North American farmers to drag a large brush made from birch branches over a freshly ploughed field, in the belief that this would encourage germination.

Bog Rosemary

Andromeda polifolia
Bog Rosemary

Height • 1–1½ feet (30–46 cm)

Spread • 2–3 feet (61–91 cm)

Flowers • tiny, light pink flowers in mid-spring

Fruit • capsules

Growth Rate • slow

Lifespan • short

Zone Rating • 2

The name of this small evergreen shrub says it all: bog rosemary thrives in moist to wet bog-like sites, and it looks a lot like herb rosemary, with similar stiff, leathery, needle-like leaves. Its botanical name also refers to its love of water. Carl Linnaeus, the Swedish botanist who in the 1700s master-minded the now-internationally accepted system of nomenclature for plants and animals, named this shrub Andromeda. In Greek mythology, Andromeda was a princess who was rescued from a sea-monster. Linnaeus wrote that bog rosemary 'is always fixed on some hilly turfy hillock in the midst of the swamps, as Andromeda herself was chained to a rock in the sea, which bathed her feet as the fresh water does the roots of this plant.'

Bog rosemary is a lovely, uncommon little shrub for moist sites.

GROWING

Sun to partial shade; moist to wet soil.

Alongside garden ponds, in rock gardens, as edging.

Fertilize with an acidic or evergreen fertilizer, such as 30-10-10, once a month from May to August.

RECOMMENDED SPECIES OR VARIETIES

'Blue Ice': 8–12 inches (20–30 cm) tall and 1½ feet (46 cm) wide; unique, icy-blue foliage; looks particularly stunning growing next to silvery-leaved plants.

TIPS

Add generous amounts of peat moss, compost or other organic matter when planting to help improve the soil's water retention. Bog rosemary does best in slightly acidic soil with lots of organic matter.

Prune bog rosemary after flowering to shear or shape the bush.

If you have a garden pond, grow bog rosemary around the edge. These shrubs do well even when grown in very wet soil.

A good snowcover throughout winter helps prevent the evergreen foliage from browning, but too much heavy snow can cause this shrub to have an open centre.

Although the leaves look like needles, they are not. Their needle-like appearance is due to the tightly curled leaf edges.

TOP: Bog rosemary blooms in spring, with clusters of tiny, nodding, urn-shaped, pink flowers that last for a couple of months. BOTTOM: Bog rosemary grows wild from Newfoundland to Manitoba and north past the tree-line to the Arctic coast. This evergreen shrub has been cultivated since 1829, although it is still rather uncommon in gardens around my area.

Boxwood

Buxus microphylla var. *koreana*
Korean Boxwood

Height • 2–3 feet (61–91 cm)

Spread • 2–4 feet (61–120 cm)

Flowers • small, creamy flowers in late spring

Fruit • seed capsules

Growth Rate • slow

Lifespan • average

Zone Rating • 4 [3]

Boxwood is a small evergreen shrub that is often clipped or sheared into formal shapes. It makes a very attractive, low hedge for lining flowerbeds, garden paths, driveways or herb gardens. The foliage is dark green—glossy on some varieties—and remains dark green in winter. Most types of boxwood are best suited to milder climates; even Korean boxwood is not considered hardy in my area. Experimenting with 'not hardy' plants is something that I really enjoy. Often, plants that are considered 'not hardy' for a region have, in fact, never been tried there. Our nursery manager, Shane Neufeld, planted his first Korean boxwood years ago, and today he has a lovely formal boxwood hedge.

GROWING

Sun to shade; needs a moist, cool soil.

Foundation planting, edging herb gardens or small flowerbeds, small hedges.

Boxwood is a naturally tidy shrub that needs little pruning other than to shape or shear. Prune either in late winter to early spring, or after it blooms in summer.

RECOMMENDED SPECIES OR VARIETIES

Korean: 2–2½ feet (61–76 cm) tall and wide; the hardiest variety.

'**Winter Beauty**': 3 feet (91 cm) tall and 3–4 feet (91–120 cm) wide; a mounded shrub with dark green foliage; one of the hardiest varieties.

TIPS

Boxwood is rated as hardy to zone 4, but it has performed well in zone 3. If you live in a lower zone, plant this shrub in a sheltered site where it will be protected from sun and wind, and where it will have good snowcover throughout winter.

Boxwood is a dense, slow-growing shrub that is good for clipping into short, formal hedges and topiary.

To help keep the soil cool and moist, use a fine-textured mulch around these shrubs. Shredded fir bark is a suitable mulch.

Boxwood's roots grow very close to the soil surface. Avoid cultivating too close to these shrubs to avoid damaging the shallow roots.

To grow as a formal hedge, space the shrubs 1 foot (30 cm) apart.

Boxwood can be shaped and sheared as an accent shrub.

Boxwood's tiny, fragrant flowers are irresistible to bees. Florists often use boxwood for greenery in floral arrangements.

TOP: Boxwood is one of the few hedges with bright, glossy green foliage.
BOTTOM: Boxwood is also great as an accent plant.

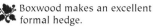

Boxwood makes an excellent formal hedge.

Buffaloberry

Shepherdia canadensis
Russet Buffaloberry
Soapberry

Shepherdia argentea
Silver Buffaloberry

Height • 6–15 feet (1.8–4.5 m)

Spread • 6–15 feet (1.8–4.5 m)

Flowers • small, yellow flowers in late spring

Fruit • small, reddish-orange berries in fall

Growth Rate • slow

Lifespan • short

Zone Rating
Russet: 1
Silver: 2

If you have a hot, dry area of the yard where nothing seems to grow well, buffaloberry may be the perfect solution. This silvery shrub is very drought tolerant and grows well in poor, salty or alkaline soil. When buffaloberry is grown on sun-baked slopes or banks, its roots hold the soil in place and reduce erosion. Buffaloberry spreads quickly and can be used to cover a wide area. This shrub blooms in spring with small, yellow flowers that are not terribly showy. Its small, reddish-orange berries look decorative in fall among the silvery leaves, and they attract birds to your garden. Buffaloberry is a very low-maintenance, undemanding shrub.

GROWING

Hot, dry, sunny location; does well in alkaline, salty or poor soil.

Background shrub, screens, on slopes; good for naturalizing.

Prune in late winter to early spring, before the leaves appear.

LEFT: Shepherdia *is an extremely tough plant that was named after John Shepherd, who was a curator of the Liverpool Botanical Garden. RIGHT: Native Peoples used the bitter berries of silver buffaloberry to flavour buffalo meat.*

RECOMMENDED SPECIES OR VARIETIES

Russet Buffaloberry

6–10 feet (1.8–3 m) tall and wide; silvery-green foliage.

Silver Buffaloberry

7–15 feet (2.1–4.6 m) tall and wide; silvery-grey foliage; young stems are silver and turn brown and flaky with age; branches lined with 1–2-inch (2.5–5.1 cm) spines.

TIPS

Buffaloberry 'fixes' atmospheric nitrogen, enriching the surrounding soil and helping nearby plants to grow better.

This shrub spreads by suckers, which is great if you want the shrub to spread and fill in gaps. If you don't want it to spread, plant it in a confined area, such as between a sidewalk and driveway.

For best fruit production, plant three or more of these shrubs: buffaloberry has separate male and female plants. The male shrubs act as pollinators, and the female shrubs produce the berries.

Buffaloberry can be trained to grow as a small tree. See *How to Prune Shrubs to 'Tree' Form* on page 64.

Although buffaloberries were used by some Native Peoples to make a foamy dessert, which resembled whipped cream, they were disliked by others because of their sour taste.

If eaten in ***large*** amounts, buffaloberries can cause intestinal distress.

Burning Bush

Euonymus nanus var. *turkestanica*
Turkestan Burning Bush
Dwarf Burning Bush
Dwarf Euonymus

Euonymus alatus
Winged Euonymus

Height • 4–20 feet (1.2–6.1 m)

Spread • 5–20 feet (1.5–6.1 m)

Flowers • pink-and-orange or yellow-green flowers in mid-summer

Fruit • orange or red capsules in fall

Growth Rate • slow

Lifespan • short to average

Zone Rating
Turkestan: 2
Winged: 4 [3]

If you want a nice shrub to add fall colour to your flowerbed or shrub border, choose a burning bush. As you might guess from the name, these shrubs blaze with colour in fall. The foliage of winged euonymus, in particular, becomes such a brilliant shade of red that the shrub appears fluorescent. The fall foliage of Turkestan burning bush is less brilliant but still showy; it turns purplish red. Turkestan has impressive, pink-and-orange flowers in summer, followed by lovely, bright red seedpods. Winged euonymus's small, greenish-yellow flowers and the orange seedpods that follow are hardly noticeable among the leaves. This shortfall is forgotten during winter, when its corky ridged branches catch the snow, creating a magnificent display.

GROWING

Sun or shade; best in moist, well-drained soil.

Feature or accent shrub, foundation plantings, screens, hedges, in groups.

To keep shrubs dense, prune in late winter to early spring before leaves appear. Winged euonymus requires a fair bit of cleaning up in spring.

TOP: The Provincial Museum of Alberta in Edmonton uses Turkestan extensively in its landscape.
BOTTOM: Turkestan has unusually attractive pendulous flowers.

RECOMMENDED SPECIES OR VARIETIES

Turkestan Burning Bush

Turkestan: 4–5 feet (1.2–1.5 m) tall and 5–6 feet (1.5–1.8 m) wide; bluish-green foliage turns red in fall; showy, pink-and-orange flowers similar to bleeding hearts; a beautiful, medium-sized shrub; great for fall colour.

'**Nana**': 2–3 feet (61–91 cm) tall and wide; a dwarf variety similar to Turkestan except in size.

LEFT: Winged euonymus gets its name from the corky, wing-like ridges along its stems.
RIGHT: During fall, Compact burning bush lives up to its name with its flame-red foliage.

Winged Euonymus

Winged: 15–20 feet (4.5–6.1 m) tall and wide; very attractive, rounded shrub; medium to dark green foliage turns fluorescent crimson in fall; cork-like, winged bark; for best colour, don't grow in shade.

Compact (*E. alatus* 'Compactus'): 5–6 feet (1.5–1.8 m) tall and 6–8 feet (1.8–2.4 m) wide; beautiful bright red in fall; a very rounded outline; yellow-green flowers are not showy; winged ridges on branches are less pronounced; also called Compact burning bush or Compact winged euonymus.

Burning bush can be sheared and shaped into a formal hedge.

TIPS

Burning bush has shallow fibrous roots that can dry out quickly. Use a mulch to help keep soil cool and retain moisture, particularly if the shrub is planted in a hot, dry site.

Although winged euonymus is rated as hardy to zone 4, it grows well in zone 3 if it is planted in a sheltered site. Provide good snowcover throughout winter.

With their distinctive form, the branches of winged euonymus are prized for floral arrangements.

Burning bush is one of the best shrubs for fall colour.

Butternut

Juglans cinerea
Butternut

Height • 40–50 feet (12–15 m)

Spread • 30–40 feet (9.1–12 m)

Flowers • catkins, not showy

Fruit • edible nuts
ripen in late September

Growth Rate • slow

Lifespan • average

Zone Rating • 3

Butternut is related to walnut and looks quite like it, except that butternut is a smaller tree. Butternut quite often has a forked or crooked trunk with low branches, making it a good tree for kids to climb. Butternut trees don't have much fall colour, but the foliage looks lovely all summer. Butternut is native to eastern North America and is rather uncommon in the West. It is also known as the white walnut tree, and its wood is not as heavy as that of the black walnut.

GROWING

Sun; prefers deep, rich, moist soil; tolerates fairly dry, hard soil, but growth is slower.

Shade tree.

Prune in late winter to early spring, before leaves appear.

RECOMMENDED SPECIES OR VARIETIES

Butternut

LEFT: Butternut in full bloom has great foliage in summer.
RIGHT: Butternuts are about 1–1½ inches (2.5–3.8 cm) long. They taste like walnuts but are very oily.

TIPS

Butternut prefers a moist, rich, deep soil but will tolerate drier conditions. The better the soil conditions, however, the more vigorous the growth.

To prevent the foliage from browning, plant in a sheltered location away from drying winter winds.

The roots of black walnuts secrete a chemical called 'juglone,' which acts as a natural herbicide to other plants.

The edible nuts are sweet and very oily, with thick shells and a distinctive flavour. Squirrels love them.

Butternut is a type of walnut, and the cold hardiest of the North American nut trees.

Caragana

Caragana arborescens
Common Caragana
Common Pea Shrub

Caragana frutex
Globe Caragana
Russian Caragana
Globe Pea Shrub

Caragana pygmaea
Pygmy Caragana
Pygmy Pea Shrub

Height • 2–20 feet (61 cm–6.1 m)

Spread • 2–18 feet (61 cm–5.5 m)

Flowers • bright yellow, 1-inch (2.5 cm) flowers in late spring

Fruit • small, slender seedpods

Growth Rate
Common: fast
Globe: slow
Pygmy: slow

Lifespan • average

Zone Rating • 1

It's interesting to know that caraganas were extensively grown on the Prairies during the drought of the 1930s—a fact that attests to their hardiness and drought tolerance. Traditionally, caraganas were often grown as windbreaks and to control soil erosion. Today caraganas are still popular; they establish quickly from seed, which makes them a good, inexpensive choice for covering large areas. Caraganas, however, are more than just hedges and windbreaks. As feature shrubs in residential gardens, I prefer the named varieties to common caragana: Fernleaf caragana adds interesting texture with its misty foliage; 'Sutherland' provides a formal look with its upright form; and the weeping varieties serve as garden centrepieces in flowerbeds. Globe caragana is rounded and more tidy than common caragana; it looks superb in mixed shrub beds. Pygmy caragana is a smaller, compact shrub that makes a superb low hedge. All caraganas are handsome, low-maintenance shrubs. Their branches are lined with a profusion of bright pea-flowers in late spring.

LEFT: Remember to consider foliage texture when planning your garden. With its narrow, needle-like leaves, Fernleaf is one of the finest-textured shrubs. The coarser foliage of the mugo pine growing around the base provides a splendid contrast.
RIGHT: A pair of 'Sutherland' caraganas provide an impressive accent near the front entrance of a home. Several of these shrubs planted in a row provide an effective screen. 'Sutherland' is an excellent, tough shrub that can lend an air of formality to a front yard or garden.

GROWING

Sun; does well in poor soil and in hot, dry conditions.

Hedges, feature shrubs, screening. Common caragana and its varieties also as windbreaks. Grafted varieties as feature shrubs. Ungrafted weeping varieties as groundcovers.

RECOMMENDED SPECIES OR VARIETIES

Common Caragana

Fernleaf (*C. arborescens* 'Lorbergii'): 15–20 feet (4.6–6.1 m) tall and 12–18 feet (3.7–5.5 m) wide; a very fine-textured version with misty foliage resembling that of an asparagus fern; soft, needle-like leaves are medium to light green; almost spineless; introduced in 1906 from Germany; often sold in 'tree' form, grafted onto a single stem.

'**Sutherland**': 12–15 feet (3.7–4.6 m) tall and 3–4 feet (91–120 cm) wide; a very impressive, tall, narrow, upright shrub; few spines.

Caragana has the ability to 'fix' atmospheric nitrogen—it takes nitrogen from the air, and, with the help of soil bacteria, changes it into a compound that plants are able to use. Because of this ability, caragana grows well in poor soil and gets by with little maintenance. By enriching the soil, caragana benefits other plants that are growing nearby.

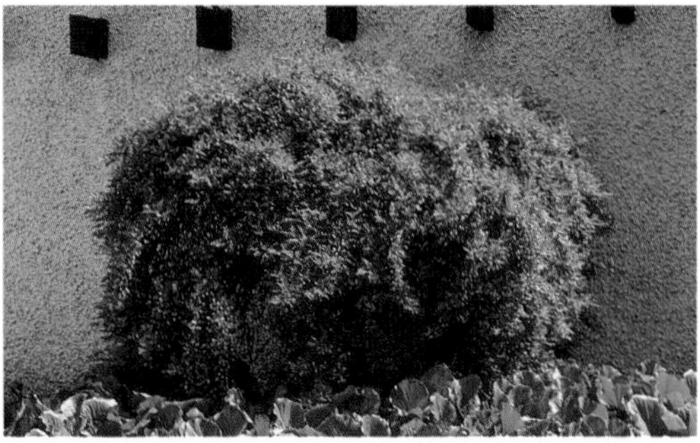

LEFT: Walker's Weeping caragana came from a cross between Fernleaf and Weeping caragana. It is a Canadian variety from Agriculture Canada's Morden, Manitoba research station.
RIGHT: Weeping caragana is absolutely stunning in full bloom. The shrub pictured here is 15 to 20 years old. The perennial elephant-ears growing beneath it provides an interesting contrast.

Walker's Weeping (*C. arborescens* 'Walker's'): sometimes listed simply as Walker; 3–6 feet (91–180 cm) tall and 6–8 feet (1.8–2.4 m) wide when grafted; often sold grafted atop a single trunk, forming a small weeping tree, but may also be available as a sprawling, mounding shrub suitable as a groundcover; fine, ferny foliage, like Fernleaf.

Weeping (*C. arborescens* 'Pendula'): 3–6 feet (91–180 cm) tall and 6–8 feet (1.8–2.4 m) wide; a dwarf, weeping variety with thick, heavy branches and a stout grafted stem; an interesting and very hardy feature shrub.

Globe Caragana

Globe (*C. frutex* 'Globosa'): 2–3 feet (61–91 cm) tall and wide; an excellent feature shrub; medium to light green foliage; slow growing and extremely hardy; introduced in 1752 from Siberia; unlike most caraganas, this variety is spineless.

Pygmy Caragana

3–4 feet (91–120 cm) tall and 3 feet (91 cm) wide; one of the best shrubs for a small, formal hedge; has a very attractive vase-shape when not formed into a hedge; dark green foliage; spiny.

The seedpods are thin, about 1 1/2–2 inches (3.8–5.1 cm) long, and yellow-green, maturing to brown in late summer. When ripe, they pop open with a fairly loud 'snap,' and the seeds go flying. A entire hedge of caragana can be quite noisy, sounding a lot like popcorn popping!

TIPS

These low-maintenance, adaptable shrubs grow well in difficult conditions, including windy sites, extremely cold sites and poor, alkaline or salty soils. They are generally untroubled by disease or insects.

Caraganas generally need little pruning. When necessary, prune after flowering or in early spring. When pruning spiny varieties, protect your skin by wearing a long-sleeved shirt and gloves.

Grafted varieties need a little more pruning. Remove any shoots that sprout from the base of the trunk or below the graft (a prominent lump on the lower trunk). Basal shoots grow from the rootstock variety (which you don't want), and if they are allowed to grow unchecked, they will outgrow the grafted variety (which you do want). Basal shoots should be snipped off as soon as they appear.

Caraganas, especially weeping varieties, are often sold as 'standards'—grafted onto a single trunk to create a miniature 'tree.' Grafted forms make splendid showpieces in flower gardens or shrub beds.

Caragana flowers are attractive to hummingbirds.

TOP LEFT: Globosa is Latin for 'globe-shaped.' Globe caragana has a naturally neat, rounded form and needs little pruning. It is sometimes available as a grafted tree, with a tidy ball of foliage atop a 2–4-foot (61–120 cm) trunk.
TOP RIGHT: Caraganas have excellent heat and drought tolerance. Pygmy caragana is one of the most drought-tolerant types, and it thrives near the radiated heat of a brick wall. Its dense, spiny branches create a formidable barrier to intruders.
BOTTOM: Pygmy caragana is sometimes also sold in grafted form. This variety originates from Siberia and was cultivated in 1751.

Caragana is one of the most drought-tolerant shrubs.

Cedar

Thuja occidentalis
Eastern White Cedar
American Arborvitae
Eastern Arborvitae

Height
$1\frac{1}{2}$–40 feet (46 cm–12 m)

Spread
$1\frac{1}{2}$–15 feet (46 cm–4.6 m)

Flowers • not showy

Fruit • tiny, brown cones in summer

Growth Rate • slow to medium

Lifespan • medium to long

Zone Rating • 2

Cedars are dense evergreen trees and shrubs with flat sprays of foliage. One of the most common uses for cedars is in foundation plantings or shrub beds against the front of the house. Although some cedars are just fine for growing around house foundations, many are simply too large and inevitably grow into the eavestroughs. Fortunately, many cedar varieties are suitable for tight spots. The cedars we grow on the Prairies are native to North America and are not true cedars. True cedars belong to the genus Cedrus *and are native to the Mediterranean.*

GROWING

Sun to partial shade; best in a moist, humid site.

Be sure to water during extremely dry periods, especially when cedars are young.

Accent or feature: 'Brandon,' 'Degroot's Spire,' 'Emerald Green,' 'Golden Champion,' 'Techny,' 'Wareana.'

Foundation planting: 'Danica,' 'Emerald Green,' 'Little Giant,' 'Woodwardii,' 'Wareana.'

Hedge: 'Brandon,' 'Danica,' 'Golden Champion,' 'Holmstrup,' 'Little Giant,' 'Techny,' 'Woodwardii.'

Rock garden: 'Danica,' 'Degroot's Spire,' 'Holmstrup,' 'Little Giant.'

Screen: 'Brandon,' 'Golden Champion.'

Shrub bed: 'Degroot's Spire,' 'Little Giant,' 'Woodwardii.'

RECOMMENDED SPECIES OR VARIETIES

'**Brandon**': upright; 30–40 feet (9.1–12 m) tall and 6–10 feet (1.8–3 m) wide; medium to dark green foliage; effective planted in groups; tolerant of heat and drought once established; medium growth rate.

'**Danica**': a slow-growing, dwarf variety; $1\frac{1}{2}$ feet (46 cm) tall and $1\frac{1}{2}$–2 feet (46–61 cm) wide; very bright green, dense foliage.

'**Degroot's Spire**': slow growing, upright, narrow; grows 6–10 inches (15–25 cm) per year; after 15 to 20 years, becomes 12–15 feet (3.7–4.6 m) tall and 2–3 feet (61–91 cm) wide; dark green, dense, fine-textured foliage; an excellent variety for small spaces.

TOP LEFT: 'Brandon' grows faster than most cedars. It is one of the largest, hardiest varieties.
TOP RIGHT: 'Degroot's Spire' has a unique, twisted form. This variety was discovered in Ontario.
BOTTOM: 'Danica' is a small cedar that is ideal for rock gardens. A row of these cedars lining the driveway makes an effective display.

TOP LEFT: 'Emerald Green' has beautiful foliage and good heat tolerance.
RIGHT: In northern gardens, few golden evergreens make good hedges. 'Golden Champion,' however, is one of the best for this use. A single shrub makes a stunning accent in a shrub bed.
BOTTOM LEFT: 'Little Giant' is one of the smallest cedars, but it has a big impact in a flowerbed, rock garden or small shrub bed.

'**Emerald Green**': very narrow, compact, pyramidal; 10–15 feet (3–4.6 m) tall and 5–6 feet (1.5–1.8 m) wide; vertical sprays of bright green foliage; makes an interesting small specimen tree; medium growth rate; excellent heat tolerance; also more tolerant of shade than other varieties; foliage does not discolour in winter; introduced in 1950; needs a protected site (see page 30) in zone 3.

'**Golden Champion**': globular; 7 feet (2.1 m) tall and 7–8 feet (2.1–2.4 m) wide; usually wider than tall; yellow-green; new foliage is extremely yellow-gold—almost fluorescent; slow growing; more tolerant of bright sun than most cedars.

LEFT: Have patience after planting 'Techny.' This variety often takes a few years to look its best, but it's worth the wait—'Techny' is a superb tree.
RIGHT: Slow-growing 'Holmstrup' makes a great addition to rock gardens.

'**Holmstrup**': compact, upright, pyramidal; 5–6 feet (1.5–1.8 m) tall and 1–3 feet (30–91 cm) wide; slow growing; resistant to wind-burn.

'**Little Giant**': a slow-growing, dwarf variety; 3½ feet (1.1 m) tall and 1½–2 feet (46–61 cm) wide; beautiful, dense, medium green foliage; somewhat columnar; very attractive.

'**Techny**': also known as 'Mission'; broad-based, pyramidal; 10–15 feet (3–4.6 m) tall and 6–7 feet (1.8–2.1 m) wide; very dark green foliage; slow growing; good as a hedge; tolerant of pruning; extremely hardy.

Native Peoples on the West Coast still carve magnificent canoes and totem poles from cedars.

A 'Wareana' is a good variety for growing near the house because it won't tower up past the eaves-troughs. Even after 30 or 40 years, 'Wareana' remains under 10 feet (3 m) tall.

'**Wareana**': small, broad-based, pyramidal; 8–10 feet (2.4–3 m) tall and 5–7 feet (1.5–2.1 m) wide after 30 to 40 years; very dense; dark green foliage; slow growing; tolerant of hot and dry conditions; usually does not brown in winter; the hardiest variety.

'**Woodwardii**': globe-shaped; 7 feet (2.1 m) tall and 7–8 feet (2.1–2.4 m) wide; usually wider than tall; holds its foliage all the way to the ground; takes well to pruning—good for hedges and topiary.

TIPS

The ideal site for evergreens like cedar is one that is sunny in summer and shaded in winter (see page 30 for more details).

Certain varieties, such as 'Brandon,' are particularly susceptible to desiccation (drying-out of foliage) if they are planted too close to a heat-reflecting wall. Avoid planting cedars against the south side of a house or in exposed, windy sites, which also causes brown foliage in summer or winter.

'Woodwardii' looks great planted in groups or grown in large shrub beds.

To promote density and to shape cedars, prune them lightly in early summer.

When planted in too shady a site, cedars tend to become 'leggy'—rather thin with less foliage.

A mulch around the base of cedars helps to maintain moisture and to keep soil cool, especially during warm stretches in summer.

The tiny, green cones, 3/8–1/2 inch (1–1.3 cm) long, appear in August, and turn brown by the end of summer. Although most people expect cones from evergreens, such as pine and spruce, they don't seem to expect cones from cedars. Quite often a concerned gardener will ask me if his cedar is dying. What appears to be a disease is merely the clusters of cones.

After a particularly bad winter, foliage tips may turn brown and die. Rest assured; these brown tips are usually shed during the coming summer and are replaced by healthy, new, green growth.

If you plan to grow cedars in dry or windy areas, spray the foliage in fall with an anti-desiccant (a horticultural spray that prevents moisture loss).

See pages 68–69 for tips on protecting cedars over winter.

Cedar is also known as 'arborvitae,' which in Latin means the 'tree of life.'

Cherry

Prunus tomentosa
Nanking Cherry
Manchu Cherry

Height • 6–10 feet (1.8–3 m)

Spread • 6–10 feet (1.8–3 m)

Flowers • white, 3/4-inch (1.9 cm) blossoms in early spring

Fruit • bright red berries, 1/2 inch (1.3 cm) or less, ripen in mid-summer

Growth Rate • medium

Lifespan • short

Zone Rating • 2

Nanking cherry serves a dual purpose in my garden: in early spring its beautiful blossoms provide a glorious display, and later on, in summer, its branches supply an abundance of small, tasty cherries. These bright red cherries are delicious in pies and jam—that is, of course, if I can get to them before the birds do! If you want to attract birds to your garden, Nanking cherry is a good shrub to grow; you'll have lots of birds visiting as soon as the cherries ripen. I use this shrub to teach my grandchildren about the ways of nature. Birds have good colour vision but a poor sense of smell, and because birds are the best way for a cherry tree to spread its seeds, the fruit turns bright red to attract the birds. Cherry stones—the seeds—are indigestible, so the birds inadvertently scatter them after they eat the fruit. Nanking cherry is the earliest-blooming cherry, and one of the best fruit-producers for northern areas.

Nanking cherry is one of the earliest-blooming cherries.

The species name *tomentosa* means 'hairy,' and refers to the leaves and new stems, which have woolly undersides—an unusual feature for cherries.

GROWING

Sun.

Informal hedges, mass planting in large shrub beds, background shrub in small beds.

RECOMMENDED SPECIES OR VARIETIES

Nanking Cherry

Also called Manchu cherry.

TIPS

Nanking cherry makes a beautiful hedge and continues to bloom and bear fruit even when clipped.

Prune after flowering to promote fruit production for the following season. The most berries are produced on second-year wood.

If you are willing to do a little annual pruning, this shrub can be grown as a small tree. See *How to Train Shrubs to 'Tree' Form* on page 64.

Cross-pollination is essential for good fruit production. Most members of the genus *Prunus* will cross-pollinate with each other, as long as their blooming periods overlap. Pincherry, Nanking cherry, chokecherry and sandcherry all cross-pollinate.

Nanking cherry can self-pollinate, but cross-pollination provides for greater fruit production.

Birds love these tiny cherries, so the fruit doesn't last long. My shrub is usually picked clean within two weeks.

If you can beat the birds to the harvest, you will have lots of these sweet cherries, which are excellent for pies and jams, and eating out of hand. Nanking cherry is very productive—a single bush yields 10–20 pounds (4.5–9 kg) of fruit.

Snip off a few flowering stems for spring bouquets.

TOP: Nanking cherry is stunning in full bloom. In early spring, the pink flowerbuds open to fragrant, white blossoms that cover the branches before the leaves open.
MIDDLE: Nanking cherry has been cultivated since 1870.
BOTTOM: Nanking cherry is a truly versatile shrub with beautiful flowers, fruit and orange-red foliage in fall.

Cherry Prinsepia

Prinsepia sinensis
Cherry Prinsepia

Height • 6–10 feet (1.8–3 m)

Spread • 6–10 feet (1.8–3 m)

Flowers • small, pale yellow flowers in spring

Fruit • orange-red to red-purple berries ripen in late summer to early fall

Growth Rate • slow to medium

Lifespan • short to average

Zone Rating • 2

Cherry prinsepia is an uncommon shrub that makes a wonderful hedge. When sheared, it has the graceful appearance of bamboo, with long, arching new shoots and thin, drooping, bright green leaves. Cherry prinsepia is one of the first shrubs to leaf out in spring. The small, yellow spring flowers aren't terribly showy, but the bright cherry-like berries provide a splendid display later in the season. The foliage turns golden in fall, offsetting the ripened orange-red to red-purple berries. This exceptional shrub is almost entirely pest-free.

GROWING

Sun to light shade.

Hedges, screens; middle to back of shrub border.

RECOMMENDED SPECIES OR VARIETIES

Cherry Prinsepia

TIPS

Generally, prune cherry prinsepia after flowering in spring. Prune hedges two to three times during the growing season to keep them well shaped, but don't prune later than early to mid-August.

Cherry prinsepia can be sheared and shaped into a formal hedge. Keep in mind that if you trim your hedge throughout the growing season or in late winter to early spring, you may not have flowers or berries that year.

Cherry prinsepia blooms on old wood.

Hedges should be thinned out periodically to promote young, vigorous growth. Old hedges that are becoming thin or 'leggy' can be brought back to life by severe pruning. See *Pruning to Rejuvenate Hedges* on page 66. This type of pruning can greatly extend the life of a hedge.

With its spiny branches, prinsepia makes a great barrier. Protect your skin by wearing gloves and long sleeves when pruning.

Cherry prinsepia can be trained to grow as a small tree. See *How to Prune Shrubs to 'Tree' Form* on page 64.

The berries can remain on bare branches into winter, provided birds don't eat them all first.

TOP LEFT: This large bed of cherry prinsepia grows at the University of Alberta in Edmonton.
TOP RIGHT: Cherry prinsepia makes a superb, long-lasting hedge. This hedge was planted in 1952, and it still blooms profusely every spring.
BOTTOM: The very tart, juicy, 1-inch (2.5 cm) berries ripen in late summer. Eat them fresh or use them for jelly.

Chokecherry

Prunus maackii
Amur Chokecherry
Manchurian Cherry

Aronia melanocarpa
Black Chokecherry

Prunus virginiana
Common Chokecherry

Height • 4–45 feet (1.2–14 m)

Spread • 4–45 feet (1.2–14 m)

Flowers • clusters of white flowers in spring

Fruit • clusters of purple-black berries ripen in late summer

Growth Rate
Amur: fast
Black: slow to medium
Common: fast

Lifespan • short

Zone Rating
Amur: 2
Black: 3
Common: 2

Although they make great jam and jelly, the berries are not the primary reason to plant a chokecherry tree. Chokecherries are marvellous trees that are the ideal size for smaller yards. They bloom profusely but briefly in spring, with long, dense clusters of creamy white flowers. The fruit ripens to dark purple-black in late summer. Amur chokecherry is noted for its striking coppery bark. The best ornamental variety of common chokecherry is 'Schubert,' a small tree with lovely purple-red leaves throughout the season. Black chokecherry, although not a true chokecherry, is a showy shrub that blooms slightly later than the others, with masses of fragrant flowers. Its plentiful berries are very showy, especially against the red fall foliage.

One of Amur chokecherry's best features is its polished bark, which, like birch bark, peels from the trunk in layers.

GROWING

Sun. Amur and common chokecherries grow well in alkaline soil. Black chokecherry grows well in sun or shade, in wet or dry sites, and it prefers neutral to slightly acidic soil.

Feature trees or shrubs. Common chokecherry also for screening. Black chokecherry at the back of a shrub bed.

RECOMMENDED SPECIES OR VARIETIES

Amur Chokecherry

35–45 feet (11–14 m) tall and wide; beautiful cinnamon-gold bark; a very dense, round-headed tree; 2–3-inch (5.1–7.6 cm) long clusters of white flowers in spring; very tart, purple-red berries mature to black in August; amber foliage in fall; usually available as a single- or multi-stemmed tree.

As its name suggests, the variety 'Autumn Magic' has spectacular fall foliage that highlights the black berries.

Black Chokecherry

'**Autumn Magic**': 4–6 feet (1.2–1.8 m) tall and wide; masses of long, slender, white flower clusters in spring; abundant clusters of small, edible but bitter, black-purple berries; glossy, rich green leaves turn fluorescent red in fall; berries hang on branches well into winter.

Common Chokecherry

'**Schubert**': 20–25 feet (6.1–7.6 m) tall and 16–20 feet (4.9–6.1 m) wide; white flowers in slender clusters 3–6 inches (7.6–15 cm) long; blooms profusely in spring; leaves are green in spring, turn deep wine-red by mid-summer, and turn purple-red in fall; tiny, dark purple, juicy cherries are good for making wine, excellent for jelly.

With its colourful foliage throughout summer, 'Schubert' is the showiest variety of common chokecherry.

TIPS

Black chokecherries are one of the most versatile shrubs, thriving in sun or shade, in poor soil, on slopes and in hot, dry conditions. More berries are produced when the shrub is grown in full sun.

Prune chokecherries in late winter to early spring, before leaves appear, or, if you wish to enjoy the flowers, prune immediately after the shrub leafs out.

Black chokecherries also thrive in moist soil. Grow these shrubs in low-lying, moist or wet areas of the garden, or alongside a pond or stream.

Because of its size and shade tolerance, black chokecherry thrives as an 'understorey' shrub, growing near larger trees.

Common chokecherries tend to produce suckers or watersprouts (shoots at the base of the trunk or branches). Just cut these shoots off as they appear.

'Schubert' is usually grafted, and it may produce green-leaved basal shoots that should be removed.

Chokecherries provide food, shelter and nesting sites for birds.

The chokecherry fruit is quite sour, but it is great for making jam, jelly, syrup and wine.

Coralberry

Symphoricarpos orbiculatus
Buckbrush
Indian Currant

Height • 2–5 feet (61–150 cm)

Spread • 4–8 feet (1.2–2.4 m)

Flowers • creamy white flowers in late spring to early summer

Fruit • tiny, purplish-red berries from fall through winter

Growth Rate • medium

Lifespan • short

Zone Rating • 3

If you have a bare spot in your yard beneath the shade of mature trees, and want an undemanding, attractive plant to fill it, coralberry is ideal. In its native habitat, this shrub grows in dappled woodland shade, and it will thrive in a similar environment in your garden. Coralberry blooms in spring, with dense clusters of tiny, yellow flowers flushed in rose-pink. Green leaves cover tidy arching branches right through fall. The abundant, tiny, purplish berries appear in fall, and are particularly decorative on bare branches in winter. Coralberry is an extremely adaptable, hardy shrub that flourishes in sun or shade, and needs little pruning.

GROWING
Sun or partial shade.

Feature shrub, foundation plantings, in containers, as an informal hedge, front to middle of the border.

Coralberry is an uncommon, striking shrub for shady sites.

RECOMMENDED SPECIES OR VARIETIES

Buckbrush

Also called Indian currant.

TIPS

Coralberry blooms on new wood. If your shrub is becoming unruly, you can prune it rather severely in late winter, and still expect flowers the following spring.

Prune coralberry in late winter to early spring, before leaves appear.

Because it needs so little attention, coralberry is a great shrub to grow in the garden at your summer cottage.

Birds don't care for these berries, so they can last for months.

TOP: The botanical name Symphoricarpos orbiculatus *means 'clusters of rounded berries.' BOTTOM: Coralberry's bright fruit is particularly attractive in winter, when displayed against a snowy background.*

Cork Tree

Phellodendron amurense
Amur Cork Tree

Height • 35–45 feet (10–14 m)

Spread • 35–45 feet (10–14 m)

Flowers • small, yellowish-green flowers in spring; not showy

Fruit • female trees have black berries in fall

Growth Rate • slow

Lifespan • average to long

Zone Rating • 3

The cork tree's name is derived from its corky bark. However, this tree is not the source of cork wood, which comes from the cork oak (Quercus suber)*, a tree native to the Mediterranean region. Cork tree is beautiful, with broad spreading branches and glossy, dark green, divided leaves that turn yellow in fall. Both the leaves and berries have a pleasant smell. The berries ripen to black in fall, and they often remain on bare branches into winter, hanging in 4–5-inch (10–13 cm) long clusters! Cork trees are dioecious, which means that male and female flowers are on different plants; thus a male tree and a female tree are both needed for berry production.*

GROWING

Sun; grows well in hot, dry sites and in acidic or alkaline soil.

Feature tree, shade tree.

LEFT: Amur cork tree is native to northern China and Japan. It was introduced to the nursery trade in 1856.
RIGHT: The thick bark of the Amur cork tree is soft and spongy, like the cork used for bulletin boards and wine-bottle stoppers. It is used medicinally in China. The bark doesn't become cork-like until trees are mature.

RECOMMENDED SPECIES OR VARIETIES

Amur Cork Tree

TIPS

This tree has a wide-spreading, shallow, fibrous root system that can be easily damaged. To avoid root damage, don't plant in a site where you are likely to dig, such as near a vegetable garden.

Once established, Amur cork tree is a tough tree. It grows well in hot, dry sites and is very insect and disease resistant.

Little pruning is required, but if necessary, prune cork trees in late winter to early spring, before leaves appear.

Although Amur cork trees are rarely identified by sex when sold by nurseries, most nurseries propagate only male trees, which are tidy trees that are good for planting near walkways, decks or swimming pools.

Amur cork tree is an unusual, large tree with attractive, cork-like bark and lovely foliage. Old trees have low spreading branches that are inviting for children to climb.

Cotoneaster

Cotoneaster apiculatus
Cranberry Cotoneaster

Cotoneaster adpressus
Creeping Cotoneaster
Ground Cotoneaster

Cotoneaster acutifolius
Peking Cotoneaster

Height • 1–10 feet (30 cm–3 m)

Spread • 4–10 feet (1.2–3 m)

Flowers • tiny, pinkish-white flowers in spring

Fruit • small, red or black berries in summer

Growth Rate
Cranberry: slow
Creeping: medium
Peking: medium

Lifespan • short

Zone Rating
Cranberry: 4 [3]
Creeping: 4 [3]
Peking: 2

Cotoneaster hedges are very common in my hometown; it seems that at least one yard on every street has one. Well-kept hedges are lovely in summer, and when the deep green foliage turns fiery orange and red in fall, the streets blaze with colour. Peking cotoneaster is a favourite for hedges. The two other types of cotoneaster are less often seen in gardens in my area. Both cranberry cotoneaster and creeping cotoneaster are shorter, wide-spreading shrubs with beautiful red berries. All cotoneasters bloom in spring, with clusters of tiny, pinkish-white flowers.

GROWING

Sun to light shade (to partial shade for Peking cotoneaster); moist, well-drained soil; avoid planting in wet sites.

Cranberry cotoneaster in foundation plantings, borders, large shrub beds. Creeping cotoneaster in rock gardens, as a groundcover. Peking cotoneaster as a hedge, screen or fall accent in a shrub bed.

RECOMMENDED SPECIES OR VARIETIES

Cranberry Cotoneaster

2–3 feet (61–91 cm) tall and 5–6 feet (1.5–1.8 m) wide; cranberry-red berries ripen in late summer and remain on branches through winter; particularly showy in fall, with a mix of berries and orange-red foliage.

Creeping Cotoneaster

1–1½ feet (30–46 cm) tall and 4–6 feet (1.2–1.8 m) wide; long-lasting display of dark red berries; resistant to fireblight; forms a looser mat than cranberry cotoneaster.

TOP: Creeping cotoneaster roots wherever its branches touch soil. It is an ideal groundcover for growing on slopes.
BOTTOM: Cranberry cotoneaster is named for its decorative, ¼-inch (0.6 cm) berries. This low-growing shrub prefers a dry site.

Peking cotoneaster is one of the most popular shrubs for hedges.

Peking Cotoneaster

6–10 feet (1.8–3 m) tall and wide; dark green foliage; excellent red-orange fall colour; black berries.

TIPS

Although both creeping and cranberry cotoneaster are rated as hardy to zone 4, we have successfully grown them for several years in zone 3. Plant them in a protected site where they will have good snowcover throughout winter.

Generally, prune cotoneasters in late winter to early spring, before the leaves appear. Prune hedges two to three times during the growing season to keep them well shaped, but don't prune later than early to mid-August.

Cotoneasters are easy-to-grow, undemanding shrubs with great fall foliage colour.

Cranberry cotoneaster tends to need more pruning than other cotoneasters because it forms a dense, thick mat. Inner branches sometimes die out, and should be removed.

Hedges should be thinned out periodically to promote young, vigorous growth. Old hedges that are becoming thin or 'leggy' can be brought back to life by severe pruning. See *Pruning to Rejuvenate Hedges* on page 66. This type of pruning can greatly extend the life of a hedge.

Crabapple

Malus x
Flowering Crabapple
Ornamental Crabapple

Malus baccata
Siberian Crabapple

Height • 15–50 feet (4.6–15 m)

Spread • 5–40 feet (1.5–12 m)

Flowers • pink, red, purple or white blossoms in spring

Fruit • tiny, red, purple or yellow crabapples

Growth Rate • slow to medium

Lifespan • average to long

Zone Rating
'Red Jade': 4
Siberian: 1
other varieties: 3

A crabapple tree in full bloom is breathtaking. Ornamental crabapples are grown for their showy blossoms, form, foliage and decorative—rather than edible—fruit. The apples look appealing on the branches, but they tend to be tart, dry and very small. Crabapple trees burst into bloom in early spring, their branches lined with red, purple, pink or white, single to double flowers. The fragrance is quite sweet but light. These trees have dense foliage, and the leaves range from green to bronze to deep wine-red. Most crabapple trees are wide spreading and rounded, but some varieties are weeping and some are narrow and columnar. Siberian crabapple is the hardiest type. It is often used in breeding programs to improve the hardiness of new apple varieties.

GROWING

Sun.

Shade tree, feature tree, screening.

Few trees rival a 'Kelsey' in full bloom. This Canadian variety was introduced in 1969 and is named after the explorer Henry Kelsey.

RECOMMENDED SPECIES OR VARIETIES

Flowering Crabapple

'**Big River**': 18–20 feet (5.5–6.1 m) tall and 10–12 feet (3–3.7 m) wide; green foliage; deep rose-pink flowers; very showy, purple-black fruit; excellent disease resistance; pyramidal tree of an ideal size for small yards; a very hardy variety from Saskatchewan; fruit remains on branches well into winter.

'**Kelsey**': 18 feet (5.5 m) tall and wide; bronzy red-green leaves; beautiful, purplish-red, semi-double blossoms; tiny, dark-fleshed fruit is excellent for colouring jellies but too small for eating; a smaller crabapple tree that fits easily into any landscape.

TOP: 'Makamik' has one of the largest flowers of all crabapples—each blossom is 2 inches (5.1 cm) across.
BOTTOM: 'Makamik' is one of the heaviest bloomers of the crabapple family.

'**Makamik**': 40 feet (12 m) tall and 35–40 feet (11–12 m) wide; bronze foliage; dark red flowerbuds open to single, purplish-red flowers; fruit is purplish red and 1/2 inch (1.3 cm) in diameter; fruit stays on tree longer than most crabapples; scab resistant; slightly susceptible to fireblight; a large, rounded tree; a Canadian variety introduced in 1921.

'**Red Jade**': 15–16 feet (4.6–4.9 m) tall and wide; medium to dark green leaves; single, deep pink flowerbuds open to white blossoms; fruit is glossy red and 1/2 inch (1.3 cm) in diameter; mildly susceptible to fireblight; a beautiful weeping crabapple tree that is absolutely stunning when in full flower.

'**Strathmore**': 20 feet (6.1 m) tall and 5–8½ feet (1.5–2.6 m) wide; new leaves are reddish green, maturing to green; dark red flowers; red-purple fruit; susceptible to fireblight; a very narrow, vase-shaped tree; excellent for smaller spaces.

'**Thunderchild**': 20–25 feet (6.1–7.6 m) tall and 16–25 feet (4.9–7.6 m) wide; deep purple-red leaves; rose-pink flowers; dark red-purple fruit; resistant to fireblight; a popular tree for its deep purple foliage; an award-winning variety.

The carbonized remains of a sour crabapple, dating back to 6500 BC, were found in Switzerland.

TOP: 'Red Jade' is the most popular weeping crabapple. Its fruit seems to be irresistible to birds. BOTTOM: 'Strathmore' crabapples have everything: beautiful pink flowers, a nice columnar shape, good fall colour and pretty red fruit.

Siberian Crabapple

Siberian: 25–50 feet (7.6–15 m) tall and 20–40 feet (6.1–12 m) wide; green leaves; pink flowerbuds open up to fragrant, white flowers; fruit is bright red to yellow and tiny (3/8 inch [1 cm] in diameter); slightly susceptible to fireblight; a very wide-spreading, rounded tree that is extremely hardy and long lived—more than 100 years!

Columnar (*M. baccata* 'Columnaris'): 30–35 feet (9.1–11 m) tall and 8 1/2–10 feet (2.6–3 m) wide; green leaves; bears fewer flowers than most crabapples; creamy white flowerbuds open to pure white, single blossoms; fruit is yellow with red cheeks and 1/2 inch (1.3 cm) in diameter; susceptible to fireblight.

TOP: Siberian crabapple is one of the few apple trees with highly fragrant flowers—most apple blossoms have only a light scent. BOTTOM: Columnar crabapple is a distinctive tree that grows at least three to four times as tall as it is wide.

LEFT: Many crabapples provide beautiful fall colour.
RIGHT: The pink flowers of 'Thunderchild' show up against a background of new green leaves. The foliage turns deep purplish red during summer.

TIPS

White-flowering crabapples generally have more brightly coloured fruit than pink-flowering varieties.

Avoid planting crabapple trees in low-lying areas of the yard where water tends to pool; it can cause damage to the roots.

Prune crabapples immediately after flowering. Don't wait too long, because next spring's flowerbuds form in early summer.

Rake up leaves and fallen fruit from around the bottom of the tree to help prevent disease.

The colourful little crabapples often remain on the branches well into winter, providing a decorative display as well as food for birds.

Cut one or two small flowering branches to display in a vase indoors, where the delicate fragrance of the blossoms can be appreciated.

Crabapples are one of the most beautiful flowering trees in spring.

Cranberry

Viburnum trilobum
American Highbush Cranberry

Viburnum opulus
European Cranberry
European Highbush Cranberry

Height • 2–12 feet (61 cm–3.7 m)

Spread • 3–12 feet (91 cm–3.7 m)

Flowers • clusters of white flowers

Fruit • bright red, tart berries

Growth Rate
American Highbush:
slow to fast
European: slow

Lifespan • short to average

Zone Rating
American Highbush: 1 or 3
European: 3

Cranberries are attractive, compact shrubs that are ideal for small gardens, low hedges or feature plantings. Tidy clusters of white flowers decorate the shrubs in spring, followed by bunches of bright red berries. The shiny, dark green leaves of cranberry bushes are shaped somewhat like maple leaves. Some varieties have spectacular, red fall colours, while the foliage of others turns a mix of yellow, red and purple. Cranberries are splendid, undemanding shrubs that are both tough and beautiful. They are very hardy and require little maintenance.

GROWING

Sun to partial shade.

Small gardens, low hedges or as a feature shrub. American highbush also for screens.

HIGHBUSH CRANBERRY JELLY

For jelly making, cranberries should be picked in the yellow stage, as they are just turning red. Carefully wash and pick over the berries and put in a large saucepan with just enough water to cover. Cook gently until the fruit is tender. Strain through a cheesecloth bag. Add equal amounts of sugar to the strained juice, bring to the boiling point and simmer gently until it gels. Pour into hot sterilized jars. Cool and seal.

(Blue Flame Kitchen)

LEFT: *An American highbush in full bloom is a lovely addition to any yard.*
RIGHT: *Highbush cranberries are not true cranberries, but they have a similar flavour and are high in vitamin C.*

RECOMMENDED SPECIES OR VARIETIES

American Highbush Cranberry

American Highbush: 8½–12 feet (2.6–3.7 m) tall and wide; spectacular in bloom, with abundant, large flower clusters; lots of edible berries; fall colour ranges from yellow to red and reddish purple.

LEFT: The fruit of 'Bailey's Compact' ripens in August and September. RIGHT: 'Alfredo' is a shorter shrub.

Cranberries have striking flowers and colourful, edible berries.

'**Alfredo**': 5–7 feet (1.5–2.1 m) tall and wide; very attractive clusters of white flowers; flowers and berries are less profuse than the species American highbush; a broader, denser, shorter shrub; fall colour ranges from yellow to red and reddish purple.

'**Bailey's Compact**': 5–7 feet (1.5–2.1 m) tall and wide; very compact growth habitat; unlike the others, the foliage of this variety turns deep red in fall.

'**Wentworth**': $8^{1}/_{2}$–12 feet (2.6–3.7 m) tall and wide; consistent, superior red fall colour.

European Cranberry

Dwarf (*V. opulus* 'Nanum'): 2–3 feet (61–91 cm) tall and 3–5 feet (91–150 cm) wide; rarely blooms or produces berries; no fall colour; a very compact, small shrub excellent for low hedges or as a filler plant; good for shady sites.

TIPS

Prune cranberries in late winter to early spring. Rejuvenate shrubs every few years by removing the oldest stems to keep the plant tidy and to encourage new growth.

Many viburnums hold their berries through winter, providing an attractive display as well as food to attract birds to the garden.

For the best berry production, grow several shrubs close together in a group. One gardener's 12-year-old cranberry bush never bore berries until a second cranberry bush was planted next to it.

The best berries for eating come from American highbush cranberries; the berries of European cranberry are too bitter for my taste, and they are best left for the birds.

The fruit of most cranberries is great for making jams and jellies.

TOP: Dwarf European cranberries contrast wonderfully with 'Goldmound' spirea.
BOTTOM: 'Wentworth' cranberry produces consistently brilliant orange-red fall foliage.

Currant

Ribes alpinum
Alpine Currant

Ribes aureum
Golden Flowering Currant

Height • 4–7 feet (1.2–2.1 m)

Spread • 4–7 feet (1.2–2.1 m)

Flowers • greenish-yellow or golden-yellow flowers in late spring

Fruit • small, red or black berries in summer

Growth Rate • medium

Lifespan • short

Zone Rating • 2

With its thick, lustrous foliage and dense, ball shape, alpine currant makes a superb hedge. Space plants 1½–2 feet (46–61 cm) apart.

Alpine currant makes a great hedge. This dense, bushy shrub has distinctive, three-lobed, dark green leaves and full branches right down to ground level. Alpine currant hedges are attractive both when sheared for a more formal look, or left unpruned in their natural form. Golden flowering currant has lovely green foliage and bright yellow flowers in late spring. (Alpine currant flowers aren't as showy.) The black berries of golden currant stand out against its bright foliage, which turns reddish bronze in fall. Both types of currant are low-maintenance, tidy shrubs that need little pruning and are rarely bothered by pests.

GROWING

Sun; does best in a rich soil.

Hedge; as filler in shrub border, in foundation planting.

RECOMMENDED SPECIES OR VARIETIES

Alpine Currant

'**Schmidt**': 4–5 feet (1.2–1.5 m) tall and wide; a slow-growing, more compact variety.

Golden Flowering Currant

5–6 feet (1.5–1.8 m) tall and wide; rich yellow, fragrant flowers in May; good scarlet fall foliage.

TIPS

Although some people recommend currants for sun or shade, I disagree. In shady sites, they tend to be less vigorous, not as dense and prone to powdery mildew.

To reduce chances of powdery mildew, avoid wetting the foliage. Water at the base of the shrub rather than from overhead. Also, thin old stems regularly to maintain a more open centre and to improve air circulation.

Prune currants regularly to maintain a compact shape, especially if they are growing as a hedge. Prune immediately after flowering. Do not prune after July to allow the shrubs time to prepare for winter.

Alpine currants produce male and female flowers on separate plants. Male plants have small, greenish-yellow flowers that are not showy, and female plants produce berries. Most shrubs sold through nurseries are male, but occasionally you may find one or two plants in your hedge with a few red berries.

Alpine currant will root wherever its branches touch the ground. To reduce this, use a mulch around the shrubs, or prune off the lower branches.

Currants are a good choice for urban gardens because they are tolerant of air pollution.

TOP: Alpine currant makes an extremely cold-hardy, beautiful hedge.
BOTTOM: Golden flowering currant produces masses of yellow blossoms.

Daphne

Daphne x burkwoodii
Burkwood Daphne

Daphne mezereum
February Daphne

Daphne cneorum
Rose Daphne
Rock Daphne
Garland Flower

Height • 6½ inches–4 feet (17–120 cm)

Spread • 2–4 feet (61–120 cm)

Flowers • pink flowers in spring

Fruit • bright red berries in summer (yellowish brown on rose daphne)

Growth Rate • slow

Lifespan • short

Zone Rating • 4 [3]

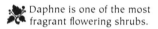

Daphne is one of the most fragrant flowering shrubs.

One of our employees' favourite 'events' is the early spring arrival of our annual shipment of daphnes. The fragrance of 100 pots of daphnes in full bloom is amazing—you can smell the sweet, spiced-honey fragrance throughout the nursery and right into the parking lot. Daphnes in full flower are almost irresistible. Their bewitching perfume and plentiful flowers entice almost every gardener to take one home. After its spring flowers are finished, daphne's fine-textured foliage offsets the flowers of nearby plants, making it a welcome, pest-free addition to borders and rock gardens.

GROWING

Ideally, four to five hours of sun each morning; avoid hot afternoon sun.

In borders, rock gardens, flowerbeds. Rose daphne also as a groundcover.

RECOMMENDED SPECIES OR VARIETIES

Burkwood Daphne

'**Carol Mackie**': 3 feet (91 cm) tall and 3–4 feet (91–120 cm) wide; variegated foliage; green leaves edged in cream; profusion of highly fragrant, pale pink, starry flowers in late spring to early summer; often has bright red berries in fall; a very hardy, compact shrub; considered one of the most beautiful and unusual daphnes.

February Daphne

3–4 feet (91–120 cm) tall and wide; blooms earlier than others; extremely fragrant, tiny, rose-pink flowers cover entire shrub before leaves open; bright red berries in summer; upright branches.

Rose Daphne

'**Ruby Glow**': 6–12 inches (15–30 cm) tall and 2–3 feet (61–91 cm) wide; short clusters of very fragrant, bright rose-pink flowers in spring; often blooms again, less profusely, in late summer; dense, dark green foliage; a very popular variety.

TOP: February daphne is a very compact shrub.
MIDDLE & BOTTOM: Rose daphne is a terrific aromatic groundcover.

TIPS

Rose daphnes are commonly found and have flourished for years in gardens throughout my region, which is zone 3, although they are sometimes listed as hardy to zone 4.

Most daphnes are fragrant, but February daphne is even more so than other types. A single cut flowering branch fills an entire room with its sweet scent.

Daphnes generally need little pruning. When necessary, prune shortly after flowering, but don't wait too long, because next spring's flowerbuds form during summer.

Rose daphne can serve as a groundcover. To grow a new plant, lay one of its flexible branches on top of bare soil (called 'trench layering'). Place a rock just behind the old flowerhead to hold the branch in place. The branch will slowly grow roots and develop into a new plant. Daphne cannot be divided or split to produce new plants. Propagate mostly by cuttings.

Use a mulch to help retain soil moisture and to keep daphne's roots cool.

Burkwood and rose daphne are evergreen: their foliage remains green all year, even underneath snow. February daphne is semi-evergreen: it may naturally drop some, but not all, of its leaves.

Because they have evergreen leaves, daphnes do best in a site where they have good snowcover throughout winter. To prevent breaking the thin branches, use only a layer of light snow on top of these shrubs.

Dogwood

Cornus racemosa
Grey Dogwood

Cornus alternifolia
Pagoda Dogwood

Cornus sericea
Red Osier Dogwood
Red Twig Dogwood

Cornus alba • Tatarian Dogwood

Height • 2–25 feet (61 cm–7.6 m)

Spread • 2 1/2–30 feet (76 cm–9.1 m)

Flowers • creamy white flowers in spring

Fruit • white to blue-black berries in summer

Growth Rate
Grey: slow
Pagoda: slow to medium
Red Osier, Tatarian: fast

Lifespan • short to average

Zone Rating
Grey, Pagoda: 3
Red Osier, Tatarian: 2

Dogwoods are attractive year-round. They bloom in spring, with clusters of creamy white flowers, followed by bright bunches of berries in summer. The fall colour of the foliage can be spectacular. It is in winter, however, that I most appreciate dogwoods, with their bright, colourful stems in the snowy landscape. Red osier and Tatarian dogwoods are the most common types. Grey dogwood is a larger shrub; it is often sold pruned to 'tree' form, with a single trunk. Pagoda dogwood, on the other hand, naturally grows as a small tree with striking horizontal branches. It spreads readily and looks splendid in mass plantings. The berries attract birds.

GROWING

Sun to partial shade.

Accent or feature shrubs, in groups or mass plantings.

RECOMMENDED SPECIES OR VARIETIES

Grey Dogwood

12–15 feet (3.7–4.6 m) tall and wide; grey-green leaves turn purplish in fall; white flowers in spring; white berries in summer; red stems; wood turns grey with age; very ornamental in winter.

TOP LEFT: Grey dogwood has pearl-like berries that stand out against the crimson stems. It is excellent for mass plantings because it spreads readily.
BOTTOM LEFT: Kelsey is excellent for mass plantings.
RIGHT: Pagoda dogwood displays fragrant flowers for about 7 to 10 days in spring, followed by bunches of blue-black berries in summer.

Pagoda Dogwood

15–25 feet (4.6–7.6 m) tall and 20–30 feet (6.1–9.1 m) wide; fragrant, creamy white flowers in spring; green leaves sometimes turns purple in fall, although colour is inconsistent; blue-black berries; attractive horizontal branches provide elegant winter interest.

Red Osier Dogwood

Kelsey (*C. sericea* 'Kelseyi'): 2–2½ feet (61–76 cm) tall and 2½–3 feet (76–91 cm) wide; dark green foliage, with purple tinge in fall; white berries in late summer and fall; needs little pruning; excellent for mass plantings and border; very fast growing for its size; stem colour very attractive in a winter landscape.

TOP & BOTTOM LEFT: For the most vibrant foliage colour, prune Golden Variegated dogwood annually.
RIGHT: The vivid yellow twigs of Yellow-twig dogwood are outstanding in a winter landscape.

Yellow-twig (*C. sericea* 'Flaviramea'): 7–9 feet (2.1–2.7 m) tall and 8–10 feet (2.4–3 m) wide; medium to dark green leaves; white berries; many upright, bright yellow stems provide beautiful winter colour; attractive informal hedge, especially in winter.

Tatarian Dogwood

Golden Variegated (*C. alba* 'Gouchaultii'): also known as Gold Variegated dogwood and Golden-edged dogwood; 4–6 feet (1.2–1.8 m) tall and wide; bright green leaves with creamy yellow edges; white berries produced in clusters.

LEFT: Siberian has lovely fall colour. RIGHT: The berries of 'Siberian Pearls' start out pale blue and turn bright white tipped in purplish black.

'**Kesselring**': 4–6 feet (1.2–1.8 m) tall and wide; dark green leaves, with a lustrous purple tinge; white berries, with a blue tinge; dark, brownish-red stems are showy in winter.

Siberian (*C. alba* 'Sibirica'): 8–10 feet (2.4–3 m) tall and wide; green leaves; showy berries vary from bright blue to bright white; berries really stand out on this shrub; brilliant red stems stand out against snow; especially appealing when planted in groups.

'**Siberian Pearls**': 8–10 feet (2.4–3 m) tall and wide; creamy white flowers in spring; white berries with blue-black tips; deep green foliage; red stems.

LEFT: Silver-leaf dogwood is an attractive contrast plant in a mixed shrub bed.
RIGHT: Yellow-leaf dogwood has bright golden leaves in summer that look excellent mixed with purple and deep green foliage shrubs.

Silver-leaf (*C. alba* 'Argenteo-Marginata'): also known as Elegantissima; 6–8 feet (1.8–2.4 m) tall and wide; silvery-green leaves with creamy edges; white berries; bright red stems; extremely showy, especially when planted in groups.

Yellow-leaf (*C. alba* 'Aurea'): 6–8 feet (1.8–2.4 m) tall and wide; bright yellow foliage all season; white berries, red stems.

Dogwoods add winter colour to the landscape.

TIPS

Prune dogwoods in late winter to early spring, before the leaves appear. Except for those in 'tree' form, dogwoods do best when one-third of the oldest stems are removed annually to encourage bright, colourful, young growth.

Dogwoods make great additions to mature landscapes. They grow well underneath larger trees, as long as the shade is not dense.

Grey dogwood spreads readily. Plant it on slopes to hold soil in place, as long as the site is not too hot and dry.

Dogwoods have shallow fibrous roots that can dry out quickly. Use a mulch to keep the roots cool and improve the soil's moisture retention.

Grey dogwood can be trained to grow as a small tree. See *How to Train Shrubs to 'Tree' Form* on page 64.

For fresh, brightly coloured stems, prune off the older, less colourful stems every three to four years.

TOP: The brilliant red stems of red osier dogwood add contrast to a snow-covered area.
BOTTOM: Dogwood can be pruned to form a beautiful full hedge.

Double-flowering Plum

Prunus triloba var. *multiplex*
Double-flowering Almond
Flowering Almond
Rose Tree of China

Height • 6–7 feet (1.8–2.1 m)

Spread • 6–7 feet (1.8–2.1 m)

Flowers • pink blossoms in early spring

Fruit • none

Growth Rate • slow to medium

Lifespan • short

Zone Rating • 3

Double-flowering plum is irresistible in full bloom. Every spring, customers arrive at the greenhouses asking for 'that beautiful shrub covered in pink flowers.' Double-flowering plum is one of the first shrubs to bloom in spring, with its leafless branches lined with showy, rose-pink, double blossoms, each about 1 1/2 inches (3.8 cm) across. The show lasts about two weeks, but by the time the flowers finish, the leaves have unfurled. Double-flowering plum is a shapely, medium-sized shrub. It does not bear fruit, making it a good choice for planting near a patio or deck.

GROWING

Sun. Needs at least six hours of direct sunlight to bloom well.

Feature shrub, back of the border, informal hedge.

RECOMMENDED SPECIES OR VARIETIES

Double-flowering Almond

Also called flowering almond or rose tree of China.

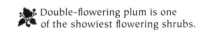

Double-flowering plum is one of the showiest flowering shrubs.

TIPS

Don't confuse double-flowering plum with Russian almond. Both shrubs are commonly called 'flowering almond.' Double-flowering plum is a larger shrub with double, unscented flowers. Russian almond is smaller, and it has fragrant, single flowers.

Prune double-flowering plum immediately after it leafs out. It often needs tidying up in spring, and to be thinned out occasionally to promote new growth.

Double-flowering plum blooms about the same time as forsythia, cherry and plum trees. Grow any of these with double-flowering plum for a stunning display of spring flowers.

Double-flowering plum is a great background shrub. Because it blooms before most other shrubs get their leaves in spring, the display of flowers is unobstructed. Later in the season, the other shrubs can take centre stage.

After a particularly harsh winter, double-flowering plum will bloom only on branches that were beneath the snowline. It seems that if the temperature drops below -31° F (-35° C), the flowerbuds will almost surely die. Extreme temperatures in early spring can also kill exposed flowerbuds. Plant your shrub in a sheltered site to keep it in the best condition.

If your mature shrub is not blooming well after an average winter, it may be in need of pruning. Double-flowering plum blooms best on one- to three-year-old wood.

Double-flowering plum has a naturally rounded shape. With pruning, double-flowering plum can be trained to grow as a small tree. For instructions, see *How to Train Shrubs to 'Tree' Form* on page 64. It is often sold grafted in 'tree' form.

Snip off a few flowering stems for spring bouquets, and later use the foliage to accent cutflowers.

You can also 'force' flowers indoors. See page 359 for details.

TOP: Double-flowering plum blooms early with masses of showy flowers. Its profuse blossoms provide a much-appreciated welcome to spring.
MIDDLE: Two double-flowering plums with a white potentilla create an elegant shrub bed.
BOTTOM: Double-flowering plum has the added benefit of foliage with warm yellow tones and orange accents.

Elder

Sambucus nigra
Common Elder
European Elder

Sambucus racemosa
Red-berried Elder
European Red Elder

Sambucus canadensis
Sweet Elder
American Elder

Height • 3–25 feet (91 cm–7.6 m)

Spread • 3–18 feet (91 cm–5.5 m)

Flowers • clusters of yellow-white to white flowers in spring

Fruit • clusters of red or black berries in summer

Growth Rate
Common: slow
Red-berried: slow to fast
Sweet: fast

Lifespan • short

Zone Rating • 3

Elders are grown for their showy foliage, which adds both bright colour and interesting texture to gardens. The colourful berries of the red-berried elder provide an eye-catching display and attract birds to your yard. As well as supplying beauty, elders are also supposed to bring luck. According to folklore, an elder will never be struck by lightning and will protect your home from evil influences. Elder leaves can be cast upon the wind as a blessing to whomever you name. Before pruning an elder, however, it is traditional to first ask the elder's permission, to avoid offending the spirits said to be living within the shrub. Regardless of whether or not you believe in their reputed powers, elders are attractive, undemanding, fast-growing shrubs with few pest problems.

GROWING

Sun to light shade. Golden elders tend to be greener in shaded sites.

Moist soil; all elders are drought tolerant.

RECOMMENDED SPECIES OR VARIETIES

Common Elder

Madonna (*S. nigra* 'Marginata'): 10–25 feet (3–7.6 m) tall and 10–18 feet (3–5.5 m) wide; large clusters of heavily scented, white flowers; small, black berries; dark green leaves with creamy edges.

Red-berried Elder

Red-berried: 8–12 feet (2.4–3.7 m) tall and wide; yellowish-white flowers; red berries in summer; dark green, cut-leaf foliage; a very vigorous, attractive, fine-textured shrub.

TOP LEFT: The fragrant flowers of Madonna elder show off well against its variegated leaves.
TOP RIGHT: Red-berried elder is a drought-tolerant shrub. The impressive 25-year-old specimen shown here is 'self-sown'—it grew from a seed that was likely dropped by a bird.
BOTTOM: Red-berried elder has clusters of yellowish-white flowers in late spring.

TOP LEFT: Golden Plume elder has bright gold, tropical-looking foliage.
TOP RIGHT: 'Goldenlocks' is a dwarf variety with dense fern-like foliage and clusters of bright red berries.
BOTTOM: 'Adams' has the brightest white flowers of all the elders.

Golden Plume (*S. racemosa* 'Plumosa Aurea'): also known as Cut-leaf Golden elder; 5–8½ feet (1.5–2.6 m) tall and wide; yellowish-white flowers in spring; red berries in summer; bright yellow foliage provides excellent contrast in a shrub bed; very vigorous, attractive, finely textured shrub.

'**Goldenlocks**': a miniature variety; 4–5 feet (1.2–1.5 m) tall and wide; dense, bright yellow foliage; masses of white flowers and bright red berries; a great shrub for rock gardens.

Sweet Elder

'**Adams**': 5–12 feet (1.5–3.7 m) tall and 12 feet (3.7 m) wide; white flower clusters from 6–10 inches (15–25 cm) across; plentiful berries in large clusters.

Golden (*S. canadensis* 'Aurea'): 5–12 feet (1.5–3.7 m) tall and 6 feet (1.8 m) wide; white flower clusters approximately 6 inches (15 cm) across; bright yellow leaves show off the red berries; foliage colour holds extremely well throughout the growing season.

Elders have been cultivated for hundreds of years.

Golden elder looks great mixed with perennials.

TIPS

Elders need regular pruning to keep them dense, compact and bushy. Prune in late winter to early spring, before the leaves appear. 'Goldenlocks' is an exception—it needs little pruning.

Elders grow well in moist, well-drained locations, and they even put up with standing water for short periods of time.

Golden elder has its best foliage colour when it grows in full sun. Its leaves contrast well with evergreens, such as pine, cedar or yew.

Elders need rejuvenation pruning if they thin out, lack vigour, have poor colour or are extremely overgrown.

The edible berries are traditionally used to make elderberry wine, as well as jams, jellies and pies.

Elder is one of the fastest-growing shrubs.

Elm

Ulmus americana
American Elm
White Elm

Ulmus pumila
Siberian Elm

Height • 50–100 feet (15–30 m)

Spread • 35–60 feet (11–18 m)

Flowers • not showy; blooms in spring

Fruit • pods, as leaves open in spring

Growth Rate • fast

Lifespan • long

Zone Rating • 2

The majestic, vase-shaped elm is one of the best shade trees—fast growing, long lived and tough. At the far end of the lawn in front of our old family farmhouse, there stands an immense elm that must be about 80 years old. My two sons and their boyhood friends climbed all over that tree, and used its branches as a goal post during years of football games. One year the tree was hit by lightning, but it survived with few tell-tale signs. On a summer morning a few years later, I discovered that our favourite tree had been hit by lightning again—but this second time its entire centre had been blown out! The elm survived, and, still thriving 20 years later, it is a grand tree that will likely live to be well over 100 years.

American elms grow to be immense trees; they are too big for most residential lots but look impressive in large open areas. Siberian elms are about half the size. The greatest problem with American elms is Dutch elm disease: a virulent fungal disease that has already wiped out entire American elm populations in many parts of North America. I am fortunate enough to live within one of the last regions in North America that is still free of Dutch elm disease. Even so, most municipalities keep a vigilant eye out for the beetles that spread this disease.

GROWING

Sun; best in moist, well-drained soil, but adapts well to most soils.

Shade tree; in parks or boulevards. Siberian also for screens.

RECOMMENDED SPECIES OR VARIETIES

American Elm

80–100 feet (24–30 m) tall and 45–60 feet (14–18 m) wide; a popular, fast-growing shade tree; native to most of North America; dark green leaves turn yellow in fall.

Siberian Elm

50–55 feet (15–17 m) tall and 35–40 feet (11–12 m) wide; ascending branches with somewhat pendulous branchlets; very fast growing; dark green leaves; resistant to Dutch elm disease.

TOP: This American elm is my family's favourite tree—it was twice struck by lightning but still thrives. When my son Bill and his wife Valerie built their house, they made sure to design it around the 80-year-old elm.
BOTTOM: A Siberian elm is a handsome shade tree suited to most fairly large yards.

LEFT: The city of Edmonton, Alberta, has the greatest population of elms in North America. There are over 60,000 elm trees in its parks, boulevards and roadside plantings, as well as many others on private property.
RIGHT: A boulevard planted with American elms is breathtaking in fall.

Elms are impressive shade trees with large canopies.

TIPS

Elms flourish even in sites where there is standing water in spring and fall.

Prune elms every year in late winter to early spring, before the leaves appear.

The bark beetles that spread Dutch elm disease breed in any kind of dead elm wood—whether broken branches or cut logs—so it is imperative to immediately remove dead or broken branches, at any time of the year. Diseased or dying branches should be removed annually. Ensure that all cut elm wood is promptly destroyed—do not store it for firewood. Elm firewood should never be transported across provincial, state or international borders.

There is no cure for Dutch elm disease, and control is very, very expensive. Preventing its spread is the only hope. Keep your elm trees in the best possible health. Water regularly, and fertilize once a month until the end of July. Also, have mature or maturing trees pruned annually.

A long, unpruned Siberian hedge is an impressive feature in any yard. Ensure that there is enough room to grow it.

Dutch elm disease is a notorious killer of elm trees. It is a fungus that blocks the sap flow and can kill healthy elm trees within one or two seasons. The fungus is spread from tree to tree by elm bark beetles. In North America, Dutch elm disease was first identified in Ohio in 1930. In Winnipeg, Manitoba, 24,000 American elm trees have died since Dutch elm disease was first reported in 1975; a further 76,000 elms were removed to prevent its spread. In Great Falls, Montana, approximately 10,000 elms—half that city's inventory—have succumbed since 1980.

Euonymus

Euonymus fortunei
Wintercreeper Euonymus

Height • 2–4 feet (61–120 cm), taller if climbing

Spread • 3–4 feet (91–120 cm)

Flowers • not showy

Fruit • pink and orange

Growth Rate • slow to medium; much faster in milder climates

Lifespan • short

Zone Rating • 4 [3]

Euonymus is a rather strange plant. It grows as either a small, mounding shrub, or as a vine, if it can cling to something. A small plant can grow to completely cover a 16½ x 20 foot (5 x 6 m) wall in about 10 years in milder climates. In my region, however, it tends to remain a smaller vine because the branches often die back over winter. Euonymus has striking, glossy foliage, either deep green or variegated green and yellow. The leaves are evergreen—they stay on all year, even while hidden under snow. The flowers are next to invisible, but the pink and orange fruits that follow can be quite showy if the flowerbuds are not damaged during winter.

GROWING

Grows anywhere—sun to heavy shade; tolerates moist, but not wet, soil.

Groundcover, self-clinging vine, wall covering in mild climates, beside large rocks.

RECOMMENDED SPECIES OR VARIETIES

'**Emerald Gaiety**': 3–4 feet (91–120 cm) tall and wide, but may spread more; leaves have a pronounced white margin and often show tinges of pink in fall and winter; a very compact variety.

'**Gold Prince**': up to 2 feet (61 cm) tall and 3–4 feet (91–120 cm) wide but may spread more; a vigorous, mounding variety; leaves of each shrub vary tremendously in colour but are usually solid green with yellow new growth; considered the hardiest variety of wintercreeper euonymus.

TIPS

Since it is not fully hardy in my region (zone 3), I grow euonymus behind a group of evergreen trees. These trees protect it from drying winds and sun in winter, and they keep it well covered in snow all winter. A hedge or retaining wall would also provide effective protection.

Euonymus requires little pruning, other than to remove any dead growth in spring or to contain its growth.

Euonymus can grow 2–3 feet (61–91 cm) per year, but in my area it tends to grow more slowly.

If you like, you can cut branches to use as greenery in floral arrangements. Florists often use euonymus greens because they are attractive and long lasting in bouquets. The foliage remains fresh looking for about two weeks.

Euonymus is a small, easy-to-grow, broad-leaved evergreen. It can be grown as a vine or shrub.

TOP: With its attractive variegated foliage, 'Gold Prince' is an interesting, broad-leaved, evergreen feature plant.
BOTTOM: 'Gold Prince' usually grows in shrub form.

Falsecypress

Chamaecyparis pisifera
Japanese Falsecypress
Sawara Falsecypress

Height • $1^1/_2$ inches–50 feet (3.8 cm–15 m)

Spread • 8 inches–20 feet (20 cm–6.1 m)

Flowers • not showy

Fruit • small cones

Growth Rate • slow to medium

Lifespan • long

Zone Rating
'Golden Pin Cushion': 4
'Sungold,' Thread-leaf: 3

The species name *pisifera* means 'pea-like,' referring to the tiny, round cones produced by female falsecypress.

Falsecypress is an unusual evergreen with attractive, soft, fine-textured foliage. Given the right spot in the garden, falsecypress will thrive with very little maintenance. It is, however, a little fussier about growing conditions than many other plants. Falsecypress likes a spot that is sunny but not hot, and soil that remains constantly cool and moist. Once you provide the ideal site, falsecypress requires little attention. These evergreens are rarely troubled by pests or disease, and they need little pruning.

GROWING

Sun to light shade; prefers a cool, moist, well-drained, acidic soil. Do not plant in hot sites.

Thread-leaf as a feature or specimen tree. Others as accents in small shrub beds or borders, feature shrubs, in rock gardens and Japanese-style gardens.

Fertilize with an acidic evergreen fertilizer in late spring and early summer.

Use a mulch to keep soil cool and to help retain soil moisture.

RECOMMENDED SPECIES OR VARIETIES

'**Golden Pin Cushion**': also known as 'Golden Dwarf Moss Cypress'; $1^1/_2$–2 inches (3.8–5.1 cm) tall and 6–8 inches (15–20 cm) wide after 8 to 10 years; mature plant may be 3–4 inches (7.6–10 cm) tall and 12–14 inches (30–36 cm) wide after many, many years; a very slow-growing miniature shrub that looks like moss; new growth is brightest gold, oldest growth is green; prized variety for rock gardens; alternate common name is 'cypress' rather than 'falsecypress.'

'**Sungold**': 6–10 feet (1.8–3 m) tall and wide after 35 years; slow growing; extremely attractive, cord-like, ascending branches; newest growth is the brightest gold, becomes green as it ages; more tolerant of sun than others.

Thread-leaf (*C. pisifera* 'Filifera'): 40–50 feet (12–15 m) tall and 10–20 feet (3–6.1 m) wide; a beautiful tree with feathery foliage.

TIPS

Plant falsecypress in a site that is sheltered from winds, to prevent the foliage from browning. Dwarf varieties do best when they have good snowcover throughout winter.

Because of their slow-growing habit, falsecypresses need little pruning. Prune them when they are actively growing to maintain their shape and density.

In warmer areas, Thread-leaf falsecypress grows into a fairly large tree, but in my region (zone 3) it has remained a small shrub.

With its striking appearance and preference for moist, cool conditions, falsecypress is ideal for planting alongside a garden pond, where it can take advantage of the higher humidity.

TOP: With its long, drooping strings of foliage, Thread-leaf falsecypress adds unique texture to the garden.
BOTTOM: 'Sungold' turns green as it ages.

Fir

Abies lasiocarpa
Alpine Fir
Rocky Mountain Fir
Sub-alpine Fir

Abies balsamea
Balsam Fir
Dwarf Balsam Fir

Abies concolor
Blue Fir
Colorado Fir
Silver Fir
White Fir

Pseudotsuga menziesii
Douglas Fir

Height • 1½–70 feet (46 cm–21 m)

Spread • 3–35 feet (91 cm–11 m)

Cones • dark purple

Growth Rate
Alpine, Balsam, Douglas: slow
Blue: slow to medium

Lifespan • average to long

Zone Rating
Balsam: 1
Alpine, Blue, Douglas: 3

I think firs are among the nicest of evergreens. These trees are less common in yards than are spruces and pines—in my region, at least—but that relative scarcity may be partially because fewer people know much about firs and because they are less readily available at many tree nurseries. Firs are strong, tidy, large trees that are ideal if you have lots of space. Their trunks are thick and straight, with smoother bark than many other evergreens. Their soft needles form a dense pyramid of foliage beneath a narrow, pointed crown, resulting in a stately look. An added highlight is the presence of decorative, dark purple cones. The only drawback to firs is that they don't fare well in dry, windy areas, but within town or city limits a sheltered site usually isn't too hard to find.

Balsam fir is rich green with fragrant foliage; the dwarf variety is very compact and, unlike most firs, grows well in shade. Blue fir is a compact tree with, as its name suggests, blue needles. Because blue fir holds its needles longer than others, it is one of the densest fir trees. Alpine fir has pale silvery needles. Douglas fir is not a true fir, although it is related and looks quite similar to true firs.

GROWING

Sun; prefers moist soil and grows well in average soil. Dwarf balsam fir grows well in sun to mostly shade, with moist, cool soil.

Dwarf balsam fir in rock gardens, borders and small shrub beds; taller firs as specimen plants, for naturalizing. All do best in a site that is sheltered from prevailing winds.

Use a mulch to keep soil cool and help retain moisture. Balsam and alpine firs, in particular, drop needles rapidly in dry conditions.

RECOMMENDED SPECIES OR VARIETIES

Alpine Fir

Alpine: 60–70 feet (18–21 m) tall and 15–20 feet (4.6–6.1 m) wide; pale blue needles with silvery undersides; a slow-growing, adaptable tree; attractive dark purple cones are 2–4 inches (5.1–10 cm) long; introduced in 1863; a good choice for large lots.

Compact (*A. lasiocarpa* 'Compacta'): 7–8 feet (2.1–2.4 m) tall and 5–6 feet (1.5–1.8 m) wide; silvery-blue needles; a dwarf, compact, pyramidal tree with short, densely covered branches; long, dark purple cones; an ideal variety for rock gardens and small yards.

Balsam Fir

Dwarf (*A. balsamea* 'Nana'): 2–2½ feet (61–76 cm) tall and 3–3½ feet (91–110 cm) wide; dark green when mature, new growth is soft lime-green; a very hardy, globe-shaped dwarf fir; a densely branched shrub smothered in short, broad, soft, flat needles; no cones; grows horizontally rather than upward; a popular choice for rock gardens.

TOP: Compact alpine fir has a lovely pyramidal shape and outstanding silvery-blue foliage. BOTTOM: The needles of balsam fir have a delicious spicy fragrance. Native Peoples used every part of this tree for different medicines.

Firs are rarely bothered by pests.

Although 'fir' is the Scandinavian word for pine, fir trees look more like spruces than pines. The easiest way to distinguish between the two is by their needles: fir needles are flat and spruce needles are round.

LEFT & RIGHT: Blue fir (silver fir) is unusual because of its long, steely blue-silver needles.

Blue Fir

40–50 feet (12–15 m) tall and 20–25 feet (6.1–7.6 m) wide; blue to blue-grey needles; a very attractive tree with beautiful, smooth, silver-grey bark and purple cones; introduced in 1872; more tolerant of heat and drought than other firs; bluer and narrower, and usually denser than the more common blue spruce.

Douglas Fir

Rocky Mountain (*P. menziesii* var. *glauca*): 50–80 feet (15–24 m) tall and 25–35 feet (7.6–11 m) wide; dark blue-green needles; thick, attractive bark covered in wide, reddish-brown ridges; distinctive cones are 2–4 inches (5.1–10 cm) long, with three-pronged 'tails.'

True firs have upright cones perched high up on the branches, whereas Douglas fir cones hang down below the branches. Unlike spruce and pine cones, which fall to the ground intact, fir cones (except Douglas fir) break up while they are still on the tree.

LEFT & RIGHT: Douglas fir's scientific name Pseudotsuga *means 'false hemlock.' Its common name refers to David Douglas (1799–1835), a Scottish botanist who is said to have introduced more North American plants to Europe than any other man. The wood is exceptionally strong, and the bark can be as thick as 2 feet (61 cm)! At one time, Douglas fir was the most important tree in the North American lumber trade.*

TIPS

Firs do best in sheltered sites, because wind dries out their foliage, causing the needles to turn brown and drop. Most yards in established neighbourhoods with large, older trees are protected from wind, so firs do fine.

Firs are tidy trees that rarely need pruning.

When shopping for a Douglas fir, be sure to choose the Rocky Mountain type (variety *glauca*). It is smaller than the Coastal Douglas fir (variety *menziesii*), which is the largest tree native to Canada, growing up to 330 feet (100 m) tall.

You can use fir branches in floral arrangements. They last up to three weeks in the vase, but you may need to mist them frequently to prevent the needles from dropping.

Flowering Raspberry

Rubus odoratus
Flowering Raspberry
Ornamental Raspberry

Height • 8½–10 feet (2.6–3 m)

Spread • 8½–10 feet (2.6–3 m)

Flowers • purple flowers in late spring to mid-summer

Fruit • tiny, red berries in late summer

Growth Rate • fast

Lifespan • short

Zone Rating • 3

Grow flowering raspberry for its showy blooms rather than for its berries. Unlike other raspberries, this shrub has big, purple flowers, each about 2 inches (5.1 cm) across, followed by tiny, flat, red berries less than 1 inch (2.5 cm) in size. Although these raspberries taste just as good as regular raspberries, they are so small that I leave them for the birds to enjoy. Flowering raspberry is an upright shrub with huge, dark green, five-lobed leaves that vary from 4–12 inches (10–30 cm) across. It grows well in sun or shade.

GROWING

Sun or shade; needs a moderately moist, well-drained soil.

Flowering raspberry is one of the few flowering shrubs for shady areas.

Shade gardens, as a background plant in a shrub bed.

ALL: *Flowering raspberry has huge, purple flowers with large, maple-like leaves, even in the shade.*

RECOMMENDED SPECIES OR VARIETIES

Flowering raspberry

Also called ornamental raspberry.

TIPS

Tidy up flowering raspberry in spring, before the leaves appear, by removing any dead tips or branches. Regular pruning is recommended to keep this shrub compact and tidy.

Avoid planting flowering raspberry in low-lying, wet sites where water tends to pool for extended periods. Such wetness can cause the roots to rot and the shrub to die.

Flowering raspberry is native to Nova Scotia. It is widely grown in European gardens.

Forsythia

Forsythia x
Forsythia

Height • 6–9 feet (1.8–2.7 m)

Spread • 6–9 feet (1.8–2.7 m)

Flowers • bright yellow flowers in early spring

Fruit • not showy

Growth Rate • fast

Lifespan • short

Zone Rating • 4 [3]

Forsythia is one of the most stunning spring-flowering shrubs. It blooms early—about the same time as cherries and double-flowering plums—providing a bright splash of yellow among the pale pink blossoms of the other species. Before the leaves emerge, forsythia flowerbuds burst into bloom along the entire length of the bare branches. Bright yellow, 1-inch (2.5 cm), tubular flowers appear in clusters of two to four. I particularly like this shrub because it provides a source for gorgeous bouquets at a time when there is little else available in the garden.

Unfortunately, in my zone 3 garden, forsythia will not bloom spectacularly every year because the flowerbuds are not entirely hardy—although the shrub itself is hardy. But since forsythia is so lovely, I grow it anyway, and I minimize the risk of losing flowerbuds by piling snow on top of the shrub to protect it from the cold. For the best chance of success, always choose a site that is protected from winter winds; a south or southwest exposure is best.

Forsythia is a spectacular spring-flowering shrub, and it is one of the earliest bloomers.

GROWING

Sun to light shade; prefers a loose, moist, well-drained soil, but does well even in heavy clay soil; the sunnier the site, the more flowers it will produce.

Background shrub, informal hedge.

RECOMMENDED SPECIES OR VARIETIES

'**Meadowlark**' (*F. x intermedia*): 6–9 feet (1.8–2.7 m) tall and 6–6½ feet (1.8–2 m) wide; flowerbuds hardy to at least -27° F (-33° C).

'**Northern Gold**' (*F. x* 'Northern Gold'): 6–8 feet (1.8–2.4 m) tall and wide; introduced in 1979; blooms slightly earlier than 'Meadowlark'; flowerbuds hardy to at least -35° F (-37° C).

TIPS

Choose only the hardiest varieties or you will have inconsistent flowering. Even with cold-hardy varieties, flowerbuds can be killed by low temperatures. (The buds are not hardy to zone 3.) In some years, as with double-flowering plum, there will be flowers only on the bottom branches—the ones that were below the snowline.

Prune forsythias after flowering. They can become rather scraggly, so to promote new growth and more flowers, remove a few of the oldest, thickest stems every year.

Forsythia is a great cutflower. Snip stems with pruning shears when the flowers are showing a bit of colour but are still closed. The flowers last two weeks or longer after cutting.

You can also cut bare stems in late winter to 'force' the flowers to bloom indoors. See page 359 for details.

Although North Americans tend to call this shrub 'for-SITH-ia,' the correct pronunciation is 'for-SYE-thia,' as it is pronounced in England. Forsythia was named in honour of the royal gardener William Forsyth (1737–1804), a Scotsman who, reportedly, never laid eyes on it.

TOP: Forsythia will do quite well in zone 3 if planted in a well-protected area.
BOTTOM: After flowering, forsythia produces very dense, deep green foliage.

Genista

Genista lydia
Dwarf Genista

Genista pilosa
Genista
Silky-leaf Woadwaxen

Genista tinctoria
Genista
Dyer's Greenwood
Common Woadwaxen

Height • 1–2 feet (30–61 cm)

Spread • 2–3½ feet (61–110 cm)

Flowers • small, bright yellow flowers in spring

Fruit • small, pea-like pods

Growth Rate • slow

Lifespan • short

Zone Rating • 3

*Genista is very similar to broom (*Cytisus *sp.). These two shrubs are often confused, which is not surprising because the difference in classification comes down to a small protuberance on the seed! Why botanists decided to split up the two, I'll never know. At one time, both broom and genista were called 'Planta Genista.' Genista explodes into bloom in spring, with its bare branches becoming completely covered in small, bright golden-yellow flowers. The flowers are held on 1–3-inch (2.5–7.6 cm) long, upright stalks, and they look a bit like miniature sweet peas (but without the fragrance). Genista is an excellent flowering groundcover for hot, dry areas, for slopes and for sites with poor soil.*

GROWING

Hot, dry, sunny areas; best in poor, gravelly or alkaline soil.

Groundcover, in rock gardens, at the front of the border.

RECOMMENDED SPECIES OR VARIETIES

Dwarf Genista

2 feet (61 cm) tall and 3–3½ feet (91–110 cm) wide; bright yellow flowers; blooms longer than most others; an eye-catching shrub in full bloom.

***Genista* (G. pilosa)**

'**Vancouver Gold**': 1 foot (30 cm) tall and 3–3½ feet (91–110 cm) wide; masses of bright golden-yellow flowers; flowerspikes are 2–6 inches (5.1–15 cm) long; blooms later than others; greyish-green foliage; extremely showy groundcover; also excellent for mass plantings.

Genista (G. tinctoria)

'Royal Gold': 2 feet (61 cm) tall and wide; profusion of bright golden-yellow flowers; bright green foliage; an attractive feature plant; also looks great planted in small or large groups.

TIPS

Do not plant genistas in low-lying, wet sites or in poorly drained areas with heavy clay soil.

Genistas need little pruning. If necessary, however, prune after flowering.

Genistas perform best in poor soil, so don't fertilize these shrubs. Genistas 'fix' atmospheric nitrogen, which means, like peas, beans and clovers, they change nitrogen in the air into nitrogen compounds that can be absorbed by the roots. The surrounding soil is also enriched by this process.

Genistas are excellent as cutflowers; they are often used by florists. Cut them for bouquets when most of the flowers on a branch have begun to open. Cutflowers last up to two weeks.

TOP: 'Vancouver Gold' is perfect for covering a sun-baked slope. MIDDLE: Dwarf genista blooms from about the end of May to the end of June in my region. BOTTOM: A shrub of 'Royal Gold' acts as a good feature plant.

Ginkgo

Ginkgo biloba
Ginkgo
Maidenhair Tree

Height • 50–80 feet (15–24 m)
Spread • 30–40 feet (9.1–12 m)
Flowers • catkins on male trees
Fruit • none on male trees
Growth Rate • slow
Lifespan • long
Zone Rating • 4

Ginkgo is the most amazing tree. It is the sole surviving species of a prehistoric tree that grew in swamps over 150 million years ago, when dinosaurs still walked the earth. The species nearly became extinct, but about 300 years ago, a single ginkgo tree was discovered growing in the garden of a Japanese temple. By 1730 ginkgo had been reintroduced to Europe, and by 1784, to North America. A ginkgo's foliage is soft green in spring and turns a lovely, bright daffodil-yellow in fall. This exceptional tree grows well in poor soil, and it survives in areas with heavy air pollution.

Ginkgo is the oldest surviving tree species. Botanists often call ginkgo a 'living fossil' because it remains in a stage of evolution that occurred millions of years ago, when fern-type trees were evolving into broad-leaved trees.

GROWING
Sun.

Feature tree; in large yards, on acreages, in parks.

Water well in late fall and mulch the soil around the base of the tree to help insulate the roots during winter.

From the earliest times, the Chinese have held ginkgo in high regard for its medicinal properties. Extract of ginkgo is one of Europe's most widely prescribed medicines. It is thought to have the potential to reduce senility and short-term memory loss by increasing blood flow to the brain. In Germany alone, $364 million Cdn worth of ginkgo extract was sold in 1991.

RECOMMENDED SPECIES OR VARIETIES

Ginkgo
Also called maidenhair tree.

TIPS

In gardens, expect ginkgo to grow to a size of 30–40 feet (9.1–12 m) tall and 20–25 feet (6.1–7.6 m) wide after 50 to 60 years. Gingko grows even more slowly in colder climates. In zone 3, where I live, it grows less than 6 inches (15 cm) a year.

Ginkgo requires very little pruning. When necessary, prune it in late winter to early spring.

Although it is rated as hardy only to zone 4, ginkgo can be grown in lower zones if it is planted in a protected site, such as behind a windbreak of evergreens. There is a 10-foot (3 m) tall ginkgo tree on the grounds of the University of Alberta, Edmonton (zone 3); it was planted over 10 years ago and has shown little winterkill.

Ginkgo has separate male and female trees. Usually, only male trees are sold by nurseries because female trees bear fruit that smells terrible as it decays. It is interesting, though, that female trees don't produce fruit until they are 20 to 50 years old.

In fall, the leaves of this tree tend to change colour all at once, and then drop off all at once. If there is a heavy frost, they can drop overnight.

Ginkgo leaves have a similar shape to maidenhair fern (known to most people as a tropical houseplant), which is why ginkgo is sometimes known as maidenhair tree.

It belongs to a class of plants called gymnosperms; most other trees in this category are conifers—cone-bearing evergreens such as pine and spruce.

Ginkgo grows very slowly. A famous ginkgo at Kew Gardens in England—planted in 1762—had grown to only about 55 feet (17 m) in height after 128 years.

TOP: Ginkgo differs from most broad-leaved trees in that its seeds are 'naked' rather than encapsulated (like a berry, fruit or nut). BOTTOM: This one-of-a-kind, 140-year-old bonsai ginkgo was available for sale at the Montreal Botanic Gardens, Quebec.

Hackberry

Celtis occidentalis
Common Hackberry

Height • 40–60 feet (12–18 m)

Spread • 40–60 feet (12–18 m)

Flowers • not showy; blooms in spring

Fruit • orange-red to purple berries ripen in fall

Growth Rate • medium

Lifespan • long

Zone Rating • 2

Hackberry is a lovely tree that grows as wide as it does tall. It is also a tough tree, thriving in almost every imaginable situation, from windy areas with dry soil to sites that are periodically flooded. The saw-toothed leaves of this tree are large—from 6–9 inches (15–23 cm) long—and they are attractive throughout summer. Hackberry's fall display is not very showy—the foliage often merely turns yellowish green, or sometimes yellow.

Hackberry and elm are related trees, although their leaves look quite different, and they have a similar shape and size. Hackberry is not affected by Dutch elm disease, however, and it is becoming widely accepted as a substitute for elm. Hackberry trees are common along urban streets and boulevards in Saskatchewan and Manitoba.

Hackberry is a very adaptable, low-maintenance shade tree.

GROWING

Sun.

Shade tree; in boulevards, parks or large properties.

RECOMMENDED SPECIES OR VARIETIES

Common Hackberry

TIPS

Hackberry is extremely adaptable to varying soil and climactic conditions. This tough tree performs remarkably well even in dry soils and windy conditions.

Prune hackberry in late winter to early spring, before the leaves appear.

Hackberry is a good tree to grow beside decks.

The berries are sweet and taste somewhat like dates, and they also contain a hard, date-like seed that could shatter a tooth, so be careful. In my region, the berries ripen in late September.

TOP: Hackberry has been cultivated in North America since 1636. BOTTOM: Hackberry 'drupes'—what the seedpods are called—contain extremely hard seeds. These drupes turn orange-red to dark purple in fall.

Harry Lauder's Walkingstick

Corylus avellana 'Contorta'
Harry Lauder's Walkingstick
Contorted Hazel
Corkscrew Hazel
Barking Bush

Height • 8–10 feet (2.4–3 m)

Spread • 8–10 feet (2.4–3 m)

Flowers • showy catkins in spring

Fruit • usually none

Growth Rate • slow to medium

Lifespan • average

Zone Rating • 4

If you want an unusual-looking shrub for your garden, Harry Lauder's Walkingstick may be just the answer. It looks somewhat like curly willow (which is not winter-hardy), and like that shrub, it is popular with florists for creating dramatic floral arrangements. In the garden, Harry Lauder's Walkingstick is a conversation piece. Its drooping leaves and stems curl and twist, resulting in a strangely attractive display. The renowned English gardener Edward Augustus Bowles (1865–1954) described this shrub as 'a collection of various crooks and corkscrews from root to tip.' It seems that Mr. Bowles was slightly twisted himself, at least in his sense of humour: he created a 'home for demented plants' in his garden called the 'Lunatic Asylum'; Harry Lauder's Walkingstick was the first resident.

GROWING

Sun to light shade; prefers a well-drained, loamy soil.

Feature shrub, as an accent in shrub border, for screens.

LEFT: Harry Lauder's Walkingstick is particularly striking in winter, with its distinctive branches silhouetted against the sky. RIGHT: Not surprisingly, the botanical name Contorta *means 'twisted or contorted' in Latin, referring to this shrub's attractive, intertwining stems.*

RECOMMENDED SPECIES OR VARIETIES

Harry Lauder's Walkingstick

Also called contorted hazel, corkscrew hazel or barking bush.

TIPS

Give this shrub a prominent location in your garden, so you can admire its bizarre beauty year-round. In late winter, attractive catkins dangle from the squiggly branches.

Prune Harry Lauder's Walkingstick in late winter to early spring, before the leaves appear, to thin or shape it.

Harry Lauder's Walkingstick is usually sold in grafted form. Sometimes long, straight stems shoot up from the rootstock; remove these suckers as they appear.

The fantastically curled branches add an unusual look to floral arrangements.

Although it is a form of European hazelnut, Harry Lauder's Walkingstick rarely produces nuts.

Harry Lauder's Walkingstick is superb for floral arrangements.

Hawthorn

Crataegus x mordensis
Morden Hawthorn

Height • 20 feet (6.1 m)

Spread • 15–20 feet (4.6–6.1 m)

Flowers • clusters of pink or white, double flowers in spring

Fruit • 1/2-inch (1.3 cm), crabapple-like fruit in mid-summer

Growth Rate • medium

Lifespan • short

Zone Rating • 3

If you have a small yard with room for only one tree, make it a hawthorn. Hawthorns are beautiful, compact trees with abundant, fragrant flowers, bright green leaves and colourful fruit. The botanical name Crataegus *comes from the Greek word* kratos, *meaning 'strength,' and it refers to the hawthorn's hard wood, strong branches and sturdy trunk. Most hawthorns have spiny branches and lots of small fruit, which are pretty but rather messy when they drop. Morden hawthorn, however, has few spines and very little fruit, making it a tidy shrub to grow close to sidewalks, patios or decks. Hawthorn generally blooms in May, and it is one of more than 100 different plants that are called 'mayflower.'*

GROWING

Sun to partial shade; well-drained soil. Feature tree; good for small yards.

RECOMMENDED SPECIES OR VARIETIES

'**Snowbird**': 20 feet (6.1 m) tall and 15–18 feet (4.6–5.5 m) wide; very beautiful in full bloom; fragrant, white, double flowers in spring; dark green leaves; few berries; resistant to rust; hardier and narrower than 'Toba.'

'**Toba**': 20 feet (6.1 m) tall and wide; a low-branched, very dense, round-topped tree; fragrant, double flowers are white with a pink blush; dark green leaves; resistant to rust; few berries.

Hawthorn flowers are said to symbolize hope. Ages ago in France, Norman peasants wore sprigs of hawthorn flowers in their caps; this custom was related to the belief that Christ's crown of thorns was made of hawthorn.

TOP LEFT: Hawthorns are quite small trees and fit easily into almost any yard. Hawthorn belongs to the same plant family as apple trees. Its fragrant flowers look and smell similar to apple-blossoms.
TOP RIGHT: 'Snowbird' is a very hardy, disease-resistant variety.

TIPS

Do not plant hawthorns in heavy clay soils or low-lying areas of the garden, where water tends to pool.

Hawthorn is a vigorous tree that benefits from annual pruning. Prune it after it flowers.

These trees sometimes produce 'watersprouts' (shoots at the base of trunks or along branches that are often mistakenly called 'suckers'). Trim them off as they appear. When trees are kept in good health, watersprouts are less likely to occur.

The sparse red berries (technically called 'pomes') attract birds, and the twiggy branches provide good cover for nesting.

Neither 'Snowbird' nor 'Toba' produce a lot of fruit, but what they do produce can be used to make jelly, or fermented and mixed with brandy.

In England, hawthorn is popular for hedgerows, because it grows in a variety of soils.

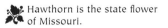

Hawthorn is the state flower of Missouri.

MIDDLE: The 1/2-inch (1.3 cm) wide fruit looks somewhat like the fruit of crabapples, but tends to be drier and to have more seeds.
BOTTOM: If it is a long and warm fall, hawthorn provides a splendid display of colour; in other years, the leaves remain green until they fall.

Hazelnut

Corylus americana
American Hazelnut
American Filbert

Corylus avellana
European Hazelnut
European Filbert

Height • 10–20 feet (3–6.1 m)

Spread • 7–12 feet (2.1–3.7 m)

Flowers • showy catkins in spring

Fruit • nuts ripen in fall

Growth Rate • medium

Lifespan • average

Zone Rating
American: 2
European: 4

Most kinds of nuts grow on large trees in mild climates. Hazelnut is one of the few nuts that grows in northern regions. It is a large, dense shrub that requires far less space than nut-bearing trees. American hazelnut is hardier and a bit smaller than European hazelnut; it grows wild from Maine to Saskatchewan, and south to Georgia. European hazelnut is very productive and is grown for commercial nut production. At one time, it was believed that a forked hazelnut twig had supernatural powers. The twigs were used as divining rods to find underground water or gold.

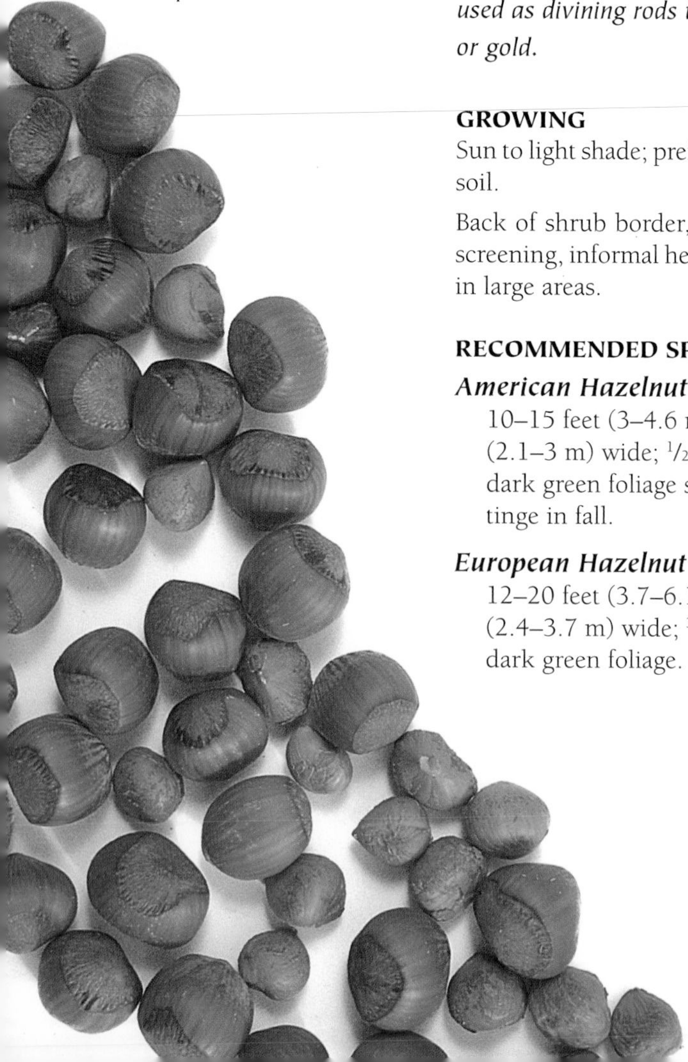

GROWING

Sun to light shade; prefers a well-drained, loamy soil.

Back of shrub border, in large shrub beds, for screening, informal hedges or naturalizing. Best in large areas.

RECOMMENDED SPECIES OR VARIETIES

American Hazelnut

10–15 feet (3–4.6 m) tall and 7–10 feet (2.1–3 m) wide; 1/2–inch (1.3 cm) nuts; dark green foliage sometimes has a red tinge in fall.

European Hazelnut

12–20 feet (3.7–6.1 m) tall and 8–12 feet (2.4–3.7 m) wide; 3/4-inch (1.9 cm) nuts; dark green foliage.

LEFT: Hazelnut has a nice, compact growth habit.
RIGHT: American hazelnut is very showy in early spring with its yellowish-brown catkins, which are 1½–3 inches (3.8–7.6 cm) long.

TIPS

Hazelnuts spread by basal shoots, and they can form very dense thickets. They are often mixed with honeysuckle vines for cottage garden hedges.

To prevent hazelnuts from spreading, thin by pruning annually in late winter to early spring, and by removing basal shoots as they appear.

A hazelnut screen or hedge protects other plants against the elements.

A hazelnut bush can be trained to grow as a small tree. See *How to Train Shrubs to 'Tree' Form* on page 64.

Hazelnuts can be eaten raw or used in baking. The oil extracted from these nuts is used in dressings and for cooking.

Hazelnut is a low-maintenance shrub that attracts wildlife. Its dense foliage and twiggy branches provide good hiding spots for birds, while the nuts attract squirrels and other wildlife.

Hazelnut was sacred to some Irish groups who believed that a brook or stream that ran by a thicket of hazel was blessed and was capable of great healing.

Hemlock

Tsuga canadensis
Canadian Hemlock
Eastern Hemlock

Height • 8 inches–2 feet (20–61 cm)

Spread • 1–2 feet (30–61 cm)

Flowers • not showy

Fruit • cones

Growth Rate • slow

Lifespan • long

Zone Rating • 4 [3]

Hemlocks can grow to become huge trees, 100 feet (30 m) tall or more, but in my Alberta garden, I grow only dwarf varieties. These small, mounding evergreens have soft, dark green, glossy needles on elegantly drooping branches. You can always tell a hemlock by the top branch of its crown: the slender 'leader' gracefully droops down. As indicated by its species name canadensis, *hemlock is native to Canada. This evergreen has been cultivated since 1736. The hemlock tree shares its common name with an entirely unrelated European weed (*Conium *sp.) that is highly toxic. Early North American settlers apparently called the evergreen tree 'hemlock' because they thought its crushed needles smelled like the European hemlock. The evergreen hemlock is not poisonous; in fact, Native Peoples once made bread from its bark. The young branch tips can be used to make tea, and an oil derived from its twigs and foliage is used to flavour root beer and chewing gum.*

GROWING

Partial to full shade; prefers a moist, well-drained, acidic soil.

In rock gardens; Japanese gardens.

RECOMMENDED SPECIES OR VARIETIES

'**Gracilis**': a very slow-growing dwarf form; grows about 1–3 inches (2.5–7.6 cm) a year; after 10 to 15 years, it will be 8–12 inches (20–30 cm) tall and 1½–2 feet (46–61 cm) wide; a very attractive feature shrub.

'**Stockman's Dwarf**': another very slow-growing dwarf form; grows about 1–3 inches (2.5–7.6 cm) a year; after 10 to 15 years, it will be 1–2 feet (30–61 cm) tall and wide; upright growth habit spreads more with age; short, thick, compact foliage; very attractive.

The variety 'Gracilis' has graceful, arching branches that make it look somewhat like a miniature weeping tree. Gracilis *is Latin for 'slender' or 'graceful.'*

TIPS

Although hemlock is rated hardy to zone 4, it grows well in a sheltered site in zone 3.

Hemlock grows slowly, so little—if any—pruning should be done.

Hemlocks have shallow roots and can dry out quickly. They prefer moist soil and humid air, so it helps to mulch them with a mixture of pine or spruce needles and shredded fir bark. The mulch keeps the roots cool, reduces moisture loss and acidifies the soil.

Protect these shrubs from drying winter winds by covering them in late fall with spruce or pine boughs, which also help collect and hold snow overtop of the shrubs.

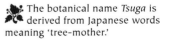

Hemlock is one of the most beautiful evergreens.

The botanical name *Tsuga* is derived from Japanese words meaning 'tree-mother.'

Ilex x meserveae
Meserve Hybrid

Mahonia aquifolium
Oregon Grapeholly
Oregon Hollygrape
Oregongrapeholly

Ilex verticillata
Winterberry
Michigan Holly

Height • 3–4 feet (91–120 cm)

Spread • 3–4 feet (91–120 cm)

Flowers • small, white or yellow flowers in summer

Fruit • red or blue berries late summer to fall through winter

Growth Rate • slow

Lifespan • short

Zone Rating
Meserve Hybrid: 4
Oregon Grapeholly: 3
Winterberry: 3

Holly

The name 'holly' is derived from the word 'holy.' For centuries, it was believed that this plant provided protection from evil spirits if grown close to the house. Hollies range from 1 foot (30 cm) shrubs to 80 foot (24 m) trees. Few hollies are winter-hardy in northern gardens.

Meserve hybrid is a newer type of holly and the hardiest evergreen holly yet developed. Winterberry is deciduous and its leaves are finely serrated, not pointed. Oregon grapeholly is not a true holly. Although this shrub closely resembles holly, the two plants are not related. It produces bunches of blue-black berries that hang like grapes from the branches, hence the name.

GROWING

Sun to light shade; moist, rich, acidic soil. Winterberry also grows in wet sites.

Meserve hybrid and Oregon grapeholly as feature shrubs, foundation plantings. Winterberry also in shrub borders, mass plantings, as an informal hedge.

RECOMMENDED SPECIES OR VARIETIES

Meserve Hybrid

'**Blue Boy**': 10–12 feet (3–3.7 m) tall and 5–6 feet (1.5–1.8 m) wide; dense, thick, dark green foliage; does not produce berries; spiny leaves; evergreen variety introduced in 1964.

'**Blue Girl**': 8–10 feet (2.4–3 m) tall and 6–8 feet (1.8–2.4 m) wide; foliage the same as 'Blue Boy'; bright red berries; needs 'Blue Boy' as pollinator.

Oregon Grapeholly

3–6 feet (91–180 cm) tall and 3–5 feet (91–150 cm) wide; yellow flowers in spring; blue-black berries in late summer and early fall; smooth, mostly shiny, dark green leaves; foliage turns purple-red in fall.

TOP: Oregon grapeholly is the state flower of Oregon.
BOTTOM: This 'Blue Girl' holly was planted three years ago in our zone 3 garden. In a sunny, sheltered spot next to a large spruce tree, it has survived just fine despite two harsh winters.

'Winter Red' has no rival in the winter landscape. The attractive, bright red berries hang on bare branches well into winter.

Winterberry

'**Winter Red**': 6–9 feet (1.8–2.7 m) tall and 6–8 feet (1.8–2.4 m) wide; flowers are not showy; dark green foliage; masses of bright red berries that remain on bare branches well into winter; both a male and female shrub needed for berry production; a deciduous holly.

In mild climates, holly's unique foliage and colourful berries add interest to gardens.

TIPS

Because holly plants are either female or male, you need at least one plant of each sex for the production of berries. Only female plants have berries. Generally, one male holly plant suffices for eight to nine female plants. For best results, grow them side by side.

Prune holly in early spring when it is dormant. Prune evergreen varieties just before 'bud break' to remove winter damage.

Holly is sometimes sold with one plant of each sex grafted or planted together.

Because Oregon grapeholly is not a true holly (*Ilex*), a single shrub will produce berries. To prevent foliage from browning, plant it in a site that is sheltered from winter winds or has good snowcover.

Winterberry was rated highly at the Canadian Hedge Trials, when trimmed to a height of 5–6 feet (1.5–1.8 m). It was given a zone 3b hardiness rating.

Keep holly well watered during extended dry spells, and add a thick mulch to help retain moisture. The mulch will also inhibit weeds and there will be less chance of damaging the shallow roots while cultivating.

In zone 3, holly will grow well if planted in a sheltered site, but it remains smaller. 'Blue Boy' and 'Blue Girl,' for example, will reach about one-quarter to one-half of their potential height, because of winter dieback.

In warmer climates, the blue hollies are evergreen; in cooler climates, they act deciduous—the leaves on branches above the snowline turn brown and die, but the dormant leafbuds often survive. In my zone 3 area, therefore, it may be best to grow them as a short hedge or as a feature shrub in a sheltered site away from winter winds.

'Blue Girl' has 'traditional,' brilliant red berries and glossy green foliage.

Honeysuckle

Diervilla lonicera
Dwarf Bush Honeysuckle

Lonicera xylosteum
European Fly Honeysuckle

Lonicera maximowicii var. *sachalinensis*
Sakhalin Honeysuckle

Lonicera caerulea var. *edulis*
Sweetberry Honeysuckle

Lonicera tatarica
Tatarian Honeysuckle

Height • 2–12 feet (61 cm–3.7 m)

Spread • 3 1/2–10 feet (1.1–3 m)

Flowers • red, purple, yellow or white flowers in spring

Fruit • most have red berries in summer

Growth Rate • slow to medium

Lifespan • short

Zone Rating
Dwarf Bush, Sakhalin, Tatarian: 3
European Fly: 4 [3]
Sweetberry: 2

Honeysuckles are wonderful additions to flower gardens. Although they perform best in moist soil, all honeysuckles are drought tolerant. 'Arnold Red,' a Tatarian honeysuckle, is a large, vigorous shrub that looks spectacular in bloom. Of the types listed here, 'Arnold Red' has the darkest flowers and is the only fragrant variety. It produces a splendid display of red berries. Dwarf bush honeysuckle is a small, tidy shrub with very attractive foliage. It has greater shade tolerance than most and thrives even in dry soil. 'Emerald Mound' is a tough, tidy shrub with attractive foliage. A group of 'Emerald Mound' honeysuckles that I saw growing in a shrub bed in the middle of a parking lot looked splendid despite the heat and little maintenance they received. Sakhalin honeysuckle is a larger, shade-tolerant shrub that blooms beautifully in spring. Sweetberry is the only honeysuckle with edible berries.

GROWING

Sun to light shade; moist soil; sakhalin needs partial shade.

Middle to back of shrub border; foundation plantings, hedges; dwarf bush in groups, mass plantings, as a filler plant; 'Emerald Mound' as an informal hedge or border.

Dwarf bush honeysuckle retains its dense form with little pruning. It blooms in early to mid-summer, later than other honeysuckles.

RECOMMENDED SPECIES OR VARIETIES

Dwarf Bush Honeysuckle

$3^1/_2$–4 feet (1.1–1.2 m) tall and wide; not a true honeysuckle, but closely resembles one; tiny, yellow flowers; glossy, dark green foliage; new leaves have tinges of bronze; foliage turns burgundy-red in fall; no berries; cultivated since 1720; a very hardy and adaptable shrub.

European Fly Honeysuckle

'**Emerald Mound**': 2–3 feet (61–91 cm) tall and 4–6 feet (1.2–1.8 m) wide; yellowish-white flowers and dark red berries; a squat, mounded, compact shrub that leafs out early in spring.

Sakhalin Honeysuckle

6–8 feet (1.8–2.4 m) tall and wide; an impressive show of dark reddish-purple flowers in spring; red berries in late summer; a round-headed shrub; foliage turns golden-yellow in fall; the only true honeysuckle with consistent fall colour.

Honeysuckles are attractive, summer-flowering shrubs.

TOP: If you are looking for an attractive, low-maintenance shrub, 'Emerald Mound' is one of the best choices. It remains full, lush and compact with little pruning or supplemental watering.
BOTTOM: With its bright green foliage, sweetberry honeysuckle is attractive even without flowers or fruit.

Sweetberry Honeysuckle

4–5 feet (1.2–1.5 m) tall and wide; yellowish-white flowers; sweet, edible, blue berries; bright green foliage; a very dense, sturdy shrub; native to eastern Siberia; introduced about 1967.

Tatarian Honeysuckle

'**Arnold Red**': 10–12 feet (3–3.7 m) tall and 10 feet (3 m) wide; the darkest red flowers of all honeysuckles; bluish-green foliage; tiny, bright red berries; an upright, multi-stemmed shrub; resistant to aphids; introduced in 1962; one of the most popular varieties.

TIPS

There are over 180 species of honeysuckle, including both shrubs and vines. Only some honeysuckles are hardy enough for cold climates, and some grow like weeds, looking rather unattractive in the garden. You are best off choosing a recommended variety.

LEFT & RIGHT: The flowers of 'Arnold Red' are the darkest of any honeysuckle, and have a sweet fragrance.

Most honeysuckles need regular pruning to encourage new growth; cut out oldest stems, crossing branches and any deadwood; prune after flowering.

Dwarf bush and 'Emerald Mound' are exceptions; they need little pruning.

'Emerald Mound' does well in zone 3 although its official rating is zone 4.

If you are growing sweetberry honeysuckle for its fruit, plant it in a site that is sunny but not hot. This shrub is drought tolerant, but the most berries are produced when the shrub has moist soil and a cooler location in the yard.

Sweetberry is named for its edible, blue fruit, which ripens in late summer and can be eaten raw or used in jams, jellies and drinks.

Horse Chestnut

Aesculus hippocastanum
Common Horse chestnut
European Horse chestnut

Height • 40–50 feet (12–15 m)

Spread • 35–40 feet (11–12 m)

Flowers • showy clusters of white flowers in late spring

Fruit • large, prickly seedpods release nuts in fall

Growth Rate • medium

Lifespan • long

Zone Rating • 4 [3]

Horse chestnut is one of the oldest and most renowned ornamental trees. It is popular in European parks and gardens, and has been cultivated since 1576.

Horse chestnut is a stunning shade tree that is very popular in Europe and many parts of Canada, but rather uncommon in my area. In late spring its sturdy branches are laden with very showy candelabras of creamy white flowers. The 8-inch (20 cm) flower clusters stand upright; each little flower within the cluster is marked in the centre with a yellow blotch that eventually turns red. Horse chestnut trees have heavy foliage and spreading crowns through which little sunlight penetrates, resulting in dense shade beneath. The dark green leaves are long-stalked and palmate—five to seven leaflets join to form one leaf, like outstretched fingers on a hand. Each leaf is up to 9 inches (23 cm) long. Horse chestnuts don't have showy fall foliage, but their large, round, prickly seedpods add interest and are fascinating for children.

GROWING

Sun to partial shade. Do not plant in a dry location.

Shade tree.

RECOMMENDED SPECIES OR VARIETIES

Common Horse chestnut

Also known as European horse chestnut.

TIPS

Don't plant horse chestnut trees near white or light-coloured reflective walls. Excessive exposure to intense sunlight and heat can cause 'sun scald'—a condition characterized by brown leaf blotches and scorched leaf edges.

In protected sites, horse chestnut does well in zone 3.

Avoid planting in very dry or windy sites. Low humidity and drying winds often burn leaf margins and subsequently make them look a little tattered.

Little pruning is required. If necessary, prune in late winter to early spring, before leaves appear.

The prickly seedpods mature in fall, and split open to release one to three shiny, brown nuts (the seeds). The nuts attract deer and squirrels.

TOP LEFT & TOP RIGHT: Horse chestnut has two unique visual characteristics. In spring its branches have plenty of creamy white flowers, and during the growing season it is covered in well-armed, prickly seedpods. BOTTOM: Horse chestnut is not a true chestnut tree, and its nuts are not good for eating. Centuries ago, the Turks used the nuts to treat respiratory ailments in horses.

Hydrangea

Hydrangea paniculata
Panicle Hydrangea

Hydrangea arborescens
Smooth Hydrangea

Height • 2–8 feet (61 cm–2.4 m)

Spread • 2–8 feet (61 cm–2.4 m)

Flowers • large, showy flowerheads in late summer

Fruit • not showy

Growth Rate
Panicle Hydrangea: slow
Smooth Hydrangea: fast

Lifespan • short

Zone Rating • 3

Hydrangeas are among the showiest of flowering shrubs. Some varieties produce abundant, spectacular flowerheads that can be huge—1 foot (30 cm) or more in size. There aren't many shrubs that bloom in late summer, which makes hydrangeas all the more desirable. Their long-lasting flowerheads persist through periods when few other shrubs are blooming. Hydrangeas continue to bloom through most of summer and often into fall, with faded flowerheads remaining on branches into winter. If this feature isn't enough to make these shrubs endearing, hydrangeas are also easy to grow, untroubled by pests and one of the best suppliers of large flowers for fresh bouquets and dried arrangements.

GROWING

Partial shade to sun; rich, moist, well-drained soil essential. Do not allow soil to dry out.

Feature shrub, foundation plantings, in shrub beds or groups.

May need support when blooming.

Hydrangeas are among the showiest summer-flowering shrubs, with huge flowerheads that last for up to three months!

LEFT: The flowers of 'Kyushu' have a more open, airy look than other hydrangeas. This variety was named after the Japanese island it came from.
RIGHT: Hydrangea is sometimes called the 'chameleon flower' because its flowers change colours. 'PeeGee's' flowers start out green, mature to white and then turn pale pink, rose and rust. Cool weather deepens the colour, and the flowerheads turn rich rusty-rose in fall. Finally, they fade to beige, remaining intact on the branches throughout most of winter—a decorative effect in a snow-covered garden.

RECOMMENDED SPECIES OR VARIETIES

Panicle Hydrangea

'**Kyushu**': 6–8 feet (1.8–2.4 m) tall and wide; slender, elegant, white, cone-shaped flowerheads are 6 inches (15 cm) long and 3–4 inches (7.6–10 cm) wide; most of the flowers are sterile and do not produce seedheads; smooth, dark green leaves that show off the flowers.

'**PeeGee**': also known as 'Grandiflora'; usually 5–6 feet (1.5–1.8 m) tall and wide but can grow much larger if planted in a protected site; huge, pinkish-white, cone-shaped flowerheads up to 1½ feet (46 cm) long and 1 foot (30 cm) wide; extremely attractive when in full bloom; the lightest green leaves of any hydrangea; a very popular, adaptable variety that grows well in gardens across North America.

With its huge flowerheads, the variety 'Annabelle' is one of the most popular hydrangeas. These shrubs continue to bloom until the first hard frost in fall.

The name 'hydrangea' is derived from the Greek word for 'water.' In keeping with this fact, never allow these moisture-loving shrubs to dry out. Keep them well watered, especially when blooming.

Hydrangeas can vary tremendously from stated sizes. One man brought an immense flower into our nursery for identification, from a shrub that he had seen blooming on a golf course in Kelowna, B.C. It was from an 'Annabelle' hydrangea, and the flower measured almost 16 inches (41 cm) across!

Smooth Hydrangea

'**Annabelle**': 2–3 feet (61–91 cm) tall and wide; very large, showy, white flowerheads are 6–12 inches (15–30 cm) across; blooms mid-summer to early fall; more shade tolerant than other hydrangeas, but blooms best in full sun; leaves are medium green and large, up to 8 inches (20 cm) long and 6 inches (15 cm) wide; flowers are sterile and do not form seedheads.

TIPS

The variety 'PeeGee' is said to eventually grow as large as 15–25 feet (4.6–7.6 m) tall and 10–20 feet (3–6.1 m) wide! In most gardens that I've seen, it averages about one-third of that size. There is, however, a splendid 'PeeGee' hydrangea growing at Lacombe, Alberta, which is now 8–10 feet (2.4–3 m) tall.

Cut back smooth hydrangeas to 3–4 inches (7.6–10 cm) above ground level in early spring. This step is not necessary with panicle hydrangeas; just remove any dead branch tips.

The flowerheads of these shrubs are so large and heavy that they can cause branches to bow down to the ground, especially with the variety

'Annabelle.' If you don't like this effect, use a peony ring; put it in place in early spring. In warmer climates, hydrangeas tend to form woodier stems and need less support.

Cut flowers for bouquets when most of the florets (the little flowers that make up the flowerhead) are just starting to open. Like poppies, hydrangeas have a milky sap that can seal the cut end. Prevent this by re-cutting the stem indoors and immediately immersing the stem ends in boiling water for 20 to 30 seconds. Cutflowers last 7 to 10 days.

Cut flowers for drying after they are fully open. Place them in a vase with about an inch (2.5 cm) of water in it. As water evaporates, the flowers dry slowly. They keep their colour better with this method than by air-drying. Cut flowers in the morning rather than in mid-day heat; it helps to prevent them from shrinking as they dry.

Gardeners sometimes ask me why their hydrangeas aren't blooming. Most often it is because of pruning at the wrong time of year. Any pruning should be done in late winter to early spring. Panicle hydrangeas often need rejuvenation pruning, which involves removing a few of the oldest stems at ground level each year. You can easily tell which are the oldest shoots; they have the most side branches.

Unfortunately, many of the lovely big-leaf hydrangeas with the blue flowers (*H. macrophylla*) are hardy only to about zones 5 and 6. I do know of one woman, however, who lives in my zone 3 area and has grown a big-leaf hydrangea in her garden for at least 10 years. If you are trying to grow one of these shrubs, choose a protected site up against the house, where the shrub will get some winter protection from it. These hydrangeas bloom on old wood, so in late fall mulch as high up the stems as possible with dry peat moss, and throw fresh snow overtop whenever you can.

The variety 'PeeGee' was introduced from Japan in 1862. Although I've never confirmed the following information, it seems logical that the name 'PeeGee' refers to the initials of this variety's botanical name: paniculata *'Grandiflora.'*

Juniperus chinensis
Chinese Juniper

Juniperus communis
Common Juniper

Juniperus horizontalis
Creeping Juniper
Horizontal Juniper

Juniperus procumbens
Japanese Juniper
Japanese Garden Juniper

Juniperus scopulorum
Rocky Mountain Juniper

Juniperus sabina
Savin Juniper

Juniperus squamata
Squamata Juniper
Single-seed Juniper

Height • 4 inches–20 feet
(10 cm–6.1 m)

Spread • $1\frac{1}{2}$–20 feet
(46 cm–6.1 m)

Flowers • tiny; in small cones

Fruit • blue or green, berry-like cones

Growth Rate
Chinese: slow to medium
Common, Japanese, Rocky Mountain, Squamata: slow
Savin: medium

Lifespan
Most: short
Common, Rocky Mountain: long
Squamata: average

Zone Rating
Chinese, Creeping, Rocky Mountain, Savin: 3
Common: 2
Japanese, Squamata: 4 [3]

Juniper

Junipers are wonderful evergreens. They are tough, hardy and available in an enormous range of sizes, from just a few inches to 20 feet (6.1 m) or more in both height and width. Foliage can be green, gold or blue. Junipers—especially upright varieties—are often confused with cedars. Chinese junipers have a huge range of sizes and shapes; there are more named cultivars of Chinese juniper than of any other type of juniper. Common junipers tend to be low, wide-spreading and very hardy; they are native to the Rocky Mountains.

The lowest, most prostrate type is creeping juniper; it forms the densest mat of foliage, putting down roots as it spreads. Japanese juniper is less common, and its foliage has a unique, billowy texture. Rocky Mountain junipers are large, but slow growing. A 12-year-old 'Medora' in our show garden has spread to (at best) 4 feet (1.2 m)—less than half its potential size. Savin junipers tend to be wide shrubs; varieties range tremendously in height. Squamata junipers are low and slow growing; some of the best cultivars have lovely blue foliage.

Gold Coast juniper is great for foundation plantings because it remains dense and compact. It's a good choice for small settings, and looks striking in a flowerbed with flowering kale. The gold colour is intensified in winter.

GROWING

Sun; grows well in almost any situation. Most junipers are very drought tolerant and thrive in a hot, dry location. Only some varieties do well in partial shade; a minimum of six hours of direct sunlight is needed per day.

In groups, mass plantings, rock gardens. Upright varieties as informal hedges. In foundation plantings, the varieties 'Blue Star,' Compact Andorra, Gold Coast, 'Mint Julep,' Savin. As groundcovers, all creeping junipers and the varieties 'Calgary Carpet,' 'Effusa,' Gold Coast, 'Mint Julep' and 'New Blue Tam.'

RECOMMENDED SPECIES OR VARIETIES

SPREADING JUNIPERS

Chinese Juniper

Gold Coast (*J. chinensis* 'Aurea'): 3–4 feet (91–120 cm) tall and 4–6 feet (1.2–1.8 m) wide; older growth is green to greenish yellow while the new growth is extremely yellow; foliage colour intensifies in cold weather; does not produce cones; a compact, dense shrub; prefers moist soil; grows well in poor soil; can be pruned or shaped; one of the best golden junipers for this area.

Symbolic meanings are often given to different plants; a common example is an olive branch, which stands for 'peace.' 'Juniper' means 'protection,' and there are many charming myths that follow this theme. According to folklore, at one time juniper branches were burned when a woman was giving birth, to prevent the fairies from substituting a changeling for the newborn baby. During the Middle Ages, it was believed that the smoke from burning juniper branches protected people from contagious diseases, such as the plague and leprosy.

TOP LEFT: 'Mint Julep' is often sold in ornamental grafted forms, including 'pom-pom' (balls of foliage atop bare branches) or 'spiral.'
TOP RIGHT: 'Effusa' is a great choice for a low-maintenance situation because of its excellent drought tolerance.
BOTTOM: 'Blue Prince' is a wonderful contrasting groundcover; this variety is the bluest juniper.

'**Mint Julep**': 4–6 feet (1.2–1.8 m) tall and 6–8 feet (1.8–2.4 m) wide; brilliant mint-green foliage on arching, fountain-like branches; becomes 'leggy' in shade; grows well in alkaline soil, as long as moist; takes readily to pruning and shaping; variety introduced in 1971; produces cones; grafted forms make splendid garden accents; in its natural form, this variety is good in foundation or mass plantings and as a groundcover.

Common Juniper

'**Effusa**': 10–15 inches (25–38 cm) tall and 7–8 feet (2.1–2.4 m) wide; rich medium green on lower older growth, and light silvery green on newer growth; both male and female plants available—only females produce cones; tolerates light shade; grows in very poor or dry, rocky soil; foliage colour holds well in winter; one of the hardiest junipers.

P.P. 5948

Creeping Juniper

'Blue Prince': 6 inches (15 cm) tall and 3–5 feet (91 cm–150 cm) wide; rich, powdery blue foliage; selected from the wild in Alberta; does not produce cones; the best blue foliage.

Compact Andorra (*J. horizontalis* 'Plumosa Compacta'): 18–24 inches tall (46–61 cm) and 6–8 feet (1.8–2.4 m) wide; grey-green foliage turns purplish in fall; rather soft needles; does not produce cones; a better variety than the original Andorra, which tended to become open in the centre; Compact Andorra remains full in the centre even when mature; introduced in 1907; tolerates light shade.

'Mother Lode™': 4–6 inches (10–15 cm) tall and 6–8½ feet (1.8–2.6 m) wide; very low-growing, spreading juniper with a beautiful golden colour; produces cones; foliage turns a deep orange-yellow colour in fall.

TOP: 'Mother Lode™' is a creeping juniper variety.
BOTTOM: Compact Andorra is a popular, low-spreading juniper with grey-green foliage that turns a beautiful plum colour in fall. Use this variety as a groundcover, or grow in a rock garden or shrub bed with nest spruce.

TOP: 'Wiltonii' is one of the more prostrate groundcover junipers. It looks stunning with its long branches trailing over the edge of a raised bed or rock wall. This steely blue juniper gains about 6–12 inches (15–30 cm) per year. BOTTOM: 'Prince of Wales' is fast growing for a juniper; this variety is a popular groundcover.

'**Prince of Wales**': 4–6 inches (10–15 cm) tall and 10–12 feet (3–3.7 m) wide; bright blue-green foliage; often has a purplish tint in winter; native to Alberta and introduced to the nursery trade in 1967; does not produce cones; sometimes sold in grafted form as a weeping tree with long, trailing branches; grafted form is very attractive with its exposed, twisted, gnarled trunk.

'**Wiltonii**': also known as 'Blue Rug' or Wilton's Juniper; 4–6 inches (10–15 cm) tall and 6–8 feet (1.8–2.4 m) wide; intense silver-blue foliage; has a purplish tinge in winter; long, trailing branches; grows well in hard soils, on rocky to gravel slopes; heat tolerant, performing well in hot weather; fast-growing variety introduced in 1914.

Japanese Juniper

'**Greenmound**': 6–8 inches (15–20 cm) tall and 5–6 feet (1.5–1.8 m) wide; striking green foliage that billows like ocean waves; does not brown on tips; both male and female plants available; only females produce cones; tolerates a wide range of soil conditions, including alkaline soil; a beautiful, mounding variety.

LEFT: The billowing foliage of a 'Greenmound' juniper flows over the edge of a rock wall. This variety performs best in an open site.
TOP RIGHT: 'Calgary Carpet' is an extremely hardy variety that spreads up to eight times its height.
BOTTOM RIGHT: With its wide-spread 'wings,' savin stands out in a crowd.

Savin Juniper

Savin: 4–6 feet (1.2–1.8 m) tall and 5–10 feet (1.5–3 m) wide; very dark green foliage; colour is much paler in winter; shrub has a distinctive vase shape; both male and female plants sold; only females produce berries; somewhat shade tolerant but becomes 'leggy' if grown in full shade; excellent for areas where a large space needs to be filled.

'**Calgary Carpet**': 8–12 inches (20–30 cm) tall and 7–8 feet (2.1–2.4 m) wide; very soft green; produces cones; tolerates light shade; prefers dry soil; our most popular juniper.

TOP: True to its name, each branch of 'Blue Star' ends in steel blue stars. The foliage colour is often magnified by drops of rain. BOTTOM: 'New Blue Tam' is an oddity among junipers. Most junipers have separate male and female plants; female junipers produce cones, but only if there is a male juniper nearby for pollination. 'New Blue Tam,' however, sometimes has both male and female flowers on the same plant, and may produce berries.

Squamata Juniper

'**Blue Star**': 3 feet (91 cm) tall and 3–4 feet (91–120 cm) wide; bright blue foliage; low, rounded, squat shrub introduced in 1950; brightest colour on new growth; produces berries; best with good snowcover through winter; ideal for an area where a low, not too wide, shrub is required; looks super in a rock garden with a rocky mulch.

'**New Blue Tam**': 15–18 inches (38–46 cm) tall and 10–15 feet (3–4.6 m) wide; slow-growing variety that takes 15 to 20 years to spread to mature size; bluish-green foliage; very dense, mounding form; tolerant to partial shade and drought; a selected variety found growing wild in the mountains of southern Europe; bluer than the original tam juniper.

LEFT: 'Medora' is a slow-growing variety that grows 6–8 inches (15–20 cm) per year. It takes about 50 to 60 years to reach mature size. Junipers are quite tolerant of drought, and very forgiving of a wide range of conditions.
RIGHT: 'Moonglow' is one of the most drought-tolerant junipers.

Upright Junipers

Common Juniper

'**Pencil Point**': 5–10 feet (1.5–3 m) tall and 1–2 feet (30–61 cm) wide; dark green foliage; slow-growing dwarf variety; takes 15 to 30 years to reach mature size; best in a sheltered site for perfect form; the narrowest columnar juniper available.

Rocky Mountain Juniper

'**Medora**': 30–40 feet (9.1–12 m) tall and 8–10 feet (2.4–3 m) wide; blue foliage; very compact variety that needs no pruning; introduced in 1954; only male plants, which produce no berries, are sold; slender, pyramidal form.

'**Moonglow**': 20 feet (6.1 m) tall and 7–8 feet (2.1–2.4 m) wide; slow-growing variety that takes over 15 to 20 years to reach full size; silver-blue foliage; a broad pyramid; remains full and dense without pruning; one of the most silvery junipers for my region.

LEFT: 'Skyrocket' makes a splendid accent in a formal garden. This variety is one of the narrowest junipers.
RIGHT: With its mane-like foliage, 'Tolleson's Weeping' is a very unusual and striking addition to gardens.

Junipers are tough evergreens that require little care.

'**Skyrocket**': 15–16 feet (4.6–4.9 m) tall and 1½–2 feet (46–61 cm) wide; blue-green foliage; particularly striking planted in groups or rows; great for formal gardens; best in a sunny, sheltered spot to retain perfect shape; one of the narrowest junipers available.

'**Tolleson's Weeping**': 18–20 feet (5.5–6.1 m) tall and 8–10 feet (2.4–3 m) wide; silver-blue foliage hangs like a mane from the arching branches; an excellent specimen plant; a green form is also available; one of the most unique and attractive junipers.

'**Wichita Blue**': 18–20 feet (5.5–6 m) tall and 5–6 feet (1.5–1.8 m) wide at the base; brilliant silvery-blue foliage; strong cone-shape; prune and shape to keep dense and compact; great colour year-round, even in winter.

TIPS

Golden or light-tipped junipers are more prone to 'desiccation'—drying-out and browning of foliage—than other junipers. Avoid planting these junipers in hot, windswept areas.

Junipers do best in low humidity, and decline in high humidity.

Generally, junipers need little pruning, other than to remove any dead branches in spring. For a more dense and compact shrub, prune while actively growing in summer. Shorten new growth by one-third to encourage growth from older parts of plant.

In our experience, Japanese and squamata junipers can also be grown in zone 3, although they are usually rated to zone 4.

Florists often use the bright blue, berry-like cones of common juniper to add to floral arrangements. Cut branches with berries last about two weeks. Mist frequently with water to prevent needles from dropping.

The foliage can be prickly, but when watered well, the needles are softer. Whenever you need to prune or work around your junipers, water them well the day before. Otherwise, it's a good idea to wear gloves to avoid scratching your hands and arms.

Add juniper 'berries' to potpourri.

LEFT: Although they look like berries, what are commonly called 'juniper berries' are actually tiny, compact, blue cones. They are used to flavour gin, an alcoholic beverage. The name 'gin' is derived from the Dutch word 'jenever,' meaning 'juniper.'
RIGHT: The bright colours of zinnias offset the silver-blue foliage of 'Wichita Blue.' To keep this variety dense and compact, prune annually.

According to legend, a juniper planted beside the front door will keep out witches. The only way for a witch to get past the juniper would be to correctly count its needles: a next-to-impossible feat!

Larch

Larix decidua
European Larch

Larix sibirica
Siberian Larch

Larix laricina
Tamarack
American Larch
Eastern Larch

Height • 10 inches–80 feet (25 cm–24 m)

Spread • 18 inches–40 feet (46 cm–12 m)

Flowers • not showy

Fruit • tiny cones

Growth Rate
European: medium to fast
'Newport Beauty': slow
Siberian, Tamarack: slow to medium

Lifespan
European: average to long
Siberian, Tamarack: long

Zone Rating
European: 3
Siberian: 2
Tamarack: 1

In fall, as leaves on other trees turn colour, the soft needles of larch turn from green to bright golden-yellow. Larch is unusual in that it is a deciduous conifer; unlike most cone-bearing trees, it sheds its foliage in fall. Larch needles are soft to touch. If you look closely at a branch, you'll notice that the needles grow one by one, in whorls along the shoots, whereas the needles of most evergreen conifers—pine, spruce, fir—grow in bundles. Few trees are as hardy as the larch.

GROWING

Sun; moist to wet soil.

Feature tree, in groups. Dwarf varieties in shrub beds or flowerbeds, in rock gardens.

RECOMMENDED SPECIES OR VARIETIES

European Larch

Weeping (*Larix decidua* 'Pendula'): 10–30 feet (3–9.1 m) wide; height varies tremendously depending on how it is grown; unless staked, this variety will sprawl along the ground; great for rock gardens or trailing over retaining walls; when staked, makes a unique specimen tree.

Siberian Larch

'**Conica**': 40–80 feet (12–24 m) tall and 15–20 feet (4.6–6.1 m) wide; quite dense foliage gives it a more uniform appearance; a cone-shaped tree with up-reaching branches; light green foliage.

TOP LEFT: Weeping larch's height can vary enormously. This specimen's upright growth was achieved by staking it .
TOP RIGHT & BOTTOM: Siberian larch has an attractive, uniform shape. Its brilliant yellow fall colour, adds contrast and flare to any yard.

TOP LEFT: Larches have tiny cones, about a 1/2 inch (1.3 cm) long, which are pink when young and brown when older.
BOTTOM LEFT: 'Newport Beauty' is a slow-growing, dwarf variety of tamarack, which gains 1–3 inches (2.5–7.6 cm) per year.
RIGHT: Tamarack grows well in wet areas.

Tamarack

Tamarack: 40–80 feet (12–24 m) tall and 15–30 feet (4.6–9.1 m) wide; smaller in urban areas; native species from Labrador to Yukon; excellent variety for wet sites; bears cones heavily every three to six years.

'**Newport Beauty**': 10–13 inches (25–33 cm) tall and 18–24 inches (46–61 cm) wide; blue-green needles; a dwarf, very attractive, globe-shaped variety ideal for small flowerbeds or rock gardens.

Larches grow well even when pruned or shaped. Siberian larch makes an unusual and attractive formal hedge, but it requires strict attention to the pruning schedule.

TIPS

Larches grown in the shade or in dry, alkaline soil have a thin appearance, with sparse foliage. They will be less vigorous and have shorter lifespans.

Larch can adapt to wet, almost boggy soils but grows best in a moist, acidic, well-drained soil.

Because of its shallow root system, plant larch in low-traffic areas to avoid soil compaction.

Little, if any, pruning is needed.

A background of dark evergreen trees is ideal for highlighting larch's beautiful fall foliage.

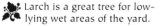

Larch is a great tree for low-lying wet areas of the yard.

Lilac

Syringa x hyacinthiflora
American Hybrid Lilac
Skinner Hybrid Lilac

Syringa x chinensis
Chinese Lilac

Syringa meyeri
Dwarf Korean Lilac
Meyers Lilac

Syringa vulgaris
French Hybrid Lilac
Common Lilac

Syringa reticulata
Japanese Tree Lilac

Syringa microphylla
Little-leaf Lilac

Syringa patula
Manchurian Lilac
Korean Lilac

Syringa x prestoniae
Preston Hybrid Lilac

*Every spring, I just can't wait for the lilacs to bloom. The alluring fragrance of these flowers invites me out to the garden, while a bouquet of cutflowers fills a room with evocative perfume. When most people think of lilacs, they mean the common one (*S. vulgaris*), which is the most widely grown. There are, however, many kinds of lilacs, ranging from dwarf, bushy types just 3 feet (91 cm) tall to mid-sized French hybrids to 30-foot (9.1 m) tall Japanese tree lilacs.*

Flowers come in seven official colours—white, violet, blue, lavender, pink, magenta and purple, with many shades of each. The florets (the tiny flowers that make up the large, clustered flowerheads) may be single (just one row of petals) or double, and vary widely in size and shape, as do the clusters.

American hybrid lilacs are the first to bloom. They are hardier, faster growing, less inclined to sucker and have more numerous, larger flowers than common lilacs. Even when young, American hybrid lilacs bloom profusely. Chinese and French hybrid lilacs begin blooming about 7 to 10 days later than American hybrids. Chinese lilacs have more flowers than French hybrid lilacs, but French hybrid lilacs have larger flowers, and are generally considered the most fragrant. Dwarf Korean and little-leaf lilac follow. Next to bloom is the Manchurian lilac.

Preston hybrids bloom in late spring, opening their first flowers about two weeks later than French hybrids. These hybrids are large shrubs with fewer flowers than French hybrid lilacs, and less fragrant, although still nicely scented. Last to bloom are the Japanese tree lilacs, which look quite different from the others. Tree lilacs bloom with abundant, musk-scented, creamy flowers in large clusters during early summer.

GROWING

Sun to light shade.

Shrub beds, specimen plant, screens, hedges. Dwarf Korean in rock gardens.

Height • 3–30 feet (91 cm–9.1 m)

Spread • 5–16 feet (1.5–4.9 m)

Flowers • showy, fragrant flower clusters in spring and summer

Fruit • capsules; noticeable; not showy, persistent

Growth Rate
- most varieties: medium
- Dwarf Korean, Little-leaf: slow

Lifespan • long

Zone Rating
- American Hybrid, Chinese, Dwarf Korean, French Hybrid, Manchurian: 3
- Little-leaf: 4
- Preston Hybrid: 2

TOP LEFT: 'Mount Baker' is one of the showiest white lilacs. It is an American hybrid variety—which some experts consider to be the best of all lilacs.
TOP RIGHT: American hybrid lilacs are the earliest bloomers. The variety 'Pocahontas' is particularly lovely, with its maroon flowerbuds opening to deep violet flowers in clusters up to 10 inches (25 cm) long.

BOTTOM: Chinese lilacs bloom at the ends of branches, with long, graceful flower clusters. Birds often nest in this shrub—perhaps because its slender, arching branches won't support the weight of cats!

RECOMMENDED SPECIES OR VARIETIES

Early-blooming Lilacs

American Hybrid Lilac

'**Mount Baker**': 10–12 feet (3–3.7 m) tall and wide; one of the first lilacs to bloom; large clusters of white, single flowers are dramatically displayed against dark green foliage.

'**Pocahontas**': American hybrid; 10–12 feet (3–3.7 m) tall and wide; one of the first to bloom; maroon flowerbuds open to deep violet flowers; blooms abundantly; vigorous, upright variety developed in Manitoba; non-suckering.

Chinese Lilac

$8^{1}/_{2}$–15 feet (2.6–4.6 m) tall and wide; large clusters of 4–6-inch (10–15 cm) long lavender-purple flowers cover the entire shrub; a graceful, wide-spreading lilac with arching branches; non-suckering.

MIDSEASON-BLOOMING LILACS

Dwarf Korean Lilac

Dwarf Korean (*S. meyeri* 'Palibin'): 3½–6 feet (1.1–1.8 m) tall and 5–7 feet (1.5–2.1 m) wide; dark reddish-purple flowerbuds open to whitish-pink flowers in 4-inch (10 cm) long clusters; blooms profusely; very fragrant; compact, strongly multi-stemmed shrub; needs little pruning; non-suckering.

French Hybrid Lilac

'**Beauty of Moscow**': 10–12 feet (3–3.7 m) tall and 8–10 feet (2.4–3 m) wide; masses of pink, double flowers in 10-inch (25 cm) long clusters; upright shrub slightly narrower than French hybrid lilacs; considered by lilac experts around the world to be one of the finest varieties!

TOP: It takes most lilacs up to six years to reach their peak blooming potential, but Dwarf Korean lilacs provide a great show when they are just one to three years old and when they are 'as old as the hills.' BOTTOM: 'Beauty of Moscow' is considered to be one of the finest varieties of lilacs.

TOP LEFT: French hybrid lilacs are the most popular type of lilac. The name 'French hybrid' arose because many of the first varieties were bred in France. Today the more than 2000 varieties available originate from different countries—the unusual, yellow-flowered 'Primrose,' for example, is a Dutch variety introduced in 1949. TOP RIGHT: 'President Lincoln' is one of the best blue lilacs. BOTTOM: 'Charles Joly' is one of the most fragrant lilacs.

'**Charles Joly**': 10 feet (3 m) tall and wide; deep purple to purple-red, double flowers in 10-inch (25 cm) long clusters; dark green foliage; produces suckers.

'**President Lincoln**': 8–10 feet (2.4–3 m) tall and wide; fine, blue, double flowers in 10-inch (25 cm) long clusters; produces suckers; one of the best blue lilacs.

'**Primrose**': 10 feet (3 m) tall and wide; extraordinary pale yellow flowers in 10-inch (25 cm) long clusters; highly unusual colour for a lilac; dark green foliage; produces suckers.

'**Sensation**': 8–10 feet (2.4–3 m) tall and 8–12 feet (2.4–3.7 m) wide; unique, beautiful, bicoloured flowers in 10-inch (25 cm) long clusters; deep purple flower-buds open to deep purple flowers dramatically edged in white; dark green foliage; produces suckers.

Little-leaf Lilac

6 feet (1.8 m) tall and 9–12 feet (2.7–3.7 m) wide; heavily scented, delicate-looking, rosy-lavender flowers in 4-inch (10 cm) long clusters; blooms profusely in spring and usually again, but abundantly, in fall, with sporadic flowers in between; similar to dwarf Korean lilac; more heat tolerant than most lilacs; a very handsome, dense shrub.

LATE-BLOOMING LILACS

Japanese Tree Lilac

'Ivory Silk': 30 feet (9.1 m) tall and wide; a more compact and uniformly oval variety; fragrant, creamy flowers in clusters 4–8 inches (10–20 cm) long; in some years there are so many flowers that the leaves are hidden; non-suckering; reddish-brown bark; extremely beautiful in full flower!

TOP LEFT: 'Sensation' dates back to 1938, but only recently became readily available.
TOP RIGHT: 'Ivory Silk' is the best Japanese tree lilac variety. The flowers show off particularly well in front of the dark foliage of evergreen trees.
BOTTOM: The flower clusters of little-leaf lilac are rarely over 3 inches (7.6 cm) long, but there are lots of them, produced all along the branches. The Chinese use these flowers to make tea.

TOP: 'Miss Kim' is one of the most exceptional lilacs.
BOTTOM: Preston lilacs are Canadian hybrids, the result of work by Agriculture Canada employee Isabella Preston (1881–1965). The variety 'Miss Canada' was introduced in 1967.

Manchurian Lilac

'**Miss Kim**': 3–5 feet (91 cm–1.5 m) tall and wide; a slow-growing, dwarf variety; stunning, purple-blue flowers in 4–6-inch (10–15 cm) long clusters; strong, exotic, somewhat spicy fragrance; small leaves finely edged in maroon; dark green foliage turns wine-red in fall, an unusual feature; non-suckering; the smallest lilac and one of the nicest varieties.

Lilac is the state flower of New Hampshire.

Pink is a hard colour to come by in lilacs. The colour of pink flowers varies with the weather, amount of sun and pH of soil. 'James MacFarlane' is a pink-flowered Preston hybrid.

Preston Hybrid Lilac

'**Donald Wyman**': 10–12 feet (3–3.7 m) tall and wide; deep purple, single flowers in 6-inch (15 cm) long clusters; non-suckering.

'**Miss Canada**': 10 feet (3 m) tall and wide; extremely attractive, single flowers in a stunning magenta hue; flowers hang from the bush like clusters of grapes; non-suckering; introduced in 1967; blooms slightly earlier than other Preston varieties; one of the most outstanding lilacs for its colour.

'**James MacFarlane**': 10–12 feet (3–3.7 m) tall and wide; pink, single flowers; non-suckering; one of the best pink-flowering lilacs!

'**Minuet**': 10–12 feet (3–3.7 m) tall and wide; light pink, single flowers; non-suckering; similar to 'James MacFarlane' but has paler flowers.

For the longest-blooming period, grow different types. You'll have lilacs in bloom for two months or longer.

The name 'lilac' comes from the Persian word for 'blue.' The genus name *Syringa* is derived from a Greek word meaning 'reed' or 'pipe,' referring to the hollow stems. In mythology, the lilac is the flower of the goddess Venus.

The world's largest lilac collection is at the Royal Botanical Gardens in Hamilton, Ontario, where close to 800 different lilac varieties are displayed.

Lilacs are one of the longest-lived shrubs. The oldest lilacs in North America are over 300 years old, growing in New Hampshire and Michigan. Their trunks are over 20 inches (51 cm) in diameter, and have an unusual and pronounced twist.

TIPS

Despite official zone ratings, I have seen French hybrid lilacs growing in zone 1, and my little-leaf lilac has thrived for years in zone 3.

Prune just after flowering, as lilacs form next spring's flowerbuds in summer.

How to decide which lilac to choose? If you are impatient for flowers, choose American hybrid varieties—they bloom the earliest. If fragrance is a priority, choose French hybrids, which have the strongest scent. If you want distinctive flowers, good choices include Dwarf Korean, 'Miss Kim,' 'Primrose,' 'Sensation' and 'Miss Canada.' Dwarf Korean, 'Miss Kim' and 'Ivory Silk' are lilacs with a different look. Otherwise, view lilacs in bloom and go by whichever flower strikes your fancy.

Lilacs bloom for two to three weeks in spring, but by growing different types, you can have lilacs in flower for almost two months. Flowers last longest in cooler temperatures; a warm spring can shorten the blooming period.

For the longest-lasting flower colour, plant in a site that is lightly shaded during the hottest part of the day. Hot sun causes flower colour to fade. Don't, however, plant your lilacs in a site that receives less than six hours of direct sunlight, because they won't bloom well.

Lilacs are somewhat drought tolerant, but the best-looking shrubs with the most flowers are those lilacs that are grown in moist, well-drained soil.

Both little-leaf and dwarf Korean lilacs make great hedges. They have a naturally uniform shape, require very little pruning, and take more than 15 years to reach maximum size. Don't use a mulch around these types. Normally, they rarely produce suckers, but can do so when heavily mulched.

Lilacs are renowned for producing suckers, but only certain types do sucker. Suckering is not necessarily a bad thing, as it results in shrubs spreading to fill in borders. If you don't want suckers, remove them by pruning, or choose non-suckering varieties.

French hybrid lilacs do tend to sucker, although the named varieties sucker less often than the species.

Lilacs can be trained to grow as a small tree. See *How to Train Shrubs to 'Tree' Form* on page 64.

If you deadhead lilacs, the shrub will devote its energy into producing new flowerbuds (for next spring's bloom) rather than into forming seeds—resulting in a greater abundance of flowers. Cut off finished flower clusters down to the next leafbud or where a new shoot is emerging. In some years, I don't get around to deadheading, but even without this extra attention, the lilacs still put on a good show of flowers.

When grown in the wrong conditions, lilacs can be prone to powdery mildew. In a sunny site with good air circulation (don't crowd plants together), you are unlikely to encounter this problem. Thinning by pruning helps to improve air circulation. Interestingly, the type of powdery mildew that affects lilacs is different from the type that affects roses, and one won't infect the other.

Lilacs are delightful in bouquets and will scent the whole room. For longer-lasting bouquets, cut when the flowers are starting to open. Either bash the woody stem ends with a hammer, or immerse them in boiling water for a few seconds. Lilacs generally last 7 to 10 days after cutting.

In Europe, lilac flowers are eaten raw, folded into batter for 'fritters' or crystallized by coating with beaten egg-whites and sugar.

WHY LILACS FAIL TO BLOOM

- It sometimes takes three to four years after planting before lilacs bloom well.
- In shady sites, lilacs don't bloom well. They need at least six hours of direct sun.
- If your lilacs are growing too near a lawn, it could be a problem. Lawn fertilizers are high in nitrogen, and too much nitrogen results in fewer flowers. Add a handful or two of bonemeal each spring to promote flowering.
- Lilacs form next year's flowerbuds in summer. Any pruning should be done shortly after they finish blooming; pruning at other times results in your cutting off potential flowers.
- Don't prune off the branch tips when pruning or cutting flowers.

Linden

Tilia x flavescens
Hybrid Linden

Tilia cordata
Little-leaf Linden
Small-leafed Lime

Tilia mongolica • Mongolian Linden

Height • 25–50 feet (7.6–15 m)

Spread • 20–40 feet (6.1–12 m)

Flowers • clusters of small, ivory flowers in mid-summer

Fruit • woody, grey, nut-like seeds

Growth Rate • slow to medium

Lifespan • long

Zone Rating • 3

Often there is a bewitching fragrance on the summer air when no flowerbed is in sight. If you are puzzled as to the source of this heavenly perfume, have a close look at the nearby trees. If you spot one with a pyramid of dark green foliage atop a very straight trunk, that's a linden tree, and its small, ivory flowers emit a strong, sweet fragrance for about two weeks in mid-summer. Lindens are great shade trees: clean, virtually free of pests, and needing little maintenance. Because they are such tidy trees, lindens are recommended for planting beside decks, patios or swimming pools. They are fairly fast-growing shade trees and an ideal size for small yards.

GROWING

Sun; moist, well-drained, fertile soil.

Specimen tree, shade tree. Decks, patios, boulevards.

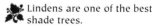

Lindens are one of the best shade trees.

LEFT & RIGHT: *The leaves of 'Dropmore' are huge compared to most other lindens.*

RECOMMENDED SPECIES OR VARIETIES

Hybrid Linden

'**Dropmore**': 40–50 feet (12–15 m) tall and 30–40 feet (9.1–12 m) wide; hardy variety bred especially for the Prairies; usually little fall colour, but sometimes turns bright yellow; slower growing than most lindens.

Little-leaf Linden

'**Glenleven**': 40–50 feet (12–15 m) tall and 30–35 feet (9.1–11 m) wide; faster growing than the species little-leaf linden; also casts lighter shade, which makes it easier to grow other plants underneath this tree; a Canadian variety.

The species name *cordata* means 'heart-shaped,' referring to the little-leaf linden's leaves.

LEFT: The linden's abundant flowers attract bees and butterflies. RIGHT: Despite its imposing growth, 'Glenleven' casts a light shade.

'**Golden Cascade**': 35–45 feet (11–14 m) tall and 30 feet (9.1 m) wide; has the usual pyramidal shape but branches cascade downwards at the tips—a striking effect; consistent, golden-yellow fall colour; a new Canadian variety that is still limited in supply.

Norlin™ (*T. cordata* 'Ronald'): 35–45 feet (11–14 m) tall and 20–25 feet (6.1–7.6 m) wide; faster growing than most other little-leaf lindens; a very hardy variety from Manitoba.

Mongolian Linden

Mongolian: 25–30 feet (7.6–9.1 m) tall and wide; a graceful tree, smaller than most lindens; introduced in 1880; bright yellow fall colour; resistant to aphids.

'**Harvest Gold**': 35–45 feet (11–14 m) tall and 20–25 feet (6.1–7.6 m) wide; a narrow, upright tree; masses of showy flowers; consistent yellow fall colour; peeling bark is an attractive, unique feature, which won't occur until the trunk is at least 2 inches (5.1 cm) in diameter.

LEFT: 'Golden Cascade' is a new variety from Manitoba that has nicely cascading branches.
TOP RIGHT: A Mongolian linden can be distinguished from other lindens by its shiny, deeply serrated leaves.

TIPS

Avoid planting linden trees in either very dry or poorly drained sites.

Lindens are noted for their good solid branching. These trees need very little pruning.

Despite the name 'little-leaf,' the leaves of this tree vary greatly in size, from 2½–4 inches (6.4–10 cm) long, and they are sometimes broader than long.

Little pruning required, but if necessary, prune in late winter to early spring before leaves appear.

Although lindens can be one of the best trees for fall colour, not all of these trees always turn bright yellow in fall. Little-leaf linden, for example, is known for its spectacular fall foliage. Nevertheless, I have seen one yard where three of these trees are planted in a row, and one just won't change colour in fall. No one knows why.

Linden flowers are sometimes sold in health food stores. The flowers are used to make a type of tea.

Maackia

Maackia amurensis
Amur Maackia

Height • 20–30 feet (6.1–9.1 m)

Spread • 20–25 feet (6.1–7.6 m)

Flowers • fragrant, white flowers in mid-summer

Fruit • 2–3-inch (5.1–7.6 cm) long seedpods in early fall

Growth Rate • slow

Lifespan • average

Zone Rating • 3

Maackia is an uncommon tree with so many redeeming qualities that I can't understand why it is not more widely grown. Its small, graceful form makes the Amur maackia ideal for small yards, and easy to fit into almost any garden landscape. Showy, upright clusters of creamy white, pea-like flowers cover the branches in summer, filling the air with a sweet scent similar to fresh-cut hay. Beautiful, golden bark offsets the lustrous green foliage on this durable, adaptable tree. Maackia has a neat appearance, grows well even in poor soil, and is rarely troubled by pests.

GROWING

Sun.

A tidy tree good for growing near walkways, decks and patios; nice feature tree for small yards.

Rarely needs pruning, but if necessary, prune only when tree is in full leaf to preserve the following season's flowers.

LEFT: Amur maackia is one of the best summer-flowering trees. RIGHT: Amur maackia performs well in poor soils.

RECOMMENDED SPECIES OR VARIETIES

Amur Maackia

TIPS

Maackia is one of the most undemanding trees. It is rarely troubled by pests, grows well in poor, acidic or alkaline soil, needs little pruning and doesn't drop messy fruit.

Amur maackia grows about 6–8 inches (15–20 cm) a year.

Maackia is named for the Russian naturalist Richard Maack (1825–86). As you are likely able to tell by its pea-shaped seedpods, this tree is a member of the legume family.

Maackia 'fixes' atmospheric nitrogen, which means that, like peas, beans and clover, it converts nitrogen gas into usable nitrogen compounds.

Magnolia

Magnolia x loebneri 'Merrill'
Merrill Magnolia

Magnolia stellata • Star Magnolia

Height • 12–15 feet (3.7–4.6 m)

Spread • 10 feet (3 m)

Flowers • white flowers in early spring

Fruit • not showy

Growth Rate
Merrill: medium
Star: slow

Lifespan • average

Zone Rating • 4

Magnolias are fabled flowers of the southern United States, but you can still grow certain varieties of these shrubs in northern regions. A few years ago, we planted a star magnolia on the west side of my son's house. It is a small shrub that blooms each spring with stunning, fragrant, white, star-shaped blossoms—provided its branches remain covered with snow all winter, since the flowerbuds are sensitive to cold weather. The leafbuds, on the other hand, are considerably tougher and can survive extreme cold very well.

I have seen young, knee-high star magnolias loaded with scented, white blooms. The plant continues to flower as abundantly when it becomes a densely branched tree. A nice feature of the magnolia is its myriad, star-shaped flowers that flutter in the faintest breeze.

GROWING

Partial shade; morning sun with afternoon shade is best. Select a very sheltered location, perhaps between buildings or among large evergreens where snow collects.

Feature tree or shrub.

RECOMMENDED SPECIES OR VARIETIES

Merrill Magnolia

20–25 feet (6.1–7.6 m) tall and 15–18 feet (4.6–5.5 m) wide; large, 4–6-inch (10–15 cm), white flowers in spring before the leaves fully open; probably the hardiest magnolia; beautiful tree or large shrub when in full flower; drought tolerant but prefers moist, well-drained soil; deep, dark green foliage.

Star Magnolia

15–18 feet (4.6–5.5 m) tall and 10–15 feet (3–4.6 m) wide; 2 3/4–4-inch (7–10 cm), white, star-shaped, scented flowers in early spring before the leaves appear; dark green leaves turn yellow or bronze in fall; a stunning, oval-shaped shrub.

TOP: Star magnolia blooms profusely provided that it is protected during cold, dry winter weather. BOTTOM: Merrill magnolia has stunning, white flowers.

TIPS

Although rated as hardy to zone 4, and sometimes reported to grow as tall as 40 feet (12 m), Merrill magnolia will likely remain a large shrub rather than a tree in my region (zone 3).

Flowerbuds form in late summer. A warm spell in winter may signal buds to break dormancy, and any cold weather and frost afterwards will kill the buds. Expect damaged flowers and even branch dieback every couple of years, usually after a warm spell in March.

Magnolias do well in acidic or alkaline soils as long as adequate moisture is provided. They do not like wet clay soils.

Prune after flowering.

Success is determined by where you place the plant in your garden. Full sun will help the plants ripen in time to go dormant for winter, and a spot sheltered from the prevailing winter winds will soften the effects of extreme temperatures.

The roots are vulnerable to cold. Locating the plant in an area that collects snow, and covering specimens with lots of mulch will help protect them.

A good way to help maintain soil fertility is provided by the plants themselves: they often drop their leaves all at once on a calm day. Leave these leaves to rot in peace, perhaps with a light cover of mulch.

Foliage is frequently used in flower arrangements, but it does not keep well.

Magnolia is the state flower of Louisiana and Mississippi.

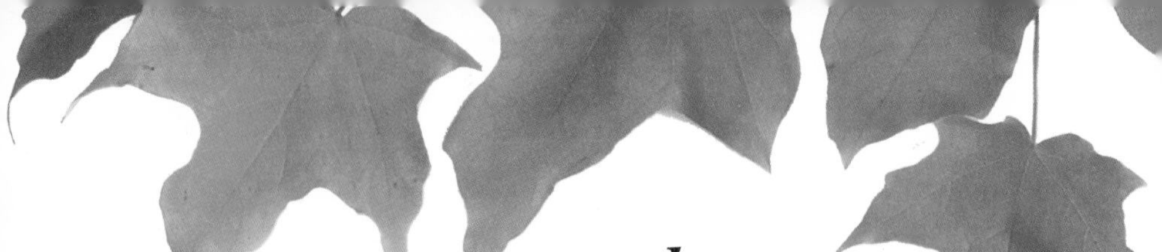

Maple

Acer ginnala
Amur Maple

Acer negundo
Manitoba Maple
Box-elder

Acer platanoides
Norway Maple

Acer rubrum
Red Maple
Scarlet Maple
Swamp Maple

Acer saccharinum
Silver Maple
Soft Maple
White Maple
River Maple

Acer saccharum
Sugar Maple
Rock Maple
Hard Maple

Height • 7–60 feet (2.1–18 m)

Spread • 7–45 feet (2.1–14 m)

Flowers • clusters of minute flowers in early spring

Fruit • winged seeds

Growth Rate
Amur, Manitoba, Norway, Silver: fast
Red, Sugar: medium to slow

Lifespan • average to long

Zone Rating
Amur, Manitoba: 2
Red, Silver, Sugar (protected site), Norway: 3

Many maples are large, imposing shade trees; others are large shrubs. With the wide range of sizes, there is sure to be a maple suited to every garden. Amur maple is a versatile shrub that adapts easily to a wide range of conditions; it is also one of the hardiest maples, one of the few maples with fragrant flowers, and one of the best for fall colour. With its open, wide-spreading branches, the Manitoba maple is a favourite with children who like to climb and build tree houses. It is a vigorous tree that withstands drought and grows well in wet soil. The Manitoba maple is too large for many urban lots but thrives on acreages and in parks and industrial areas. With its broad, dense canopy of foliage, Norway maple is one of the most striking trees. Norway maples are more common in eastern Canada than in my region, because they are less hardy than other maples. Despite this quality, they still grow well here in sheltered sites.

Red maple lives up to its name. In early spring, it blooms with dense clusters of tiny, red flowers. The leaves are red when they first unfurl in spring, before turning dark green in summer, but the leaf stalks remain bright red. In fall, this maple can't be missed—it is one of the first trees to turn colour, with a stunning display of brilliant red foliage. Silver maple is one of the fastest-growing shade trees, and when well maintained, it can be extremely beautiful. The sugar maple is famous for being the source of the sweet sap used to make maple syrup, as well as for its flaming fall foliage.

GROWING

Sun to partial shade; Amur maple needs sun to partial shade, all others in sun.

Well-drained soil is best for all maples. However, red and silver maples also grow well in wetter soil. Manitoba is the most versatile, growing in almost any conditions, from wet to dry. Amur also tolerates dry soil.

All shade trees. Manitoba, red, 'Crimson King' and 'Northwood' as feature trees near decks and patios. Amur as a feature tree, in groups, in borders, as background, for hedges and screens.

TOP & BOTTOM: An Amur maple is one of the first trees to leaf out in spring, and blazes with colour in fall.

RECOMMENDED SPECIES OR VARIETIES

Amur Maple

Amur: 15–20 feet (4.6–6.1 m) tall and 15 feet (4.6 m) wide; available multi-stemmed or with a single trunk; will be wider if multi-stemmed; sweetly scented, creamy white to pale yellow flowers in early spring; very dark green, glossy leaves; grey snakeskin bark; bright red-winged fruit; fall colour varies from shades of yellow to red.

TOP & BOTTOM: The variety 'Embers' has showy samaras, which turn bright red in early summer.

'**Bailey's Compact**': 7–8 feet (2.1–2.4 m) tall and wide; a fine-textured, compact variety; foliage consistently turns brilliant scarlet in fall; one of the best varieties for fall colour.

'**Embers**': 15–20 feet (4.6–6.1 m) tall and 15 feet (4.6 m) wide; a graceful, round-headed tree; usually available either as a single-trunked or a multi-stemmed tree; very showy, red-winged seeds in summer; fall colour is more consistent than Amur; foliage turns brilliant red; excellent variety for small yards or large shrub beds.

The winged seeds of maples are called 'samaras,' or 'keys.' Mature seeds resemble propellers that twirl and spin away from the tree during breezes; children often play with these 'helicopters.'

LEFT: Manitoba maples, such as 'Baron Manitoba,' are handsome trees that withstand periodic flooding or prolonged drought. RIGHT: Huge 'Crimson King' maple trees are common in milder areas than mine, but in a sheltered site in my region, it can still become a large tree.

Manitoba Maple

'**Baron Manitoba**': 35–50 feet (11–15 m) tall and 35–40 feet (11–12 m) wide; only male trees are sold—males do not produce seeds—meaning that no seedlings need be removed from your garden; adaptable to difficult conditions; leaves are bright green on top and lighter green underneath, with a powdery blue coating on stems and buds only; fall colour is yellow; an extremely hardy Canadian variety from Morden, Manitoba.

Maple syrup contains 15 times the calcium and one-tenth the sodium of honey.

Norway Maple

'**Crimson King**': 40–50 feet (12–15 m) tall and 35–45 feet (11–14 m) wide; one of the most stunning maples; rich maroon leaves throughout the growing season; grey bark; maroon-yellow flowers in early spring; the most vigorous of the red-leafed maples; an excellent specimen tree; introduced from France in 1946.

Many types of birds, including robins, build nests in maple trees.

TOP & BOTTOM: Norway maples are huge trees that cast heavy shade. Little rain penetrates their dense canopies to reach underlying soil. OPPOSITE PAGE: The red maple turns colour early in fall—it is usually one of the first trees to start the show. Generally, the leaves turn brilliant red.

'**Superform Norway**': 50 feet (15 m) tall and 40–45 feet (12–14 m) wide; a variety of Norway maple selected for its 'super form': a straighter trunk and better branching habit, so less pruning is required; tree has a strong, heavy appearance; great shade tree; dark green leaves; masses of frothy yellow flowers while branches are still bare in early spring.

Red Maple

Red: 40–50 feet (12–15 m) tall and 35–40 feet (11–12 m) wide; a very strong, clean-looking tree; red flowers in early spring before leaves appear; leaves are dark green on upper surface and greyish beneath; fall colour varies from green to yellow, yellow-orange and red; intolerant of air pollution; superb specimen tree.

'**Northwood**': 40 feet (12 m) tall and 35–40 feet (11–12 m) wide; a nice specimen tree with a rounded, oval shape; red flowers in early spring; dark green summer foliage; excellent yellow to red fall colours; a very hardy variety.

Silver Maple

50–75 feet (15–23 m) tall and 35–50 feet (11–15 m) wide; attractive leaves are medium green on top and silvery grey underneath; greenish-yellow to red flowers in early spring; winged seed matures in early summer; can withstand several weeks of flooding per year; does well in full sun but is very adaptable to poor conditions; don't plant it near driveways or sidewalks; introduced to the nursery trade in 1725.

THE SWEET FACTS ABOUT MAPLE SYRUP

The sugar maple is the primary source of the sweet sap used to make maple syrup. The Latin *saccharum* means 'containing sugar.' Red, silver and black maples are also sources of maple syrup. Even a Manitoba maple can be tapped, but the resulting syrup has a toffee-like flavour.

The harvesting of maple sap, known as 'sugaring-off,' occurs over a six-week period in early spring. During the harvest, about 7 percent of the maple tree's sap is harvested. Tapping sap does not harm the maple tree; many tapped trees are well over 100 years old.

It takes about 33 gallons (150 l) of maple sap to produce 14 ounces (400 ml) of pure maple syrup. The sweet sap is heated until most of the water boils away. What remains is maple syrup—so pure that little further refining is needed. If boiled longer, the syrup forms maple cream, then soft sugar and finally hard sugar.

Today, there are about 20,000 maple syrup producers in North America. All the world's maple sugar comes from North America's 'Maple Belt'—a hardwood forest area stretching from the Maritimes through Quebec, Ontario and New England to the mid-western United States. During a normal crop year, approximately 50 million pounds (23 million kg) of syrup is produced.

When the wind blows, you can see the silvery undersides of the silver maple.

Sugar Maple

40–60 feet (12–18 m) tall and 25–35 feet (7.6–11 m) wide; excellent for large, open areas; medium to dark green leaves; fall colour is brilliant yellow, burnt orange and occasionally light red; introduced to the nursery trade in 1753; one of the best maples for fall colour.

To most of the world, a red maple leaf represents Canada. The maple leaf emblazoned on Canada's national flag comes from the sugar maple.

TIPS

Maple trees should not be pruned before they are in full leaf, and better yet, not until early July. The sap runs heavily in spring, and the tree can 'bleed' excessively if pruned at this time, making it unsightly, although the tree will not be harmed.

Amur maple can be 'tailored' by pruning to 'tree' form; it withstands heavy pruning. You can often buy this maple with a single main stem rather

than its usual multiple stems. Alternatively, you can prune your Amur maple to grow as a small tree. See *How to Train Shrubs to 'Tree' Form* on page 64.

The seeds of Manitoba maples tend to sprout readily. To avoid having to remove little maple seedlings from your yard, choose a seedless variety, such as 'Baron Manitoba.'

Sugar maples, red maples and their varieties are intolerant of excessive air pollution.

If leaves are very pale, use an acidic fertilizer high in iron to lower the pH of the soil. Red maples in particular like acidic soil and a sunny, moist location.

Don't plant Norway maples close to your house because they can become huge.

'Crimson King' likes a moist location, and is susceptible to branch tip damage ('tip kill').

The sugar maple likes a well-drained, moist location with slightly acidic soil. Do not plant the tree in confined spaces. It is intolerant of high soil salt levels.

Maples are one of the best trees for fall foliage colour.

Mayday

Prunus padus var. *commutata*
Mayday Tree
European Bird Cherry

Prunus padus 'Colorata'
Swedish Mayday

Height • 30–40 feet (9.1–12 m)

Spread • 30–40 feet (9.1–12 m)

Flowers • clusters of white or pink flowers in spring

Fruit • black berries in summer

Growth Rate • medium to fast

Lifespan • short

Zone Rating • 3

Mayday trees bloom early with a spectacular display of fragrant flowers.

When maydays are blooming, many people come out to the greenhouses, asking 'What is that tree with the white blossoms and wonderful scent?' Whether or not people are aware of its name, everyone knows it by sight, for a mayday tree in full bloom can't be missed. The entire tree becomes absolutely covered in flowers; the display is stunning. To me, maydays are one of the most welcome signs of spring. They are one of the first trees to leaf out, and they bloom early—as their name suggests—filling the air with a fresh, sweet fragrance. Maydays are superb shade trees, with rich, dark green leaves forming wide-spreading canopies.

GROWING

Sun.

Shade tree for large yards, parks, public areas, acreages.

TOP LEFT: Mayday's tiny flowers form loose, dangling clusters from 3–6 inches (7.6–15 cm) long.
TOP RIGHT: Mayday is a member of the Prunus *family (cherries, plums), but its berries generally aren't eaten, except by birds—hence the name bird cherry.*
BOTTOM: Although maydays are not commonly used as boulevard trees, a street lined with them looks breathtaking in spring.

RECOMMENDED SPECIES OR VARIETIES

Mayday Tree

30–40 feet (9.1–12 m) tall and wide; white flowers; blooms two to three weeks earlier than the Swedish; leaves are dark green on top and greyish underneath; the most common type.

Swedish Mayday

30–40 feet (9.1–12 m) tall and wide; pink flowers; leaves are bronze when young and turn dark purple-green with purplish undersides; branch stems are also dark purple; rounded tree with low, up-reaching branches; an uncommon variety that may be hard to find, but is well worth the effort.

TIPS

Avoid planting near driveways, patios or sidewalks because fallen berries can be messy. Birds, however, love them.

Maydays have thick foliage and cast quite dense shade.

Prune in late winter or early spring.

Sometimes maydays produce suckers or 'watersprouts' (shoots at the base of the trunk). As they appear, just prune them off. Trees kept in good health are less likely to produce suckers.

Maydays are one of the first trees to leaf out in spring.

Mockorange

Philadelphus x
Hybrid Mockorange

Philadelphus lewisii
Lewis Mockorange

Height • 2–5 feet (61–150 cm)

Spread • 1–5 feet (30–150 cm)

Flowers • pure white flowers from late spring to early summer

Fruit • not showy

Growth Rate • medium

Lifespan • short to average

Zone Rating
Hybrid: 3–4
Lewis: 2

Mockorange is beautiful in bloom with its sweetly scented, white flowers. The flowers smell similar to orange blossoms, hence the common name. Flowers and fragrance are, however, the mockorange's best features, as these shrubs tend to fade into the background when out of bloom. Choose a spot in your garden where a nice display of plain green foliage is sufficient for most of summer, and reserve the spotlight for showier plants.

Those few weeks in late spring to early summer when mockoranges bloom and fill the air with sweet fragrance are reason enough for me to include them in my garden.

GROWING

Sun to light shade.

Accent in shrub border, background shrub, informal hedge, screen, foundation planting.

RECOMMENDED SPECIES OR VARIETIES

Hybrid Mockorange

'**Galahad**': 4–5 feet (1.2–1.5 m) tall and wide; 1–1¼-inch (2.5–3.2 cm), extremely fragrant, white flowers; a hardy variety ideal for small shrub beds and flower gardens.

'**Miniature Snowflake**': 2–3 feet (61–91 cm) tall and 1–2 feet (30–61 cm) wide; a miniature variety with a profusion of large, very fragrant, double flowers.

Lewis Mockorange

'**Blizzard**': 4–5 feet (1.2–1.5 m) tall and wide; abundant, lightly scented, white flowers in late spring to early summer; flowers fine even when pruned after flowering; scented, but not as heavily as the other varieties; foliage turns yellow and orange in fall; the hardiest variety; developed in Beaverlodge, Alberta.

TIPS

Some varieties of mockorange are hardier than others. Be sure to choose one suitable for your area.

Occasionally, however, even the hardiest mockorange varieties may not bloom well. After a particularly harsh winter, flowers may appear only on branches that were beneath the snowline. Extremely cold temperatures or early spring frosts can kill exposed flowerbuds. Plant your shrub in a sheltered site and keep it healthy to help alleviate the effects of such cold.

Mockorange needs annual pruning to keep it tidy. Prune after flowering as it blooms on last year's wood. Thin out older stems.

I just cannot resist snipping off a few sweetly scented flowering branches to display in a vase.

Mockorange is sometimes referred to as 'syringa.' This name is also the botanical name for lilac; don't confuse the two shrubs.

TOP: A 'Galahad' shrub in full bloom works well in shrub beds.
MIDDLE: 'Miniature Snowflake' is a dwarf shrub with beautiful, fragrant flowers that are almost twice the usual size.
BOTTOM: Fragrant, bright white flowers completely cover 'Blizzard's' branches for two to three weeks in early summer.

Mountain Ash

Sorbus americana
American Mountain Ash

Sorbus reducta
Dwarf Chinese Mountain Ash

Sorbus aucuparia
European Mountain Ash

Sorbus x hybrida
Oak-leaf Mountain Ash

Sorbus decora
Showy Mountain Ash

Height • 1–40 feet (30 cm–12 m)

Spread • 2–25 feet (61 cm–7.6 m)

Flowers • clusters of tiny, white flowers

Fruit • clusters of red, orange or pink berries

Growth Rate • slow to medium

Lifespan • short to average

Zone Rating • 2

At one time in England, its name was not to be mentioned. During the 15th and 16th centuries, the mountain ash—or rowan tree, as it was commonly called—was strongly associated with witchcraft and the occult. Today, however, the mountain ash has become one of our most popular ornamental trees. Mountain ash blooms in spring with showy clusters of tiny, white flowers, and throughout summer casts interesting shadows whenever the sun shines through its fernlike foliage. The decorative clusters of berries truly distinguish the mountain ash. The berries turn colour in mid- to late summer and often remain on bare branches well into winter.

GROWING

Sun; moist, well-drained soil.

Shade tree, feature tree. Dwarf Chinese as a groundcover, in shrub beds.

RECOMMENDED SPECIES OR VARIETIES

American Mountain Ash

25–30 feet (7.6–9.1 m) tall and 16–20 feet (4.9–6.1 m) wide; large flower clusters, from 3–5 inches (7.6–12 cm) across; pungent fragrance; bright orange-red berries; an open, rounded tree with dark green leaves; yellow fall foliage; very hardy.

Dwarf Chinese Mountain Ash

1–2 feet (30–61 cm) tall and 2–3 feet (61–91 cm) wide; unusual groundcover; very attractive in flower; berries turn bright pink in mid- to late summer, and remain on branches after the leaves drop in fall; glossy, dark green leaves; one of the best mountain ashes for fall colour; foliage turns bright red to bronze; an uncommon type that can be hard to find, but is well worth the search.

TOP LEFT: The berries of American mountain ash are said to taste better after a light frost.
TOP RIGHT: Dwarf Chinese is an unusual mountain ash that grows as a small shrub or groundcover.
BOTTOM: European mountain ash has large flower clusters, from 3–5 inches (7.6–13 cm) across.

European Mountain Ash

European: 25–40 feet (7.6–12 m) tall and 16–25 feet (4.9–7.6 m) wide; large clusters of white flowers; tiny orange-red berries; matte, dark green leaves; an erect, oval-shaped tree; fall foliage colour ranges from green to yellow and red.

TOP: Columnar ash is an uncommon, underused tree in my region.
BOTTOM: Oak-leaf mountain ash is a vigorous tree that is often mistaken for oak, because its leaves resemble an oak's.

Columnar (*S. aucuparia* 'Fastigiata'): 20–25 feet (6.1–7.6 m) tall and 6–8 feet (1.8–2.4 m) wide; a slow-growing columnar tree; red berries.

Peking (*S. aucuparia* 'Pekenensis'): 25–30 feet (7.6–9.1 m) tall and 15–16 feet (4.6–4.9 m) wide; large clusters of white flowers; tiny, orange-yellow berries; flat, dark green leaves; fall colour ranges from green to yellow and red.

Russian (*S. aucuparia* 'Rossica'): 25–40 feet (7.6–12 m) tall and 16–25 feet (4.9–7.6 m) wide; large clusters of white flowers; tiny, orange-red berries; resistant to fireblight; large, dark green, saw-toothed leaves; foliage turns yellow and red in fall.

Oak-leaf Mountain Ash

25–35 feet (7.6–11 m) tall and 16–25 feet (4.9–7.6 m) wide; flower clusters from 2–5 inches (5.1–13 cm) wide; large berries, much redder than many other mountain ash trees; matte green, oak-shaped leaves with white undersides, up to 3½ inches (8.9 cm) long; a pyramidal, oval-shaped tree.

Showy Mountain Ash

20–25 feet (6.1–7.6 m) tall and 15–16 feet (4.6–4.9 m) wide; white flowers in clusters 4–4½ inches (10–11 cm) across; blooms about 10 days longer than other types; red berries; dark green leaves; resistant to fireblight; a very attractive, small, slow-growing, dense tree; the hardiest mountain ash.

TIPS

These trees are often available either with a single trunk or in multi-stemmed form.

Do not plant mountain ash trees in low-lying, wet areas of the yard.

Prune in late winter to early spring, before leaves appear.

An ideal site for a mountain ash is on top of small rises or at the higher end of a yard, where excess moisture from rain or melting snow drains away quickly.

Dwarf Chinese mountain ash spreads quickly in moist, well-drained soil. It should be planted in a confined space if you don't want it to spread too far too quickly.

Mountain ash berries attract entire flocks of birds to the yard, especially during winter. I have seen flocks of cedar waxwings move in on one tree and completely clean off all the berries, and then move on to the next tree.

The berries are edible, although I have never eaten them. They are said to taste similar to cranberries, and are sometimes used for jams, wine and marmalade. Russian mountain ash is supposed to have the sweetest berries.

Decorum *means 'shapely.'* Sorbus decora, *the showy mountain ash, is considered by many to be the most attractive mountain ash species.*

Mountain ash trees are available in a range of shapes and sizes.

Nannyberry

Viburnum lentago
Sheepberry
Wild Raisin

Height • 15–18 feet (4.6–5.5 m)

Spread • 8–10 feet (2.4–3 m)

Flowers • clusters of creamy white flowers in spring

Fruit • blue-black berries in fall

Growth Rate • slow to medium

Lifespan • average

Zone Rating • 2

Nannyberry is a wonderful shrub with large clusters of white flowers in spring and decorative, edible berries in fall. The colourful berries are one of this shrub's best features; they start out green with yellow tinges, and gradually turn pink and finally to bluish black when mature. Nannyberries are sweet, juicy and make wonderful jam, but you'll have a tough time beating the birds to the harvest! This versatile shrub grows in sun to partial shade and is rarely bothered by pests. The dense, lustrous foliage is attractive throughout summer and turns purplish red in fall.

GROWING

Sun or shade; wet or dry soil. Avoid very hot, dry sites.

Feature shrubs, screens, hedges or in mass plantings.

Nannyberry is a versatile shrub that grows well in sun or shade.

RECOMMENDED SPECIES OR VARIETIES

Sheepberry

Also available as wild raisin.

TIPS

If you want lots of berries, grow more than one nannyberry. A single shrub will produce berries generously, but generally fewer of them. The flowers are wind pollinated, and will yield more berries if the shrubs are grown fairly close together.

Although it grows well in dry soil, be sure to water this shrub during summer heat waves.

Generally, it is a pretty tidy shrub, but when necessary, prune after flowering to encourage denser growth or to control size.

Nannyberry can be trained to grow as a small tree. See *How to Train Shrubs to 'Tree' Form* on page 64.

You may have to protect the berries from birds if you wish to have a good harvest. Ripe berries are bluish black, sweet and juicy. They are great eaten fresh or made into jams and jellies.

TOP LEFT: Nannyberry blooms for about two weeks in spring, with attractive clusters of creamy white flowers from 3–4½ inches (7.6–11 cm) across.
TOP RIGHT: This shrub shows nannyberry's form.
BOTTOM: Nannyberry is often one of the first shrubs to turn colour in fall.

Ninebark

Physocarpus opulifolius
Common Ninebark

Height • 15 inches–10 feet (38 cm–3 m)

Spread • 2–10 feet (61 cm–3 m)

Flowers • clusters of small, white or pink flowers in early summer

Fruit • showy, red seedpods in fall

Growth Rate • medium

Lifespan • short

Zone Rating
'Dart's Gold,' Golden: 2
'Tilden Parks': 3

Ninebark looks a lot like the gold-leaved varieties of spirea, and gardeners sometimes confuse the two shrubs. The boulevard near the entrance to our greenhouses is lined with ninebarks, and their bright foliage can't be missed. When customers at the greenhouses ask for golden spirea, I often double-check to see if it was actually those shrubs across the street that they had in mind. Ninebark is generally a larger shrub than spirea, and its flowers are less showy. Ninebark, however, makes up for its rather dowdy flowers with a stunning display of bright red seedpods that hang in clusters of three to five. The variety 'Tilden Parks' is distinct, with its low, spreading growth. It is one of the best groundcovers.

GROWING

Sun to partial shade for golden varieties; 'Tilden Parks' in sun to dense shade.

Prefers moist, well-drained soil but tolerates periods of dryness.

Accent or feature shrub; in foundation plantings, mass plantings; as a hedge, screen or groundcover.

RECOMMENDED SPECIES OR VARIETIES

Common Ninebark

'Dart's Gold': 4–5 feet (1.2–1.5 m) tall and wide; bright golden foliage; pinkish-white flower clusters; showy, red seedpods; excellent for small spaces in the shrub bed, for mass plantings or groups; more compact than most golden ninebarks; the species name *opulifolius* means 'rich leaves,' referring to the opulent foliage.

Golden (*P. opulifolius* 'Luteus'): 8–10 feet (2.4–3 m) tall and wide; golden-yellow foliage; clusters of pinkish-white flowers; red seedpods; blooms for two to three weeks in late spring, with flower clusters from 1–2 inches (2.5–5.1 cm) across.

'**Tilden Parks**': 15–20 inches (38–51 cm) tall and 2–4 feet (61–120 cm) wide; outstanding groundcover; more shade tolerant than others; rarely blooms; dark green leaves; within a year, foliage is so thick and dense that few weeds can grow through!

TOP: 'Dart's Gold' is a compact variety with intense colour.
MIDDLE: Ninebark's red seedpods are showier than its flowers. The name Physocarpus *means 'bladder fruit,' referring to the inflated seedpods.*
BOTTOM: 'Tilden Parks' is more shade tolerant than other varieties, and is the only ninebark that is suitable as a groundcover.

TIPS

Ninebark is an undemanding shrub that continues to thrive with little care, and flourishes even when planted in a sunny spot near a heat-reflecting brick wall.

Prune in late winter to early spring, before leaves appear. To encourage new growth and bright foliage on golden varieties, thin and cut back strongly every year.

For the best foliage colour, plant gold-leaved varieties in a sunny spot. The shadier the location, the greener the foliage is.

'Tilden Parks' grows well even in dense shade. One gardener grows it on the north side of a fence, underneath a mayday tree, where the shrub thrives despite receiving very little sunlight.

Few weeds grow underneath ninebarks.

Oak

Quercus macrocarpa
Bur Oak
Mossy Cup Oak

Quercus borealis
Northern Red Oak

Quercus palustris
Pin Oak
Swamp Oak

Quercus rubra
Red Oak

Quercus alba
White Oak
Stave Oak
Stone Oak
Tanner's Oak

Height • 50–100 feet (15–30 m)

Spread • 25–80 feet (7.6–24 m)

Flowers • catkins in spring; not showy

Fruit • acorns

Growth Rate • slow to medium

Lifespan • very long

Zone Rating
Bur: 2
Northern Red, Red: 3
Pin, White: 4

Oaks are one of the longest-lived, most magnificent trees. When you plant an oak, think of it as a 'heritage tree,' because an oak—often called the 'king of trees'—will reign in your yard for several generations to come, so choose its site with care. One gardener, while gazing at the huge oak tree in his front yard, said, only half-jokingly, that if the oak died, he would have to sell the house. His oak is a much-loved tree, with a well-used swing hanging from one of its strong, wide-spreading branches. Most likely, the grandchildren of the children who now climb the oak's branches will one day also enjoy a ride on its swing.

Bur oak is the hardiest type. Both bur oak and white oak—the largest oak of all—grow well in either wet or dry conditions. Northern red oak, pin oak and red oak prefer moist conditions.

GROWING

Sun; moist, acidic soil.

Shade tree.

'Mighty oaks from tiny acorns grow.'
—common adage

LEFT: Bur oak is a very hardy native tree that is becoming more popular as a boulevard tree in Alberta.
TOP RIGHT: Bur oak has distinctive acorns that are half covered with a moss-like cap or cup, hence this tree's other common name: 'mossy cup.'
BOTTOM RIGHT: Most oaks have round-lobed leaves, but the leaves of northern red, red and pin oak are narrower and more sharply pointed, while the leaves of white and bur oak are more rounded.

RECOMMENDED SPECIES OR VARIETIES

Bur Oak

70–80 feet (21–24 m) tall and 30–40 feet (9.1–12 m) wide; very impressive tree; dark green summer foliage; turns yellow to yellow-green in fall; thick furrowed bark; pollution tolerant; very adaptable and hardy.

Northern Red Oak

60–70 feet (18–21 m) tall and 30–40 feet (9.1–12 m) wide; medium rate of growth; pollution tolerant; leaves are reddish when young and turn dark green when mature; superb red colour in fall.

Pin Oak

50–60 feet (15–18 m) tall and 25–40 feet (7.6–12 m) wide; medium rate of growth; beautiful fall colour; glossy, dark green leaves turn brown, bronze or red in fall; good choice for wet areas; one of the easier oaks to transplant because of its fibrous root system (most have tap roots).

Red oak is one of the best oaks for fall colour.

Red Oak

60–70 feet (18–21 m) tall and 30–40 feet (9.1–12 m) wide; beautiful, large specimen tree; very hardy; deep, dark green foliage followed by a beautiful red fall colour; light brown acorns about 1 inch (2.5 cm) long; the provincial tree of Prince Edward Island.

White Oak

80–100 feet (24–30 m) tall and 50–80 feet (15–24 m) wide; a very durable tree; edible acorns; dark to bluish-green foliage; can have good red fall colour but not consistent; gains on average at least 1 foot (30 cm) per year for the first 15 to 20 years; because of its potential immense size, this tree is best for a large, open area.

The oak leaf has a distinctive shape, often used as a reference to describe other plants. Any plant with the species name *quercifolia*, such as *Sorbus quercifolia* (oak-leaf mountain ash), has similarly shaped leaves.

White oak is a magnificent tree that is fast growing when young but slows with age.

TIPS

Some oak trees have long tap roots that enable them to reach moisture deep down in the soil. When you buy a container-grown tree, however, the tap root has been trimmed to make it easier to plant. Mature trees are drought tolerant, but newly planted trees need to be watered well until their roots become established.

Prune in late winter to early spring before leaves appear.

Pin oak tolerates wet conditions and standing water for several weeks; it is a good choice for wet locations.

Although acorns are delicious, they are hard to get at and are usually eaten by birds and squirrels.

A mature oak tree is estimated to have about one-quarter of a million leaves.

Ohio Buckeye

Aesculus glabra
Ohio Buckeye

Height • 30–50 feet (9.1–15 m)

Spread • 30–50 feet (9.1–15 m)

Flowers • large, cream-coloured flowers in late spring

Fruit • nuts with spiny shells

Growth Rate • slow to medium

Lifespan • long

Zone Rating • 3

Ohio buckeye is the state tree of Ohio.

Ohio buckeye is a great shade tree, but only for large yards. Given abundant space, this tree is beautiful, has a nice rounded outline and shiny, dark green foliage. The leaves are shaped somewhat like large hands, with five outstretched leaflets, each about 4 inches (10 cm) long. Ohio buckeye blooms in late spring and early summer, with long, creamy, upright flowerspikes at the ends of its branches. Its nuts aren't edible, but they are interesting, encased in hard, spiny shells. Foliage turns orange in fall.

GROWING

Sun to partial shade.

Shade tree for large yards, acreages and parks.

RECOMMENDED SPECIES OR VARIETIES

Ohio Buckeye

TIPS

Avoid planting this tree in hot, dry, windy locations, or in sites near reflective walls, because too much sun and heat often cause foliage to become 'scorched.'

Prune in late winter to early spring before leaves appear.

Because of its spiny nutshells, don't plant Ohio buckeye in a site near walkways or on parts of the lawn where children often run barefoot. Squirrels love these nuts.

With its dense canopy, Ohio buckeye casts deep shade.

TOP: For large spaces, Ohio buckeye is an excellent tree. It has been cultivated since 1809.
BOTTOM LEFT: Ohio buckeye's upright flowerspikes are about 6 inches (15 cm) long.
BOTTOM RIGHT: Ohio buckeye doesn't always change colour before winter arrives, but when fall is sunny and warm, the foliage turns a lovely shade of orange.

Pincherry

Prunus pensylvanica
Pincherry
Wild Red Cherry

Height • 25–40 feet (7.6–12 m)

Spread • 18–25 feet (5.5–7.6 m)

Flowers • clusters of 1/2-inch (1.3 cm), white flowers in spring

Fruit • clusters of 1/4-inch (0.6 cm), light red cherries in summer

Growth Rate • medium

Lifespan • short

Zone Rating • 2

Pincherry provides four seasons of interest. In spring, it blooms profusely with small clusters of tiny, white flowers. In summer, the branches are decorated with clusters of tiny, light red cherries, and in fall the long leaves turn orange and yellow. In winter, the reddish-brown bark of the pincherry is especially attractive against a snowy background. Cultivated pincherries have a different form than wild pincherries; they tend to be vase-shaped with a single trunk, whereas wild pincherries grow as multi-stemmed shrubs. Pincherries look quite similar to mayday trees, but are much smaller and fit more easily into most yards. Like maydays, the fruit attracts birds. Pincherry jelly is, without a doubt, my favourite preserve, although the berries take forever to pick.

GROWING

Sun; best in a moist, well-drained, sandy soil. Do not grow in shade or allow to dry out.

Good tree for small yards and limited spaces.

RECOMMENDED SPECIES OR VARIETIES

Pincherry

Also available as wild red cherry.

Pincherry may get its name from the faint pinstripes on its berries.

TIPS

Be sure to plant pincherry in an open site where it will not become overshadowed by larger trees. In shady sites, it is much shorter lived.

Pincherry usually needs pruning only once every four to five years. Prune in late winter to early spring before leaves appear.

Pincherries provide food, shelter and nesting sites for birds.

The cherries are pretty sour for eating fresh, but they do make a nice, tart jelly, jam or pie. They are also used for syrup, sauces and wine.

LEFT: The bark has attractive, horizontal markings that are powdery orange on young trees and black on mature trees.
TOP RIGHT: Pincherry blossoms make an attractive early spring display.
BOTTOM RIGHT: Pincherry is also an attractive addition to the yard in fall with its brilliant orange colour.

Pine

Pinus nigra
Austrian Pine
Black Pine

Pinus aristata
Bristlecone Pine

Pinus strobus
Eastern White Pine

Pinus flexilis
Limber Pine

Pinus contorta var. *latifolia*
Lodgepole Pine

Pinus mugo
Mugo Pine
Swiss Mountain Pine

Pinus sylvestris
Scotch Pine
Scots Pine

Pinus cembra
Swiss Stone Pine

Height • 1–70 feet (30 cm–21 m)

Spread • 3–40 feet (91 cm–12 m)

Flowers • not showy

Fruit • purple, pink or brown cones

Growth Rate
Austrian, Eastern White, Lodgepole, Mugo, Scotch: medium
Bristlecone, Limber, Mugo (dwarfs), Swiss Stone: slow

Lifespan • long

Zone Rating
Austrian, Bristlecone, Eastern White, Swiss Stone: 3
Limber, Mugo, Scotch: 2
Lodgepole: 1

Pines come in a remarkable variety of sizes and shapes. Some pines become huge trees, while others are quite small and well suited to small gardens. Pines are the most common conifer (cone-bearing tree) in Canada. These versatile trees grow well in various soils, including poor, dry sites.

Austrian pine is a large tree with a stout trunk and lustrous needles. If you want a very interesting tree, choose bristlecone pine; the world's oldest-known living tree is a 4700-year-old bristlecone pine, growing at an elevation of 10,000 feet (3048 m) on a mountainside in California. These trees have a very distinctive, weathered look, with branches densely covered in whorls of short needles.

Pines come in a wide range of sizes, shapes and colours, making this evergreen a very versatile addition to the home landscape.

With their long, soft needles, eastern white pines stand out from other trees. Their beautiful foliage gives them an appearance that is noticeably different even from a distance. Limber pines are wide, slow-growing trees that establish themselves well in windy sites; their branches often take on interesting shapes. The lodgepole pine is a tall, slim tree; Native Peoples used its long, straight trunk for building teepees and lodges, hence the name.

Mugo pines can be either large or small rounded shrubs. Scotch pine has long, attractive, blue-green needles, and is popular as a Christmas tree. Swiss stone pine is one of the most elegant and shapely pines, and one of the best for small yards because it grows slowly.

TOP: Austrian pine is very attractive, but requires a large yard. BOTTOM: Pines have two types of cones: the smaller cones clustered at the ends of branches are male, and the larger cones further in along the branches are female. Female pine cones can remain on branches for many years before opening to release their seeds and dropping to the ground; male cones disintegrate soon after shedding their pollen in spring.

GROWING

Sun; average to dry, sandy soil.

Feature trees, screens, in groups, beside decks. Dwarf varieties in foundation plantings, shrub beds, flowerbeds, rock gardens. 'Hillside Creeper' as a groundcover.

RECOMMENDED SPECIES OR VARIETIES

Austrian Pine

50–60 feet (15–18 m) tall and 20–40 feet (6.1–12 m) wide; stout tree with a thick, short trunk and lustrous, dark green needles; tolerant of heat, drought and air-pollution; does well in heavy clay soils; extremely attractive, grey to grey-brown bark with deep, brown furrows; tawny-yellow cones that turn brown with age.

TOP LEFT: Bristlecone pine is a slow-growing tree with an intriguing irregular shape.
TOP RIGHT: A mature eastern white pine has no equal when well grown.
BOTTOM: The attractive foliage of eastern white pine is popular with florists for Christmas wreaths.

Bristlecone Pine

A slow-growing tree that gains 6–8 inches (15–20 cm) per year; after 50 to 60 years, becomes 30–40 feet (9.1–12 m) tall and 20–25 feet (6.1–7.6 m) wide; dark green foliage with white resin flecks all over the needles; irregular pyramidal shape, often more spreading than upright; dark purple, female cones may not appear until the tree is about 20 years old; an extremely long-lived tree.

Eastern White Pine

Eastern White: 50–70 feet (15–21 m) tall and 20–40 feet (6.1–12 m) wide; long, soft, light green to blue-green needles, from 3–5 inches (7.6–13 cm) long; an extremely handsome, ornamental tree; new cones are light red to pinkish green and become 4–8 inches (10–20 cm) long; cones take up to three years to mature; introduced to the nursery trade in 1705.

'**Blue Shag**': a spreading dwarf form that grows 4–6 inches (10–15 cm) per year; after 10 to 12 years, reaches $3^1/_2$–5 feet (1.1–1.5 m) tall and 4–6 feet (1.2–1.8 m) wide; soft, silvery-blue foliage; excellent for rock gardens.

Dwarf Eastern White (*P. strobus* 'Nana'): a slightly larger, spreading dwarf form that grows 3–4 inches (7.6–10 cm) per year; after 15 to 20 years, becomes 4–5 feet (1.2–1.5 m) tall and 5–6 feet (1.5–1.8 m) wide; long, soft, blue-green needles; extremely beautiful; great for rock gardens.

TOP: 'Blue Shag' works well as a feature plant.
BOTTOM: Dwarf Eastern White pine is a slow-growing, short variety with an attractive, round shape and long, soft needles similar to the needles of the taller eastern white pine.

TOP LEFT: Limber pine is named for its tough, flexible, young branches, which can actually be tied in knots without breaking.
TOP RIGHT: Young Weeping Eastern White pines can look a bit sparse but fill in nicely with age.
BOTTOM: 'Big Tuna' has a single stem and a gorgeous, oval shape.

Weeping Eastern White (*P. strobus* 'Pendula'): 15–30 feet (4.6–9.1 m) tall and wide; size varies tremendously depending on how it is grown; to limit the height, remove the 'leader'; long, bluish-green needles on long, pendulous branches; unique specimen tree!

Limber Pine

35–40 feet (11–12 m) tall and 25–30 feet (7.6–9.1 m) wide; dark blue-green needles; a dense, broad pyramidal tree when young, and a broad, flat-topped tree at maturity; light-brown cones are erect when young and pendulous when mature; very adaptable; does not wind-burn easily; introduced in 1861.

Lodgepole Pine

65–70 feet (20–21 m) tall and 15–20 feet (4.6–6.1 m) wide; green needles; a tall, narrow tree with a long, straight trunk and rather short, open crown; casts little shade; grows well in moist areas; a tidy tree that doesn't drop cones; good for growing near decks; great planted in groups.

Mugo Pine

'Big Tuna': 10–12 feet (3–3.7 m) tall and 6–8 feet (1.8–2.4 m) wide; dense, dark green needles; has a single trunk (rather than multiple stems) that is more visible with age; very compact, oval-shaped variety.

'Mops Mugo': a dwarf form that I consider to be one of the best; grows 2–3 inches (5.1–7.6 cm) per year; after 15 to 18 years, reaches 3–4 feet (91–120 cm) tall and wide; a very compact, dense form; excellent for rock gardens, foundation plantings, borders, as a feature shrub or accent in a shrub bed.

'White Bud Mugo': a very attractive dwarf variety named for its thick, white 'buds,' which will form the new growth; grows 2–3 inches (5.1–7.6 cm) per year; after 15 years, reaches 3–4 feet (91–120 cm) tall and 4–5 feet (1.2–1.5 m) wide; particularly attractive in early spring when the bright white buds appear; good for rock gardens and small settings; remains dense and compact.

TOP LEFT: A mugo pine well placed in front of a house can act as an attractive screen. TOP RIGHT: 'Mops Mugo' is well suited to everything from rock gardens to shrub beds. BOTTOM: 'White Bud Mugo' has a very compact dwarf form.

TOP LEFT & BOTTOM: Scotch pines have attractive, flaky, orange-red bark on their upper trunks and branches. The bark on the lower trunk is greyish brown.
TOP RIGHT: This four-year-old 'Hillside Creeper' is already about 8 feet (2.4 m) wide.

Scotch Pine

'French Blue Scotch': 40–60 feet (12–18 m) tall and 20–30 feet (6.1–9.1 m) wide; beautiful blue needles up to 3 inches (7.6 cm) long; excellent as a feature tree or in background plantings; the bluest Scotch pine available!

'Hillside Creeper': a fast-growing, unusually low variety of Scotch pine; 1–2 feet (30–61 cm) tall and 8–10 feet (2.4–3 m) wide; reaches full width in just four to five years; long, green needles; very attractive; excellent groundcover.

Swiss Stone Pine

50–60 feet (15–18 m) tall and 10–20 feet (3–6.1 m) wide; beautiful, shiny green needles are white-blue underneath; stunning tree with a dense columnar shape; excellent planted as a single feature tree or in groups; requires a loamy, well-drained, slightly acidic soil.

TIPS

If you are looking for a mugo pine for your front yard, it's best to choose a dwarf—especially if you plan to plant it underneath your living room window. Mugo pines have such incredible variation in growth habit that many growers refuse to commit themselves to a fixed size at maturity.

Generally, however, mugo pines range from 15–40 feet (4.6–12 m) tall and 15–30 feet (4.6–9.1 m) wide—large enough to block the view and most of the sunlight from your window. Even dwarf varieties can sometimes suddenly send up long shoots after several years.

Most pines are quite drought tolerant, but remember that young trees need to be well watered throughout the first growing season after they are planted, until their root systems become established.

Pine trees provide shelter and seed (inside the pines cones) for many birds. Chickadees, jays, woodpeckers and nuthatches will use these trees year-round.

The soil beneath pine trees is dry and can become quite acidic.

Fallen pine needles can be composted and then used as a mulch for other plants, such as hemlock, rhododendrons, azaleas, boxwood or certain perennials, that prefer to grow in acidic soil.

LEFT: Swiss stone pines are unusual in my area of the country. These beautiful trees have violet cones that remain on the branches for three to four years before turning brown and dropping. RIGHT: During spring, dusty yellow clouds of pollen arise from the male cones whenever the wind moves the branches.

Eastern white pine is the provincial tree of Ontario and the state tree of Maine. Cut branches will last over two weeks in floral arrangements, if you keep the vase filled with water and mist the foliage frequently.

Plum

Prunus nigra
Canada Plum

Prunus x nigrella
Hybrid Plum

Height • 12–18 feet (3.7–5.5 m)

Spread • 8–12 feet (2.4–3.7 m)

Flowers • pink or white blossoms in spring

Fruit • plums mature in late summer

Growth Rate • medium

Lifespan
Canada: average
Hybrid: short

Zone Rating • 2

Plum trees are absolutely spectacular in full flower. They bloom in early spring, with an abundance of fragrant blossoms that line the branches before the leaves appear. Canada plums and hybrid plums are grown for their ornamental value rather than for their fruit, because the Canada plum produces tiny plums and the hybrid bears no fruit at all. Plum trees mature quickly, making them a perfect choice for the impatient homeowner who wants a showy feature tree. Their small size makes plum trees ideal for planting in small yards and growing under power lines, while their beauty is such that they deserve a prominent place in the garden.

GROWING

Sun; moist, well-drained soil is best but does well in heavy clay soil.

Feature tree, screening; great for small yards.

The hybrid plum was developed in Manitoba in 1952, and produces a dramatic rose-pink blossom.

RECOMMENDED SPECIES OR VARIETIES

Canada Plum

'**Princess Kay**': 12–18 feet (3.7–5.5 m) tall and 8–10 feet (2.4–3 m) wide; lots of fragrant, white, double blossoms in spring; 1¼-inch (3.2 cm), yellowish-red plums ripen mid- to late summer; tree trunk is short; showy bark is purplish black with white marking, and is especially striking in winter; blooms slightly earlier than hybrid; a heavy-blooming variety, even when young.

Hybrid Plum

12–15 feet (3.7–4.6 m) tall and 10–12 feet (3–3.7 m) wide; red flowerbuds open to bright rose-pink blossoms; a sterile variety that forms no fruit; glossy, deep green foliage has a purple tinge; a cross between a Canada plum and the popular spring-flowering shrub, Russian almond; developed in Manitoba and introduced in 1952; blooming period lasts two to three weeks longer than other plums.

'Princess Kay' has showy, glossy, purplish-black bark with white, horizontal stripes, which provides a dramatic background for the white spring blossoms.

Plum trees provide colourful displays of fragrant blossoms in spring.

TIPS

Do not plant in low-lying, wet areas where puddles can form in spring from melted snow, or in any other site where water will pool around the tree's roots.

Avoid planting in open areas where the trees will be exposed to winter winds. Harsh conditions in winter can damage flowerbuds, resulting in few to no flowers the following spring.

Prune after blooming, as next year's flowerbuds form in summer.

In some years blossoms can be damaged by late spring frosts. Frost-damaged blossoms turn brown or black, and as a result, will not produce fruit.

To lessen chances of frost damage, you can delay flowering somewhat by mulching the soil around the tree, or by growing evergreens, perennials or shrubs around the base. These actions help to keep the roots cool so that the tree remains dormant a little longer and blossoms open a bit—perhaps up to a week—later in spring.

If your plum tree is not blooming well, it could be because of unusual or extreme changes in temperature during winter. Unseasonal thaws followed by sudden freezing temperatures can kill flowerbuds.

Fewer blossoms can result from aging. Like all fruit trees, ornamental plums tend to produce less as they get older. Pruning can help improve flowering.

If you want a plum tree to grow beside a deck, patio or pool, choose the hybrid plum, a sterile variety that does not produce fruit.

If you want to attract birds to your garden, choose 'Princess Kay.' Its plums are too small for us to bother eating, but the birds love them.

If you want to send someone a message, consider the ancient language of flowers. In florigraphy, plum blossoms mean 'keep your promises.' The plum tree stands for 'fidelity.'

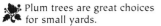

Plum trees are great choices for small yards.

Poplar

Populus x 'Griffin'
Griffin Poplar

Populus x 'Northwest'
Northwest Poplar

Populus alba
Silver Poplar
White Poplar

Populus x canescens 'Tower'
Tower Poplar

Height • 40–70 feet (12–21 m)

Spread • 8–75 feet (2.4–23 m)

Flowers • catkins in spring

Fruit • not showy

Growth Rate • fast

Lifespan
most varieties: short
Northwest: average

Zone Rating
most varieties: 2
Silver Poplar: 3

Whenever I hear people say that they don't like poplars, I try to convince them otherwise. Poplars have a bad reputation for producing enormous amounts of fluffy seeds and suckers. However, the new varieties don't have these undesirable traits, but they do retain the poplar's best attributes: fast growth and adaptability. Ted and I planted northwest poplars to create a quick shelterbelt that increased in height by a few feet every year. We have three tower poplars in the flowerbeds that line our house, and just 10 years after planting, they do indeed tower above our two-storey home. In almost any situation where you want fast growth, poplars are a reliable choice.

Silver poplar is a very striking, large, rounded tree with silvery leaves that provide great contrast against green foliage. Tower poplar is quite a narrow tree that grows at least seven times taller than its width. Such an extreme columnar form is rare in trees this tall. Griffin is a hybrid variety that is shorter than most poplars, so it is well suited to smaller yards. Northwest is an impressive, wide-spreading tree that provides quick shade, but it grows too large for most yards. In parks and the landscaped common area between condominiums, for example, northwest poplar is a superb choice.

Poplars are one of the fastest-growing trees, and 6 foot (1.8 m) saplings can reach the top of a two-storey house in just two to four years!

The griffin poplar has a nice oval growth habit and doesn't produce white, fluffy seeds.

GROWING

Sun; best in a moist, rich, deep soil but grows in just about any soil.

Windbreaks, shade trees. Because of their size, tower and griffin poplars are the best choices for smaller yards.

RECOMMENDED SPECIES OR VARIETIES

Griffin Poplar

50–60 feet (15–18 m) tall and 25–30 feet (7.6–9.1 m) wide; one of the smaller poplars; a very upright, oval tree; does not produce fluff.

LEFT: Northwest poplars are excellent shade trees.
RIGHT: Northwest poplars have brilliant fall colour.

Northwest Poplar

70 feet (21 m) tall and 70–75 feet (21–23 m) wide; an excellent tree for shade or windbreaks in large yards or parks; very strong grower; shiny, dark green leaves; wide canopy; these trees do not produce fluff, because they are male.

Silver Poplar

40–70 feet (12–21 m) tall and wide; three-lobed leaves are dark green on top, bright silvery white underneath and shimmer in the wind; extremely attractive windbreak or wide-spreading shade tree with a rounded or oval canopy; often mistaken for a maple because of the shape of its leaves; tends to produce suckers at the base; most trees sold are males, which do not produce fluff.

Young leaves of silver poplar are white and almost completely covered with hairs; older leaves are dark green on top with white, cottony undersides. The bark of silver poplars is pale silvery grey, distinguished by diamond-shaped markings on the older branches and trunk.

Tower

70 feet (21 m) tall and $8^1/_2$–10 feet (2.6–3 m) wide; very formal appearance; good for windbreaks, defining boundaries, or creating a screen around small properties; grey-green leaves; does not produce suckers or basal shoots; one of the few poplars with good yellow fall colour.

TIPS

It is important to know which type of poplar you are buying. Poplars have male and female trees; the females produce massive amounts of annoying fluffy seeds and drop sticky leaf scales everywhere. Male poplars don't make this mess. Hybrid poplars, such as tower and griffin, don't make a mess either. With northwest and silver poplars, most nurseries sell only the male trees.

Prune most poplars in late winter to early spring. A silver poplar is an exception; prune it in late summer or fall to avoid sap bleeding. A tower poplar is a tidy tree that requires little pruning.

Poplars make good 'nurse' trees in windbreaks, protecting other slow-growing trees.

Keeping these trees in the best possible state of health reduces suckering. Certain types, such as tower poplars, tend not to produce suckers unless stressed or damaged.

Unfortunately, poplars are a favourite food of tent caterpillars, but those leaf-chewing insects usually don't affect the health of the tree. Tent caterpillars tend to go in cycles and only become a problem once every seven or so years. Interestingly, the black poplar that grows in the woods in my area seems to be immune, remaining untouched while other surrounding poplars are stripped of their leaves.

TOP: Tower poplars are one of the tallest and narrowest columnar trees. BOTTOM: The leaves of silver poplars are covered with cottony hairs that help stop them from wilting in the sun.

Potentilla

Potentilla fruticosa
Shrubby Potentilla
Bush Cinquefoil

Potentilla tridentata
Wineleaf Cinquefoil

Height • 3 inches–3 feet (7.6–91 cm)

Spread • 1 inch–3 1/2 feet (2.5 cm–1.1 m)

Flowers • yellow, pink, orange or white flowers all summer

Fruit • not showy

Growth Rate • slow

Lifespan • short to average

Zone Rating • 2

Potentillas are lovely, easy-to-care-for shrubs that brighten gardens with their abundant, saucer-shaped flowers, which last all summer. These extremely adaptable shrubs grow well in most types of soil and are small enough to fit easily into almost any garden. Potentillas have fine-textured, green to silvery foliage and range from low, creeping shrubs to large, erect bushes. Most potentillas have 1-inch (2.5 cm), saucer-like flowers, but some varieties have flowers that are larger—semi-double or double. There are over 130 varieties of potentilla, but not many are winter-hardy. It's best to stick with the recommended varieties, but don't be afraid to experiment.

'Nuuk' potentilla is different. It grows just a few inches tall, and spreads to form a tight mat of dark green foliage. 'Nuuk' blooms best in June, when it glows with clusters of bright white flowers, and then goes on to bloom sporadically for the rest of summer. All potentillas, however, are tough, hardy, low-maintenance shrubs that are rarely bothered by insects or disease.

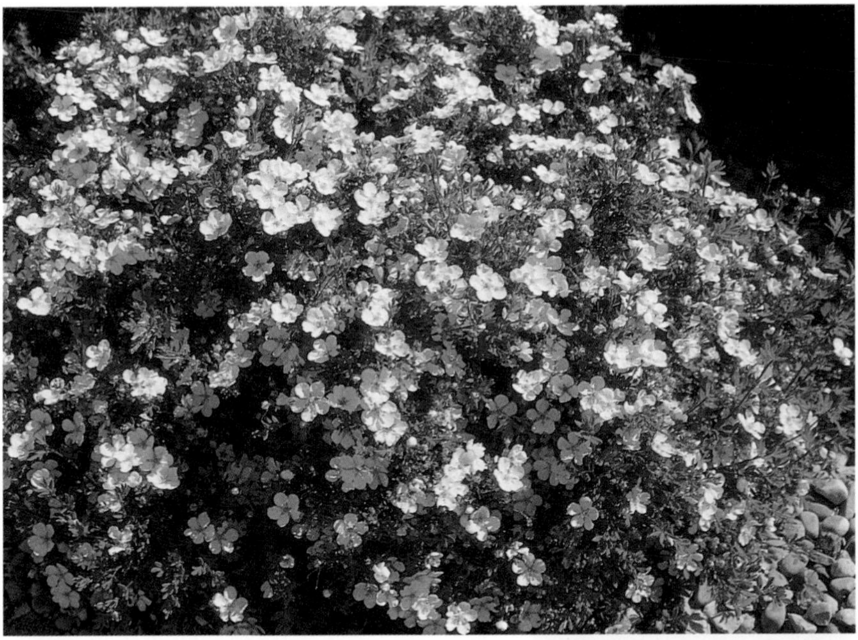

GROWING

Sun to partial shade for shrubby potentillas. 'Nuuk' prefers a sunny site.

Mass plantings, in groups, foundation plantings, borders, raised beds or large containers; certain varieties make good hedges. 'Nuuk' as a groundcover, in rock gardens or borders.

RECOMMENDED SPECIES OR VARIETIES

Shrubby Potentilla

'**Abbotswood**': 3 feet (91 cm) tall and 3–3½ feet (91–110 cm) wide; white flowers; dark blue-green foliage; makes a good hedge; can be sheared and shaped for a more formal appearance.

'**Gold Drop**': 2 feet (61 cm) tall and 2–3 feet (61–91 cm) wide; a bushy dwarf variety with leaves smaller than usual; lemon-yellow flowers; more flowers than many other varieties.

TOP: With its large flowers, 'Abbotswood' is stunning in full bloom. It is one of the best white-flowered potentillas.
BOTTOM: 'Gold Drop' is a profuse bloomer, with an abundance of lemon-yellow flowers all summer. This dwarf variety is great for mixed borders and foundation plantings.

TOP LEFT: 'Goldstar' has the largest flowers—twice the size of most potentillas. This variety tends to bloom in clusters, resulting in a very showy display.
RIGHT: 'Pink Beauty' is an exceptional variety. Pink-flowered potentillas are notorious for fading quickly to almost white, but the flowers of this new Canadian variety from the University of Manitoba remain pink for well over a month, even in temperatures of 86° F (30° C). Keep shrubs well watered for the longest-lasting flowers.
BOTTOM LEFT: 'Orange Whisper' blooms in an unusual colour for a potentilla. This colour holds well throughout summer.

'**Goldstar**': 3 feet (91 cm) tall and 2–2½ feet (61–76 cm) wide; large, deep yellow flowers in clusters; very attractive upright shrub.

'**Orange Whisper**': 2½–3 feet (76–91 cm) tall and wide; pale orange flowers; a compact, mounding variety.

'**Pink Beauty**': 2–2½ feet (61–76 cm) tall and wide; abundant, rich pink flowers with long-lasting colour; blooms a bit later than others, but continues to bloom until frost.

'**Snowbird**': 2–2½ feet (61–76 cm) tall and wide; white, semi-double flowers; slower growing than most varieties.

'**Yellow Gem**': 15 inches (38 cm) tall and 3–3½ feet (91–110 cm) wide; large, bright yellow flowers; a compact, spreading habit from the University of British Columbia.

'**Yellowbird**': 3 feet (91 cm) tall and wide; bright yellow, double flowers; young shrubs have some single flowers, but mature shrubs are consistently double; very upright form; a good variety for hedges.

LEFT: A mass planting of 'Yellow Gem' provides a bright display of flowers all summer. This variety's flowers are larger than usual, from 1½–2 inches (3.8–5.1 cm) across. TOP RIGHT: 'Snowbird's' bright white, semi-double flowers are shown off to great advantage against dark green foliage. BOTTOM RIGHT: Potentilla's five-petalled flowers look like the flowers of roses. Both roses and potentillas belong to the same plant family. 'Yellowbird' has double flowers, a rather rare feature in potentillas.

This immature 'Nuuk' will eventually bloom with abundant clusters of white flowers in late spring, and fewer flowers in summer. This low-growing, spreading potentilla is native to Greenland; it is extremely hardy.

Wineleaf Cinquefoil

'Nuuk': 3–4 inches (7.6–10 cm) tall and 1–1½ feet (30–46 cm) wide; white flowers; blooms profusely in late spring and sporadically throughout summer; an attractive, spreading evergreen potentilla; perfect for borders along walkways or in shrubs beds.

Potentilla means 'powerful,' a reference to this plant's reputed medicinal qualities.

TIPS

For the best flower colour, plant potentillas in a site that is partially shaded during the hottest part of the day. The flowers tend to fade quickly in hot sun, especially older varieties. Yellow flowers generally hold their colour better.

Potentillas are very drought tolerant, but the shrubs bloom better and have nicer-looking foliage when grown in moist, well-drained soil.

Prune as soon as leaves begin to appear in spring. Potentillas tend to need annual pruning: trim away any of last year's dead flowers from the ends of twiggy branches, cut out weak growth to ground level, and shorten strong shoots by about one-third.

Regular pruning results in more flowers and a denser bush. 'Nuuk' is an exception—it doesn't need pruning.

Potentillas bloom on new wood, so hedges can be trimmed in either fall or early spring without affecting the flower show.

For a tidier display over winter, some gardeners remove the dead flowers in fall. This step is a matter of personal preference; whether you prune in spring or fall doesn't matter to the shrub.

These shrubs look splendid growing in large containers. If the container is large enough, the roots won't dry out and freeze so the shrubs can be left in place over winter. Be sure to water well in late fall; the survival rate is far lower when plants enter winter with their roots in dry soil. 'Nuuk' potentilla won't fare so well in a container.

A potentilla hedge is particularly striking in full bloom. During winter, it acts as a wind barrier to protect nearby perennials.

Shrubby potentillas can be trained to grow as miniature flowering trees. See *How to Train Shrubs to 'Tree' Form* on page 64.

Potentilla is one of the longest-blooming shrubs, with non-stop flowers from early summer to frost.

Fruticosa means 'with a shrubby habit' in Latin. Look for shrubby potentilla (*Potentilla fruticosa*) when shopping from catalogues, because there are also non-woody potentillas that are perennials rather than shrubs.

Rhododendron

Rhododendron catawbiense
Catawba Rhododendron

Rhododendron 'P.J.M.'
P.J.M. Hybrid Rhododendron

Height • 2–6 feet (61 cm–1.8 m)

Spread • 2–6 feet (61 cm–1.8 m)

Flowers • pink, white or red flowers in late spring

Fruit • not showy

Growth Rate • slow

Lifespan • short to average

Zone Rating
Catawba: 4 [3]
P.J.M. hybrids: 3

'Rhododendron' is a huge family of plants; there are over 1000 species and several thousand varieties. Out of all those rhododendrons, only a very few are hardy enough to grow in snowy, cold-winter areas—the ones that do are particularly prized. Catawba rhododendrons are native to the southeastern United States; they are named after the Catawba River in the Blue Ridge Mountains. Despite the difference in climate, given the right site, Catawba rhododendrons will thrive in northern gardens.

P.J.M. hybrid rhododendrons are the hardiest rhododendron. The original P.J.M. was introduced in 1943, and since then, about 25 more varieties have been created from it.

Ted and I have two rhododendrons—'Roseum Elegans' and 'Henry's Red'—planted near the kitchen window of our house, where we can admire their flowers often.

Elegans *is Latin for 'elegant.' 'Roseum Elegans'* (Rhododendron catawbiense) *bears large, elegant clusters of deep lavender-pink flowers in late spring.*

GROWING

Sun to light shade; moist, well-drained, acidic soil. Keep these shrubs well watered.

Feature shrub; accent plant in small shrub border, mass plantings in large shrub border.

Fertilize once a month until the end of July with an evergreen fertilizer.

RECOMMENDED SPECIES OR VARIETIES

Catawba Rhododendron

'**Hindustan**': 5–6 feet (1.5–1.8 m) tall and wide; large clusters of pinkish-orange flowers; up to 17 flowers in each cluster; flowerbuds hardy to -40° F (-40° C).

'**Roseum Elegans**': 6–10 feet (1.8–3 m) tall and 5–8 feet (1.5–2.4 m) wide; very showy, lavender flowers; heat tolerant; a handsome shrub with dark green, leathery leaves; flowerbuds hardy to -40° F (-40° C).

P.J.M. Hybrid Rhododendron

'**Aglo**': 3–6 feet (91 cm–1.8 m) tall and wide; large clusters of light pink flowers with dark pink blotches; leaves turn mahogany in winter; a very hardy, dense, rounded shrub; flowerbuds hardy to -40° C (-40° F).

The rhododendron is the state flower of Washington and West Virginia.

TOP: Rhododendrons bloom for two to four weeks in late spring to early summer. 'P.J.M.' is one of the most popular varieties.
BOTTOM: Rhododendrons are slow-growing shrubs. After 10 years, 'P.J.M.' may be only 4 feet (1.2 m) tall but even young plants bloom well; this 'P.J.M.' was two years old in 1996.

'**Compact**': 3–6 feet (91 cm–1.8 m) tall and wide; large clusters of vibrant lavender-pink flowers; leaves turn mahogany in winter; as its name suggests, this shrub is a smaller, more compact version of P.J.M.; flowerbuds hardy to -40° C (-40° F).

'**Henry's Red**': 3–6 feet (91 cm–1.8 m) tall and wide; large clusters of very dark red flowers; dense, compact, upright shrub with dark green foliage; flowerbuds hardy to -26° F (-32° C).

'**P.J.M.**': 3–6 feet (91 cm–1.8 m) tall and wide; lots of large clusters of vibrant lavender-pink flowers; leaves turn mahogany in winter; a dense, rounded shrub; flowerbuds hardy to -40° F (-40° C).

'**Regal**': 3–5 feet (91 cm–1.5 m) tall and 4–6 feet (1.2–1.8 m) wide; rich purple-pink flowers; leaves turn mahogany in winter; a compact shrub; flowerbuds hardy to -40° F (-40° C).

TIPS

More than 100 new rhododendron varieties are introduced each year, but only a limited number are winter-hardy to zone 3. Catawba grows well in zone 3 if in a sheltered site.

Even hardy rhododendrons do best planted in a sheltered site, where they will have a fairly deep covering of snow throughout winter. Ideally, grow rhododendrons close to a house or heated building. The site should be sunny in summer but partially shaded in winter, and protected from winter winds.

A thick, light snowcover provides excellent plant protection. Every winter I cover my rhododendrons with snow as soon as enough snow is available.

Prune immediately after flowering.

Rhododendrons bloom best when grown in full sun. They will, however, still bloom with a minimum of three hours of direct sunlight each day, but with fewer flowers. Catawba varieties are a little more shade tolerant than P.J.M. hybrids.

These shrubs have shallow roots that are prone to drying. Keep the soil around rhododendrons consistently moist. Don't plant in a flowerbed underneath a house overhang, where they will receive little moisture from rain.

Rhododendrons prefer acidic soil. If your shrubs have pale leaves, few flowers and generally look unhealthy, have your soil tested.

A mulch of shredded fir bark helps retain soil moisture.

Older shrubs can become 'leggy' with bare lower branches. Pruning will rejuvenate rhododendrons.

Rhododendrons are broad-leaved evergreens; they retain their leaves year-round, even in winter. Often, the leaves curl tightly during a freezing winter; this curling is a natural adaptation that helps to prevent moisture loss.

Rhododendron means 'rose tree.'

'Henry's Red' has an unusual colour for a hardy rhododendron; few others have such dark flowers. There are 12 to 15 individual flowers in each cluster, and each flower has 10 protruding stamens.

Rhododendrons are one of the most beautiful flowering shrubs.

Rose

Rosa spp.
Hardy Shrub Rose

Height • 2–10 feet (61 cm–3 m)

Spread • 2–6 feet (61 cm–1.8 m)

Flowers • pink, red or yellow flowers all summer to frost

Fruit • red or orange rosehips in fall

Growth Rate
'Adelaide Hoodless,' 'Hansa,' 'John Davis,' 'Morden Centennial,' 'Thérèse Bugnet': medium
'Blanc Double de Coubert,' 'Frau Dagmar Hartopp,' 'J.P. Connell,' 'Morden Fireglow': slow
'John Cabot': fast

Lifespan • average

Zone Rating
'Adelaide Hoodless,' 'Blanc Double de Coubert,' 'Frau Dagmar Hartopp,' 'J.P. Connell,' 'John Davis,' 'Morden Fireglow': 3
'Hansa,' 'John Cabot': 1
'Morden Centennial,' 'Thérèse Bugnet': 2

Throughout history, roses have been one of the world's most beloved flowers, celebrated by artists, florists and poets as well as gardeners. The rose is also one of the oldest plant species; it was around long before humans. In recent years, the demand for hardy roses has increased tremendously, likely because hardy roses are as easy to grow as any other shrub, but they bloom far longer. Hardy roses need no special winter protection. More and more gardeners are discovering the carefree beauty of hardy roses; at our greenhouses, they outsell their more tender hybrid cousins by at least three to one.

GROWING

Sun.

Accents in a flowerbed or with other shrubs, as groundcovers or hedges. Climbing roses on a trellis, arbour or fence.

LEFT: 'Adelaide Hoodless' is a very hardy rose that blooms with as many as 25 flowers in a single cluster.
RIGHT: The flowers of 'Blanc Double de Coubert' have a strong, sweet scent.

RECOMMENDED SPECIES OR VARIETIES

Hardy Shrub Roses

'**Adelaide Hoodless**': a Parkland series rose; 5–6 feet (1.5–1.8 m) tall and wide; large clusters of red, 2-inch (5.1 cm), double flowers; glossy foliage; blooms continuously from early summer to frost; decorative red rosehips.

'**Blanc Double de Coubert**': rugosa hybrid rose; 4–6 feet (1.2–1.8 m) tall and 4–5 feet (1.2–1.5 m) wide; very fragrant, white, semi-double flowers from 2½–3 inches (6.4–7.6 cm) across; vigorous, arching rosebush; disease resistant; blooms repeatedly from early summer to frost; large, round, bright scarlet rosehips.

TOP: 'Hansa' makes an excellent hedge with its upright, arching shrubs.
MIDDLE: 'Frau Dagmar Hartopp' does well even with shade for half the day.
BOTTOM: 'J.P. Connell's' popularity is partly because of its thornless stems and lovely, yellow flowers.

'**Frau Dagmar Hartopp**': hardy shrub rose; 2–3 feet (61–91 cm) tall and 4–5 feet (1.2–1.5 m) wide; fragrant, silvery-pink, single flowers are 3–3½ inches (7.6–8.9 cm) across; glossy foliage; good fall colour; makes a great groundcover; blooms repeatedly from early summer to frost; very large, round rosehips.

'**Hansa**': rugosa hybrid rose; 4–5 feet (1.2–1.5 m) tall and 5–6 feet (1.5–1.8 m) wide; large, fragrant, fuchsia-red, double flowers; excellent disease resistance; blooms repeatedly from early summer to frost; large, gleaming red rosehips; one of the toughest and longest-lived roses.

TOP: Although 'John Cabot' is officially described as reddish pink, its flowers range in colour from deep orchid-pink to red-purple.
BOTTOM: 'John Davis' is one of the most popular climbing roses. It blooms non-stop all season.

'**J.P. Connell**': Explorer series rose; 2–3 feet (61–91 cm) tall and wide; fragrant, yellow, 3–3½-inch (7.6–8.9 cm), double flowers in clusters of three to eight; blooms repeatedly from early summer to frost.

'**John Cabot**': Explorer series climbing rose; 8–10 feet (2.4–3 m) tall and 5–7 feet (1.5–2.1 m) wide; fragrant, reddish-pink, 2½-inch (6.4 cm), double flowers; blooms repeatedly from early summer to frost; a beautiful, very hardy climber.

'**John Davis**': Explorer series climbing rose; 5–6 feet (1.5–1.8 m) tall and 4–6 feet (1.2–1.8 m) wide; fragrant, pink, double flowers up to 3½ inches (8.9 cm) across; blooms continuously from early summer to frost; one of the longest-blooming roses.

In early summer, 'Morden Centennial' blooms so profusely that the flowers literally hide the foliage. It continues to bloom off and on, less abundantly, until fall frost.

Roses are one of the most beautiful flowering shrubs.

'**Morden Centennial**': Parkland series rose; 4–5 feet (1.2–1.5 m) tall and 3–4 feet (91–120 cm) wide; clusters of lightly scented, bright pink, 4-inch (10 cm), double flowers; blooms repeatedly early summer to frost.

'**Morden Fireglow**': Parkland series rose; 3–3½ feet (91–110 cm) tall and 2–3 feet (61–91 cm) wide; 3-inch (7.6 cm), double, flowers are orange-red with bright scarlet on the undersides of petals; blooms repeatedly early summer to frost.

'**Thérèse Bugnet**': hardy shrub rose; 5–6 feet (1.5–1.8 m) tall and 4–5 feet (1.2–1.5 m) wide; fragrant, pink, double flowers 3–4 inches (7.6–10 cm) across; frilly petals; blooms repeatedly from early summer to frost; grey-green leaves; good fall colour; abundant, orange rosehips; one of the world's most cold-hardy varieties.

TIPS

Water roses regularly. Because they bloom over such a long period, they need more moisture than most shrubs.

LEFT: 'Morden Fireglow's' brilliant petal colour is unusual for a hardy rose.
RIGHT: 'Thérèse Bugnet' was developed over a 25-year-period by Georges Bugnet, of Legal, Alberta.

Prune in early spring, immediately after leafbuds begin to swell. 'Thérèse Bugnet' is an exception; it blooms on old wood and should be pruned after flowering.

Attach climbing roses to a trellis or another support by loosely tying canes on with a soft material, such as foam-covered wire, string or strips of cloth.

Leave climbing roses on their trellis over winter.

Deadhead regularly; removing finished flowers encourages further blooming. Stop deadheading a few weeks before the end of summer to allow rosehips to form. As well as providing a decorative display, rosehips signal plants to prepare for winter.

Hardy roses need little pruning. Just remove dead branches or branch tips in early spring.

When snipping flowers for bouquets, cut stems just above the first set of five leaves; it is from here that new shoots will grow. Make your cut at a 45-degree angle rather than straight across. Prune buds facing away from the centre of the plant.

Russian Almond

Prunus tenella
Russian Almond
Flowering Almond
Dwarf Russian Almond

Height • 2–5 feet (61–150 cm)

Spread • 5 feet (1.5 m)

Flowers • 1/2-inch (1.3 cm), bright pink flowers in spring

Fruit • furry nuts in mid-summer

Growth Rate • slow to medium

Lifespan • short

Zone Rating • 2

The seeds of Russian almond are used to make an oil that is similar to true almond oil. This shrub is native to Siberia.

Russian almond is an extremely beautiful, spring-blooming shrub. Just as the leaves start to unfurl in spring, the flowerbuds open to entirely cover the branches with bright rosy-pink flowers. Russian almond is one of the first shrubs to bloom in my garden, and I can never resist snipping off a branch or two to display in a vase on my kitchen table. After it finishes blooming, Russian almond is less prominent in the garden, but it is a nice, rounded shrub that provides an effective background for other flowers. The leaves are dark green, with paler undersides. Russian almond is an adaptable, drought-tolerant shrub that can serve many purposes: it grows well on slopes, it makes a very attractive, short, informal flowering hedge, it looks good planted with other shrubs, and it mixes well in almost any flowerbed.

GROWING

Sun to light shade.

Feature shrub, foundation plantings, as an informal hedge or in a shrub bed.

RECOMMENDED SPECIES OR VARIETIES

Russian Almond

Also called flowering almond or dwarf Russian almond.

TIPS

Russian almond tends to sucker by sprouting at the base. Plant it where you need to fill in a space in a border, or on a slope where it can stabilize soil.

If you don't want it to spread, plant Russian almond in a confined space, such as between a sidewalk and your house, or remove its mulch in early spring.

Prune Russian almond only after flowering, to shape or thin out the shrub.

In some years, the blossoms can be damaged or killed by hard frosts in late spring. Frost-bitten blossoms turn brown or black, and as a result they will not produce fruit.

Russian almond produces lots of furry nuts. The nuts are edible, but I have never tasted them; I leave them on the bush to attract and feed birds instead.

Russian almond will cross-pollinate with early-flowering plums and cherries. Without a cross-pollinator in the area, none of these shrubs will bear fruit.

Snip off a few flowering stems for spring bouquets. You can also 'force' flowers indoors. See page 359 for details. Use the foliage later in the year to accent cutflowers.

TOP LEFT: Russian almond makes a rather attractive hedge, although it is not commonly used for this purpose.
TOP RIGHT & BOTTOM: Russian almond is one of the showiest spring-flowering shrubs, and it is also one of the first to bloom.

Russian Cypress

Microbiota decussata
Russian Cypress

Height • 2–3 feet (61–91 cm)
Spread • 12–15 feet (3.7–4.6 m)
Flowers • not showy
Fruit • not showy
Growth Rate • slow
Lifespan • short to average
Zone Rating • 2

Russian cypress looks a lot like a spreading juniper, but its foliage is less prickly. These two evergreens are related and both are tough shrubs. If you want an evergreen groundcover for a shaded, moist site, however, Russian cypress is the one you want. It thrives underneath large shade trees or in sunny sites, as long as it has sufficient moisture. Russian cypress makes an attractive, spreading mat of bright green foliage with gracefully nodding branch tips.

GROWING

Sun to shade; moist, well-drained soil.

Groundcover.

This extremely hardy evergreen was originally discovered in 1921, growing near the tree-line on a mountainside in eastern Siberia.

Russian cypress looks splendid trailing over a retaining wall.

RECOMMENDED SPECIES OR VARIETIES

Russian Cypress

TIPS

To prevent the foliage from browning, plant Russian cypress in a site where it will have good snowcover throughout winter. Remove any browned foliage in early spring.

If you find that Russian cypress is outgrowing its allotted area in your garden, prune it in early summer to control its spread. Trim off the newest outer branch tips; it's best to remove only first- or second-year wood.

Russian cypress seems to be the most vigorous during hot summers. It prefers humid conditions and is not at all drought tolerant; be sure to keep it well watered.

Russian cypress is one of the best evergreen groundcovers.

The botanical name *Microbiota* is derived from Greek words meaning 'small cedar.' Russian cypress is in the same plant family as cedars, cypresses and junipers.

Russian Olive

Elaeagnus angustifolia
Russian Olive

Height • 20–30 feet (6.1–9.1 m)

Spread • 20–30 feet (6.1–9.1 m)

Flowers • clusters of 1/4–1/2-inch (0.6–1.3 cm), yellow flowers in late spring

Fruit • small, yellow, olive-like fruit covered in silver scales

Growth Rate • medium to fast

Lifespan • short to average

Zone Rating • 2

Gardeners often come out to our greenhouses asking for 'that tree with the silver leaves.' Most often they mean Russian olive, a striking, medium-sized tree with long, narrow leaves that range from silver to greyish green. As well as adding unusual foliage colour to the home landscape, Russian olive also provides heady fragrance. In late spring, its small, yellow, tubular flowers, which are barely visible amongst the leaves, emit a strong, sweet perfume. The entire boulevard along our street is lined with Russian olives, and when they are blooming, the powerful scent is quite noticeable, even when you are driving past them. I think it is one of our most beautiful trees.

GROWING

Sun; average to hot, dry sites.

Feature tree, shade tree, as a screen or windbreak near decks and patios.

RECOMMENDED SPECIES OR VARIETIES

Russian Olive

TIPS

Do not plant Russian olive in heavy clay soil or in a low-lying area of the yard where water tends to pool. Russian olives can die quite quickly in waterlogged soil.

Prune Russian olive in late winter to early spring, before the leaves appear.

Although Russian olive grows well

Russian olive 'fixes' atmospheric nitrogen, which means it has the ability to create nitrogen compounds that it can use as fertilizer.

in most soils, mature trees do not always adapt to changing soil conditions; a tree growing in dry soil will not fare well if soil conditions suddenly become wet. Keep this in mind when making modifications to your yard.

To highlight its silver foliage, plant Russian olive in front of dark green, mature pine or spruce trees.

Over-fertilized or over-watered Russian olives produce soft, weak growth and are more susceptible to insects and disease.

Russian olive is one of the last trees to leaf out in spring, but also one of the last to lose its leaves in fall. The leaves often remain on the branches well into December.

The branches of this tree are covered in 2- to 4-inch (5.1–10 cm) thorns. Be sure to wear thick gardening gloves and long sleeves or a jacket when pruning.

Although I have never tasted them, the small olive-like berries are edible and apparently sweet, though somewhat dry and mealy.

TOP LEFT: A Russian olive tree planted in a well-tended lawn—one that is fertilized often—will need no additional fertilizer, other than perhaps some bonemeal for the first few seasons.
TOP RIGHT: The olive-like berries of the Russian olive can be eaten fresh or made into jellies, sherbets and wine.
BOTTOM: The flowers of Russian olive are among the most fragrant of all trees in my area.

Salt Bush

Halimodendron halodendron
Salt Bush
Salt Tree

Height • 6–7 feet (1.8–2.1 m)

Spread • 4–6 feet (1.2–1.8 m)

Flowers • small, purple flowers in late spring

Fruit • long seedpods

Growth Rate • medium when young; then slow

Lifespan • short

Zone Rating • 3

Salt bush is a drought-tolerant, very low-maintenance shrub with attractive foliage and pretty flowers.

Salt bush offers an unusual colour combination with its pale purple flowers and silvery-grey foliage. It blooms in late spring with small clusters of flowers that resemble little sweet-peas; they have a similar, although much lighter, fragrance. This shrub is far from its native home in Turkey and Turkestan, but it will thrive in North America, if you provide the right environment. Salt bush is still rather uncommon in gardens, but there are quite a few bushes in my region. This shrub is unique in its genus: there are no other types of Halimodendron.

GROWING

Hot, dry, sunny location.

Screen, informal hedge, on slopes.

Once well established it needs little fertilizing or watering.

RECOMMENDED SPECIES OR VARIETIES

Salt Bush

Also called salt tree.

TIPS

Use a minimum of organic matter when planting salt bush. Unlike most shrubs, salt bush declines in rich soil. For the best health, colour and performance, plant in a highly alkaline soil. Horticultural lime helps increase soil alkalinity.

Prune salt bush after flowering.

Avoid planting salt bush in low-lying, wet areas of the garden. Too much moisture leads to root rot. A hot, sunny slope is an ideal site for this drought-tolerant shrub.

Salt bush can be trained to grow as a small, showy tree. See *How to Train Shrubs to 'Tree' Form* on page 64. It is sometimes sold in this form, grafted onto caragana roots. Be sure to prune off any shoots that grow from the base, to prevent the caragana from taking over.

LEFT: The downy, grey foliage of salt bush makes a lovely contrast to the usual green leaves of other plants.
RIGHT: As you might guess from its flowers, salt bush is related to caragana. Both shrubs bloom about the same time in spring.

Salt bush 'fixes' atmospheric nitrogen; it has the ability to change nitrogen gas into nitrogen compounds that it can use, thereby enriching the surrounding soil.

Sandcherry

Prunus x cistena
Purpleleaf Sandcherry

Height • 5–6 feet (1.5–1.8 m)

Spread • 5–6 feet (1.5–1.8 m)

Flowers • small, pink flowers in spring

Fruit • tiny, purple-black cherries in mid-summer

Growth Rate • slow to medium

Lifespan • short

Zone Rating • 3

Purpleleaf sandcherry is one of the first shrubs to bloom in spring. Its dark purple branches are covered in a profusion of small, fragrant, pink, single flowers before the leaves are fully open. After blooming, the deep reddish-purple foliage contrasts beautifully with other plants, so this shrub remains a garden highlight all summer. Sandcherry does get tiny, purple-black cherries, but not many; they are barely noticeable amongst the leaves, although birds will always find them. While purpleleaf sandcherry is a bit particular about its site, if you choose the right spot in your garden, this shrub can be very striking. It blooms about the same time as double-flowering plum, which has similar growing requirements. Growing these two species side by side provides a breath-taking display in spring.

GROWING

Sun; moist, well-drained soil. Sheltered site best.

Feature shrub, foundation planting, for contrast in a shrub border.

RECOMMENDED SPECIES OR VARIETIES

Purpleleaf Sandcherry

TIPS

Avoid planting this shrub in low-lying, wet areas, where water will pool around the roots.

Without regular pruning, sandcherry becomes rather sparse. To keep it dense and compact, prune it annually, immediately after flowering.

For the best foliage colour, be sure to choose a sunny site. If this shrub is grown in shady sites, its leaves tend to turn partially green, and they become prone to powdery mildew.

Dwarf mugo pines, cedars, potentillas and the small, white-flowered spireas are good partners in a shrub bed.

Although this species is one of the hardiest purple-leaved shrubs, the branches often die back in my region if the shrub is grown in exposed, windy sites. If this happens, just prune away the dead stems. For best results, plant your shrub in a sheltered spot where it will have good snowcover throughout winter, and be sure to fertilize it as recommended and to water it well in late fall.

Like most early-spring bloomers, purpleleaf sandcherry may not bloom well every year. Harsh winters or late spring frosts can kill the flowerbuds or the emerging flowers. Planting your shrub in a sheltered site helps to prevent this problem.

Sandcherries will cross-pollinate with early-flowering cherries, chokecherries and plums. Without a cross-pollinator in the area, they will bear little fruit. The cherries attract birds.

Snip off a few flowering stems for spring bouquets. You can also 'force' flowers indoors (see page 359 for details). Later in the summer, use the foliage to accent cutflowers.

TOP LEFT: Sandcherry looks great as an informal hedge.
TOP RIGHT: Purpleleaf sandcherry is one of the most attractive spring-flowering shrubs.
BOTTOM: Because of its colour, consider the background when picking a spot for purpleleaf sandcherry. It looks stunning growing in front of a larger evergreen.

Purpleleaf sandcherry is one of the hardiest purple-leaved plants.

Sea Buckthorn

Hippophae rhamnoides
Sea Buckthorn

Height • 15–30 feet (4.6–9.1 m)

Spread • 15–30 feet (4.6–9.1 m)

Flowers • yellow flowers appear before leaves in spring

Fruit • bright orange berries in fall and winter

Growth Rate • medium

Lifespan • short to average

Zone Rating • 3

Sea buckthorn is one of the best shrubs for winter colour.

Sea buckthorn blooms in early spring, with tiny, yellow flowers lining the branches before the leaves open. The bright silvery-green leaves provide great contrast in the garden throughout summer, and they look particularly attractive after the multitude of bright orange berries appear. The dense clusters of berries cling closely to the branches after the leaves drop in fall, and they often last well into late winter. As well as providing a showy display for most of the year, sea buckthorn's thorns can be formidable. One gardener that I know had a problem with deer and dogs on his acreage. To keep them away, he planted a long hedge of sea buckthorn; its thorny branches formed an impenetrable barrier.

GROWING

Hot, dry, sunny, open area.

Mass-planted in front of large evergreens, as an accent in large shrub borders, as a hedge. Good for stabilizing slopes.

RECOMMENDED SPECIES OR VARIETIES

Sea Buckthorn

TIPS

Sea buckthorn 'fixes' atmospheric nitrogen—with the help of bacteria, this shrub converts the nitrogen in the air into nitrogen that it can absorb. Most other plants that have this ability are members of the legume (pea) family, but sea buckthorn is not.

This shrub thrives in poor, alkaline, salty soil. It is a good choice for growing in sea-side gardens

A sea buckthorn grown in natural form is great for lining walkways or roadways.

or for planting alongside driveways or roads on which salt is used in winter. Sea buckthorn is widely used as a roadside shrub in Europe.

Prune sea buckthorn after it flowers. It blooms heaviest on the previous season's growth.

In my area, I have never seen a sea buckthorn much taller than 20 feet (6.1 m) but in milder climates, such as Vancouver's, these shrubs grow to 30 feet (9.1 m) or taller.

Sea buckthorn can be trained to grow as a small tree (see *How to Train Shrubs to 'Tree' Form* on page 64), a form in which it is often sold. When grown in 'tree' form, sea buckthorn is quite attractive. Its height and spread vary depending on how it is pruned, but a sea buckthorn 'tree' is generally narrower than the shrub.

Sea buckthorn is an attractive, drought-tolerant, low-maintenance shrub that thrives in dry, sandy soil where little else will grow.

The outer branches of sea buckthorn have many 1–2-inch (2.5–5.1 cm) spines. These spines provide protective cover for birds that like to nest in this shrub. When pruning, it's a good idea to wear thick gloves and long sleeves.

In order to have berries on your sea buckthorn, you'll need at least two shrubs, since the male and female flowers are on separate plants. Only the female shrubs produce berries, but male shrubs are necessary for pollination.

The tart, juicy berries are high in vitamins A and C. They are often eaten raw with cheese, cooked in sauces or made into jams and jellies.

Cut branches are attractive in floral arrangements.

Serviceberry

Amelanchier x grandiflora
Serviceberry

Height • 20–25 feet (6.1–7.6 m)

Spread • 15–20 feet (4.6–6.1 m)

Flowers • clusters of pinkish-white flowers in early spring

Fruit • clusters of small, dark blue berries in summer

Growth Rate • medium

Lifespan • short

Zone Rating • 4 [3]

Serviceberry is a very showy, small tree that is attractive year-round. It blooms earlier than most spring-flowering shrubs.

Serviceberry is normally a large, multi-stemmed shrub. I prefer the hybrid variety 'Autumn Brilliance,' a very hardy grafted form with a single trunk—it looks like a small, showy tree. In spring, profuse, drooping clusters of frothy, pinkish-white flowers cover the branches before the leaves are fully open. In summer, bunches of small, edible, dark blue berries hang among the dark green leaves, which turn brilliant bronze-red in fall. Even in winter, serviceberry is outstanding, with its bright red twigs, and the smooth, steel grey bark of its trunk lined in spiralling streaks. Serviceberry is an adaptable, low-maintenance shrub that grows well in sun to partial shade, and it is so attractive that, in my opinion, no yard should be without one.

GROWING

Sun to partial shade; best in moist, well-drained soil but adapts easily to most soils. The sunnier the location, the more flowers and berries produced.

Feature shrub, naturalizing; good for small yards.

Serviceberry needs little pruning, but if pruning is necessary, do it soon after flowering, or in very early spring while the shrub is still dormant.

RECOMMENDED SPECIES OR VARIETIES

'**Autumn Brilliance**': 20–25 feet (6.1–7.6 m) tall and 15–20 feet (4.6–6.1 m) wide; larger and hardier than other hybrid varieties; the best for fall colour—leaves turn brilliant red.

TIPS

Serviceberries are related to saskatoons, and, like saskatoons, they produce lots of small, sweet berries. Use them as you would saskatoon berries, in pies, jams, jellies and for eating fresh. Serviceberries ripen about the end of July.

Even if you don't use the berries for cooking, they won't go to waste; birds absolutely love them.

Although the variety 'Autumn Brilliance' is rated as hardy to zone 4, it has done well in my zone 3 garden for years. Avoid planting it in very exposed, windy sites. In a mature garden or a yard within an established neighbourhood, 'Autumn Brilliance' should do just fine.

TOP: Serviceberry is named for its resemblance to the service tree (Sorbus domestica), *which is grown in England but is not well known here.*
BOTTOM: The leaves of the serviceberry turn a brilliant bronze-red in fall, making it one of the best trees for fall colour.

Snowball

Viburnum opulus 'Roseum'
Common Snowball
European Snowball
Guelder Rose
Snowball Bush
Snowball Tree

Height • $8^1/_2$–10 feet (2.6–3 m)

Spread • $8^1/_2$–10 feet (2.6–3 m)

Flowers • white flowers in late spring

Fruit • none

Growth Rate • medium

Lifespan • short

Zone Rating • 3

Snowball is a popular, old-fashioned flowering shrub. Once you've seen it bloom, you'll know how it got its name: the bright white flowers form rounded clusters 2–4 inches (5.1–10 cm) across, and they look like just like snowballs! The dark green leaves are nearly 4 inches (10 cm) long, and they have downy undersides and are shaped somewhat like a maple leaf. Sometimes, the foliage turns red and orange in fall. Like all the shrubs in the Viburnum *genus, snowball is an undemanding bush that is easy to grow. Unlike the others, however, snowball does not produce berries, a feature that endears it to many gardeners.*

GROWING

Sun to partial shade; prefers a moist location; adapts to most soils.

Feature shrub, in mass plantings, as a screen.

RECOMMENDED SPECIES OR VARIETIES

Common Snowball

Also called European snowball, guelder rose, snowball bush or snowball tree; a unique variety of European cranberry (see page 144), with spectacular flowers and no fruit (sometimes sold under the variety name 'Sterile').

TIPS

For a lovely display, plant a group of three snowballs in a shrub bed behind several hydrangeas (such as 'Annabelle' and 'PeeGee'), which have similar flowers but bloom later.

Prune snowball in early summer, after its flowering has finished. Thin out older stems to rejuvenate the shrub and to keep it tidy.

Snowball looks magnificent when it is trained to 'tree' form—pruned and grown as a small flowering tree. See *How to Train Shrubs to 'Tree' Form* on page 64 for details.

Snowball flowers are stunning in bouquets. Cut them when the blooms are still light green; they will turn white as they open up in the vase. Snowball's flowers last up to two weeks after cutting.

TOP LEFT: Snowball often has deep red leaves in fall.
TOP RIGHT & BOTTOM: Snowball is one of the showiest spring-flowering shrubs, with large, rounded flower clusters that look like perfect snowballs.

Snowball is one of the oldest cultivated shrubs. It has been grown in gardens since the 16th century.

Snowberry

Symphoricarpos albus
Common Snowberry

Height • 3–4 feet (91–120 cm)

Spread • 3–4 feet (91–120 cm)

Flowers • clusters of tiny, pinkish-white flowers in mid-summer

Fruit • clusters of small, 1/2-inch (1.3 cm), white berries in late summer and early fall

Growth Rate • average

Lifespan • short

Zone Rating • 2

If you are looking for an interesting, undemanding plant to grow in difficult sites, consider snowberry. This shrub grows well in sun or shade, underneath large trees and on slopes. It tends to sucker freely, spreading rather quickly to cover a large area, and it fills in nicely as an informal hedge. Snowberry is a compact, rounded shrub with dark blue-green foliage. It blooms in summer, with small, dense clusters of bell-shaped, pinkish-white flowers at the tips of its branches. After it is finished flowering, the branches are decorated with abundant, dense clusters of white berries, which remain throughout fall and well into winter.

Snowberry is a great low-maintenance shrub for shady areas.

GROWING

Sun or shade.

Foundation plant, as an informal hedge; good 'understorey' shrub for growing in shady sites beneath larger trees.

RECOMMENDED SPECIES OR VARIETIES

Common Snowberry

Snowberries were considered to be part of the spirit world by some Native Peoples—they were believed to be 'ghost' berries or 'saskatoons of the dead' and were not to be eaten.

TIPS

Snowberry tends to produce suckers, which is useful in situations where you want the shrub to spread and fill in gaps. If you don't want it to spread, plant in a confined area, such as next to a sidewalk or driveway.

Snowberry generally needs little pruning. When necessary, prune it in late winter to early spring, before leaves open.

This shrub is prone to powdery mildew. To help prevent this disease, water your shrubs in the morning rather than at night, plant them where they'll receive filtered sunlight rather than full shade, and don't crowd the shrubs. Improve air movement by thinning the shrub (prune to remove a few of the middle stems). Good air circulation also helps to prevent powdery mildew.

The berries are occasionally attacked by a fungus. If that happens, simply remove the infected berries.

Snip off branches of berries to add to bouquets, or to display on their own in a vase. Snowberry lasts up to two weeks after cutting.

TOP: Snowberry spreads quite nicely and fills in gaps.
BOTTOM: Snowberry's glistening white berries are not edible. Birds don't care for them either, which results in a longer-lasting display. The clusters of berries remain on bare branches into early winter.

Spirea

Spiraea x bumalda
Bumald Spirea

Spiraea fritschiana
Fritschiana Spirea

Spiraea x arguta
Garland Spirea

Spiraea japonica
Japanese Spirea

Spiraea nipponica
Nippon Spirea

Spiraea x vanhouttei
Vanhoutte Spirea
Bridalwreath Spirea

Height • 8 inches–7 feet (20 cm–2.1 m)

Spread • 2–8 feet (61 cm–2.4 m)

Flowers • either white flowers in spring, or pink flowers in summer

Fruit • not showy

Growth Rate • slow to medium

Lifespan • short

Zone Rating • 3–4

Spireas are easy-to-grow flowering shrubs that come in two basic types: the white-flowered ones, which bloom for three to four weeks in spring, and the pink-flowered ones, which bloom from early summer to fall. Some varieties have such showy foliage that they would be worth growing even without the flowers. Garland spireas are first to bloom in spring, followed by Vanhoutte, Nippon and finally fritschiana. Of the summer-bloomers, bumald spireas bloom first, followed by Japanese spireas. By growing a variety of types, you could have spireas blooming in your garden for months.

GROWING

Sun to light shade.

Feature or accent; mixed borders, shrub beds, foundation plantings. Smaller varieties in rock gardens.

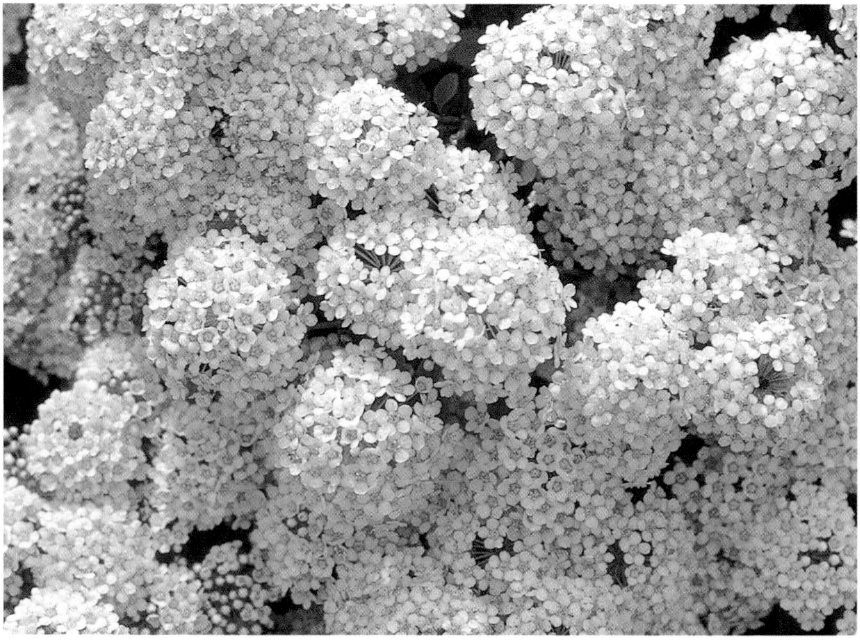

RECOMMENDED SPECIES OR VARIETIES

SPRING-BLOOMING SPIREAS

Fritschiana Spirea

2–3 feet (61–91 cm) tall and 3–4 feet (91–120 cm) wide; flat-topped clusters of bright white flowers are striking against dark green foliage; blooms in mid- to late spring; introduced in 1919; uncommon in North America; a compact, mounding shrub with larger leaves than most spireas, up to $3^1/_2$ inches (8.9 cm) long.

TOP & BOTTOM: Fritschiana has one of the largest flower clusters of the spireas, and produces beautiful yellow, purple and red colours in fall.

TOP LEFT: 'Renaissance' has a plethora of white blossoms in late spring to early summer.
TOP RIGHT: Dwarf Garland's showy blossoms make it great for accent planting.
BOTTOM: 'Snowmound' creates an attractive contrast with its white flowers and dark blue-green foliage.

Garland Spirea

Dwarf Garland (*S. x arguta* 'Compacta'): also known as 'Foam of May'; 3½–4 feet (1.1–1.2 m) tall and wide; garlands of white flowers in late spring; very showy in full bloom; light green foliage; great shrub for rock gardens or accent in border; a smaller version of the popular garland spirea—just half its size with the same profusion of flowers.

Nippon Spirea

'**Snowmound**': 3–5 feet (91–150 cm) tall and wide; arching stems covered in bright white flowers that stand out against dark blue-green foliage; blooms in late spring; attractive shrub with a clean, dense outline; a profuse bloomer.

Vanhoutte Spirea

'**Renaissance**': 5–7 feet (1.5–2.1 m) tall and 6–8 feet (1.8–2.4 m) wide; abundant, rounded clusters of white flowers on long, arching branches; blooms in late spring to early summer; dark blue-green foliage; superb red-orange fall colour; excellent disease resistance.

Summer-blooming Spireas

Bumald Spirea

'Anthony Waterer': 3–4 feet (91–120 cm) tall and 4–5 feet (1.2–1.5 m) wide; medium to dark pink flowers; new leaves are russet-red, turning dark green in summer, and red to red-purple in fall; one of the most popular varieties.

'Dart's Red': 3–4 feet (91–120 cm) tall and wide; similar to 'Anthony Waterer' but has darker flowers; despite the name, these flowers are actually deep purple-pink.

'Frobellii': 3–4 feet (91–120 cm) tall and wide; similar to 'Anthony Waterer' but with lighter, brighter pink flowers; also more drought tolerant than most spireas.

TOP: 'Anthony Waterer' is one of the most popular varieties of spirea. BOTTOM: Summer-blooming spireas have distinctive, flat-topped flower clusters, 2–5 inches (5.1–13 cm) across, in various shades of pink. 'Dart's Red' has one of the darkest hues.

TOP: 'Goldmound' is an excellent accent plant.
BOTTOM: 'Little Princess' has masses of rose-pink flowers.

Japanese Spirea

Alpina (*S. japonica* 'Nana'): 2½ feet (76 cm) tall and wide; soft pink flowers in late spring to early summer; blooms for five to six weeks, longer than most varieties; small, rich blue-green leaves just ½–1 inch (1.3–2.5 cm) long; a dainty, fine-textured shrub that is great for rock gardens and borders.

'**Goldmound**': 2½–3½ feet (76–110 cm) tall and 3–4 feet (91–120 cm) wide; pink flowers and iridescent foliage in shades of yellow and gold; forms a low, smooth mound of bright foliage.

'**Little Princess**': 2–2½ feet (61–76 cm) tall and 3–3½ feet (91–110 cm) wide; profuse, dense clusters of rose-pink flowers; a fast-growing, fine-textured, low shrub.

'**Magic Carpet**': 8–12 inches (20–30 cm) tall and 2–3 feet (61–91 cm) wide; miniature variety that forms a colourful, compact carpet of foliage in shades of red and yellow; clusters of pink flowers late spring to early summer.

'**Shirobana**': also known as 'Shirbori'; 2–3 feet (61–91 cm) tall and wide; a unique variety that produces several colours of flowers at once (although its name means 'white' in Japanese); flower clusters can be deep rose-pink, light pink, white or a combination of those colours; leaves may also be multi-coloured in light and dark shades of green.

Japanese spireas begin to bloom about 7 to 10 days later than other summer-blooming types.

TIPS

Although most spireas are rated for zone 4 or higher, they do fine in my zone 3 garden.

Prune the white-flowered, spring-blooming spireas immediately after they bloom. Prune the pink-flowered, summer-blooming spireas either in late winter to early spring, before leaves appear, or in summer, after the first flush of flowers.

Trim off the finished flowerheads, which tend to make the plants look messy. Deadheading also encourages a second flush of flowers later in summer.

Gold- or yellow-leaved varieties look terrific planted with dwarf evergreens, purpleleaf sandcherry, dwarf Korean lilac or weigela. For the best foliage colour, choose the sunniest spot. Leaves often turn greener in shade.

Older spirea shrubs that aren't blooming well and are becoming thin or 'leggy' can be brought back to life by severe pruning.

TOP: 'Shirobana' is unique in its production of several colours of flowers at once.
BOTTOM: 'Magic Carpet' is a miniature variety that is good for borders or as a groundcover.

Spireas are one of the most popular shrubs in Canada.

Spruce

Picea pungens
Colorado Spruce

Picea abies
Norway Spruce

Picea omorika
Serbian Spruce

Picea glauca
White Spruce

Height • 1–100 feet (30 cm–30 m)

Spread • 1–35 feet (30 cm–11 m)

Cones • some showier than others; pink, purple or brown

Growth Rate
dwarf forms, Serbian Spruce: slow
other varieties: medium

Lifespan • long

Zone Rating
Colorado: 2
Norway, Serbian: 3
White: 1

The spruce genus is surprisingly diverse. Many people only equate spruces with Christmas tree shapes—pyramidal evergreen trees with long, graceful branches covered in short needles—but spruces come in many other forms. My husband Ted and I have three 'Fat Albert' spruces that stand like stout sentinels at the edge of our driveway—they are the quintessential spruce. In the garden, nestled amongst the flowers, we have a low-growing Nest spruce. Next door, my son Bill and his wife Valerie grow several unusual types of spruce, including an 'Acrocona' with pretty pink cones, a Weeping Norway spruce with long, trailing branches, and a tall, very narrow Columnar Blue spruce.

Colorado spruce is one of the most popular species and also one of the most drought tolerant. Many Colorado spruce varieties have blue needles, but some are dark green. Norway spruce looks quite different; its secondary branches point downward, rather than out or upward like most spruces. Norway spruces have dark green, dense foliage. Serbian spruce is easy to identify by its two-toned needles—I think this species is one of the most beautiful spruces. White spruce trees have the usual cone-shape, and are generally dense and dark green. Tall members of this species are often used for windbreaks on farms.

GROWING
Sun to light shade; moist soil.

Feature trees, windbreaks, screens. Dwarf varieties as feature shrubs, in foundation plantings, in mixed flowerbeds and rock gardens.

LEFT: Creeping Blue spruce can be trained to trail over garden gates or retaining walls.
*RIGHT: For gardeners who like blue spruces but don't have a lot of room, Columnar Blue spruce (*P. pungens *var.* glauca *'Fastigiata') may be the perfect solution. This variety is about two-thirds as wide as the usual Colorado blue spruce. The name 'Fastigiata' means 'with upright branches growing close together' or 'columnar.'*

RECOMMENDED SPECIES OR VARIETIES

Colorado Spruce

Creeping Blue (*P. pungens* var. *glauca* 'Procumbens'): 1–2 feet (30–61 cm) tall and 15–20 feet (4.6–6.1 m) wide after 15 to 20 years; grows 3–6 inches (7.6–15 cm) a year; silvery-blue needles; a dwarf form of the popular Colorado blue spruce; eventual size varies tremendously depending on how it is grown: it can be staked upright and then trail outward; it can be trained to trail over a sturdy garden gate; or it can mound and sprawl over large rocks or retaining walls. Irregular growth habit—young branches slant upwards and older branches droop—creates a distinctive, atypical look for a spruce.

Columnar Blue (*P. pungens* var. *glauca* 'Fastigiata'): 30–60 feet (9.1–18 m) tall and 15–20 feet (4.6–6.1 m) wide in 40 to 50 years; grows 8–14 inches (20–36 cm) a year; blue needles; a much narrower version of the usual Colorado blue spruce.

Pungens is Latin for 'sharply pointed,' describing the needles of the Colorado spruce.

LEFT: The first 'Hoopsii' in Canada were brought over from the Royal Botanical Garden in Britain between the First and Second World Wars.
RIGHT: When grown in an open area, 'Fat Albert' has a perfect cone shape. This 10-year-old tree at my home has never been pruned.

'**Fat Albert**': 50–60 feet (15–18 m) tall and 20–30 feet (6.1–9.1 m) wide; blue needles; a very dense, upright, broadly pyramidal tree; nicely shaped and requires little pruning; one of the best varieties for growing as a feature tree.

'**Hoopsii**': 50–60 feet (15–18 m) tall and 30–35 feet (9.1–11 m) wide; outstanding colour—the bluest of all spruces; dense foliage; most spruces have very straight trunks, but this unusual variety often has an S-curved trunk and leader, which give individual character to each of these trees; the name, by the way, is pronounced 'hoop-see-eye.'

If you want a blue spruce, look for the word *glauca,* which refers to the 'glaucous bloom' (think of blueberries), a light blue-grey, waxy coating on the needles.

'**Mesa Verde**': 4–5 feet (1.2–1.5 m) tall and 10–12 feet (3–3.7 m) wide; deep green needles; great for large rock gardens or shrub beds; use as an alternative to junipers; a one-of-a-kind spruce.

'**Montgomery**': also known as 'R.H. Montgomery'; $8^1/_2$ feet (2.6 m) tall and 7–$8^1/_2$ feet (2.1–2.6 m) wide after 30 to 40 years; a dwarf variety that grows 3–6 inches (7.6–15 cm) a year; blue needles; compact branches and a broad pyramidal shape; great as a feature in shrub beds, rock gardens or in small yards.

Spruces are excellent evergreens, providing a huge range of size and shape.

TOP: 'Mesa Verde' has an unusual shape. As its name suggests, it looks like a green 'mesa'—a flat-topped mound with sharply sloped sides. BOTTOM: 'Montgomery' is a slow-growing, dwarf variety of Colorado spruce. The tree in my son Bill's garden is now about $3^1/_2$ feet (1.1 m) tall; it gains less than 6 inches (15 cm) in height each year.

TOP LEFT & RIGHT: 'Acrocona' is a Swedish variety of Norway spruce that dates back to 1890; it has the showiest cones of all spruces. BOTTOM: 'Cupressina' is a dwarf variety of Norway spruce; this tree is 20 years old.

Norway Spruce

'**Acrocona**': 20 feet (6.1 m) tall and wide; green needles; graceful, curtain-like tree; very attractive, unique, bright pink to reddish-purple cones; considered to be a 'dwarf' because this variety is smaller and slower growing than the species Norway spruce, a tree that can reach 50 feet (15 m) in height.

'**Cupressina**': 10 feet (3 m) tall and 3 feet (91 cm) wide in 10 years; needles are dark green in summer and tinged blue in winter; dense, narrow, columnar dwarf variety with up-reaching branches; ideal for screening; great feature tree for small yards.

'**Little Gem**': 1–1½ feet (30–46 cm) tall and 2–2½ feet (61–76 cm) wide in 10 to 25 years (the smallest dwarf); dark green needles; newest growth is lime-green; a very dense variety that looks somewhat like a bird's nest; extremely slow growing; ideal for rock gardens; one of our most popular varieties.

In Antarctica there is just one lonely tree: a Norway spruce growing on Campbell Island. It is believed to be the most remote tree in the world. The closest tree to it is on the Auckland Islands—over 120 nautical miles (220 km) away!

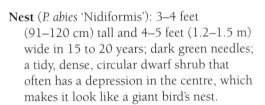

Nest (*P. abies* 'Nidiformis'): 3–4 feet (91–120 cm) tall and 4–5 feet (1.2–1.5 m) wide in 15 to 20 years; dark green needles; a tidy, dense, circular dwarf shrub that often has a depression in the centre, which makes it look like a giant bird's nest.

'**Ohlendorffii**': 2½–3 feet (76–91 cm) tall and 1½ –2 feet (46–61 cm) wide in 10 years; 12–15 feet (3.7–4.6 m) tall and 8–10 feet (2.4–3 m) wide after 30 to 40 years; a very dense, cone-shaped dwarf spruce; plant it with groups of different colour and texture, such as blue horizontal juniper, 'Little Giant' cedar, yellow potentilla, 'Magic Carpet' spirea or the perennial elephant ears; if you can't provide a sheltered site, consider this variety in place of Dwarf Alberta spruce.

*TOP: Nest spruce (*P. abies *'Nidiformis') is also known as Bird's Nest spruce because of its distinctive shape. 'Nidiformis' is from the Latin* nidis, *meaning 'nest-like.'*
BOTTOM RIGHT: Diseases can be beneficial in odd ways. The variety 'Little Gem' originated from a 'witch's broom'—a generic term for the distorted growth usually caused by a disease organism. Since then, that original witch's broom was carefully cultivated to reproduce and retain the same attractive form.
BOTTOM LEFT: 'Ohlendorffii' is a dwarf variety of Norway spruce. With its rather formal, conical shape, it looks striking in a large rock garden or beside a large rock in a flowerbed.

TOP: The variety 'Pumila' has a similar shape to Nest spruce, but its branches point upwards rather than laying flat.
BOTTOM: Because of the diverse growth habit of Weeping Norway spruce, the possible ways to grow it are almost endless. It can be trained to grow as a 'living fence' or as a weeping tree with long, trailing branches. The flexible branches take on the form of whatever they cover.

'Pumila': 3–3½ feet (91–110 cm) tall and 4–6 feet (1.2–1.8 m) wide after 20 to 25 years; dark green needles on stiff, densely covered branches; great for rock gardens; consider as an alternative to dwarf mugo pine; a unique, low-growing shrub.

Weeping (*P. abies* 'Pendula'): 1–15 feet (30 cm–4.6 m) tall and 15–20 feet (4.6–6.1 m) wide after 15 to 20 years; grows 8–12 inches (20–30 cm) a year; dwarf variety; eventual size varies tremendously depending on how it is grown (similar to Creeping Blue spruce); often sold staked as a weeping tree, but may also be sold as a mounding, spreading spruce that makes a striking, rather unique groundcover; dark green needles; super hardy; thick, dense growth that is extremely attractive.

Serbian Spruce

Dwarf Serbian (*P. omorika* 'Nana'): 3–3½ feet (91–110 cm) tall and 4 feet (1.2 m) wide in 10 to 15 years; 10–12 feet (3–3.7 m) tall and 8–10 feet (2.4–3 m) wide after 40 to 50 years; very slow growing, just 2–3 inches (5.1–7.6 cm) a year; an extremely beautiful dwarf spruce with unusual, bicoloured needles—dark green with silvery-blue undersides; shape varies from a dense mound to a globe shape to a very broad pyramid; does best in a site sheltered from wind; one of the most striking evergreens.

White Spruce

Dwarf Alberta (*P. glauca* 'Conica'): 5–7 feet (1.5–2.1 m) tall and 2½–3 feet (76–91 cm) wide in 20 to 25 years; 12–15 feet (3.7–4.6 m) tall and 4–5 feet (1.2–1.5 m) wide after 60 to 70 years; very slow growing, 1–3 inches (2.5–7.6 cm) a year; light green needles; a very dense, formal-looking, cone-shaped dwarf spruce that looks like a perfect little Christmas tree; excellent for rock gardens or at a front entranceway; originally discovered in 1904 growing at Lake Laggan, Alberta; does best in a site sheltered from winds; one of the most popular varieties.

TOP: Dwarf Serbian spruce is a graceful, very slow-growing tree. Its cones are blue-black when young and turn cinnamon-brown when mature.
BOTTOM: Because of their dense, perfect cone shape, Dwarf Alberta spruces are often grown commercially and sold for use as indoor Christmas trees. In the garden, the shape of Dwarf Alberta spruce can be accented with flowers such as annual lavatera.

Spruce trees do produce flowers, albeit without the usual look of pretty petals. Female flowers and cones form at the branch tips, while male flowers and cones form along the branches. Pollination occurs in spring, and the cones open in fall to release the winged seeds.

TIPS

For the bluest blue spruce, choose a recommended blue variety. Named varieties have been carefully selected for their desirable colour.

To intensify the blue colour, use a fertilizer that contains chelated iron. Excessive use of dormant oil for insect control can cause fading of the colour and should be avoided.

To create denser growth or to shape spruces, prune them by removing one-third of the new growth in early summer. Dwarf varieties generally don't need pruning.

Dwarf evergreens grow slowly, gaining only a few inches each year. Because they take so long to mature, dwarf varieties are grown at the nurseries for many years before they are sold. Although this slow growth makes them quite expensive, dwarf evergreens are a good investment. They add interest to the garden, they need little to no pruning, and they are very long lived.

If you want a perfectly shaped spruce, you must plant it in an open area, well away from any shade. Shaded branches grow very poorly and the spruce loses its symmetry and vigour.

Serbian spruce and the more tender varieties, such as 'Cupressina' and Dwarf Alberta, are slightly more susceptible to wind-burn and winter desiccation—drying-out of needles—than other spruces. I find that planting these trees in groups or in a protected site, which is sheltered from winds, helps to prevent the needles from browning and dropping.

Dwarf spruces are ideal for planting along walkways or beneath windows, because they won't sprawl over the path or block your view. They also add beautiful texture to flowerbeds.

White spruce is the provincial tree of Manitoba.

I think spruces look best in their natural form, with the lowest branches sweeping the ground rather than being removed to expose the bare lower trunk. When the branches cover the surrounding soil, they serve the same purpose as a mulch: keeping the soil cool. Even with the bottom branches removed, few plants will grow in the densely shaded, dry, acidic soil underneath a spruce tree.

Spruces can be shaped or sheared to form a very attractive hedge. Jasper Park Lodge, a famous resort in Alberta's Rocky Mountains, has a beautiful, sheared spruce hedge near some of its guest cabins. Most spruces, except dwarf varieties, are suitable for hedges.

Spruces make fine outdoor Christmas trees, and they look very pretty hung with Christmas lights. It is best to string lights early in the season, thereby avoiding breaking the branches in subzero weather. If a branch tip is broken off, that particular branch will start growing in a different direction, resulting in a misshapen tree. Tie lights on with a soft material rather than using metal or plastic clips.

LEFT: Serbian spruces are distinguished by two-toned needles that look as if they are permanently covered in frost. These trees are particularly attractive on blustery days when the branches flash silvery blue. The species name omorika *is the Serbian word for 'spruce.'*
RIGHT: Spruce trees can be trained to a variety of forms. This blue spruce has an upright growth.

Centuries ago, when the explorer Jacques Cartier and his men were suffering from scurvy, Native Peoples helped them get well by giving them tea made from the bark and needles of spruce.

Sumac

Rhus aromatica
Fragrant Sumac

Rhus glabra
Smooth Sumac

Rhus typhina
Staghorn Sumac

Height • 2–23 feet (61 cm–7 m)

Spread • 6–23 feet (1.8–7 m)

Flowers • green or yellow flowerspikes in spring

Fruit • furry, red fruit

Growth Rate • slow to medium

Lifespan • short

Zone Rating • 3

If you have a large area to fill and want a showy, undemanding shrub, plant a sumac. These shrubs vary from short to tall, they grow well in average to poor soil, and they thrive even on slopes. Their glossy foliage is attractive throughout summer, and blazes with colour in fall. Sumacs can add an exotic touch to gardens with their unusual, velvety red fruits, which stand out above the leaves. These shrubs have the male and female flowers on separate plants; only female shrubs produce fruit. Both smooth sumac and staghorn sumac have interesting branches that resemble a deer's antlers. Staghorn sumac has rather hairy twigs, while the branches of smooth sumac are, as the name indicates, smooth. Fragrant sumac is a smaller shrub with aromatic foliage. The variety 'Gro-low' is resistant to insects and diseases, and it does as well in sun as in shade.

GROWING

Sun to partial shade for most; 'Gro-low' in sun or shade; prefers moist soil and does well in dry sites.

Mass planting, on slopes, naturalizing, back of shrub border. 'Gro-low' as a groundcover.

General fertilizing.

LEFT: Cut-leaf has exotic, tropical-looking foliage.
RIGHT: 'Gro-low' makes a thick, carpet-like groundcover.

RECOMMENDED SPECIES OR VARIETIES

Fragrant Sumac

'Gro-low': 2 feet (61 cm) tall and 6–8 feet (1.8–2.4 m) wide; fragrant, bright yellow flowers; aromatic foliage turns red in fall; furry, scarlet fruit; a wonderful groundcover.

Smooth Sumac

Cut-leaf (*R. glabra* 'Laciniata'): 9–15 feet (2.7–4.6 m) tall and wide; green flowers; large, bright scarlet fruit; long, lacy leaves turn orange-red in fall; a beautiful, very hardy, tropical-looking shrub.

LEFT & RIGHT: Staghorn sumac is named for its picturesque branching habit, which resembles a deer's antlers. It is most noticeable in winter, after the colourful fall leaves drop.

Staghorn Sumac

Staghorn: 16–23 feet (4.9–7 m) tall and wide; green flowers; large, bright scarlet fruit; thick, velvety stems; long, lacy leaves turn orange-red in fall; very hardy; tropical-looking shrub.

Lace-leaf (*R. typhina* 'Lacinata'): 16–20 feet (4.9–6.1 m) tall and wide; similar to Staghorn, except for its lacy leaves.

The velvety red fruit of sumac is edible. It can be used to make a 'pink lemonade' drink by bruising the fruit in water, straining and adding sugar.

TIPS

The male and female flowers of sumacs are on separate plants, so you'll need at least two shrubs—one male, one female—to get any fruit. Only female shrubs bear the showy fruit.

Prune sumacs in late winter to early spring, before the leaves appear. To encourage your shrubs to become bushier, cut them back to ground level. To encourage a shrub form, remove older stems and any winterkill. If you prefer a 'tree' form, remove unwanted stems and any winterkill.

Smooth sumac and staghorn sumac can be trained to grow as small trees. See *How to Train Shrubs to 'Tree' Form* on page 64.

Sumac spreads by suckers, and it can fill in a large area very nicely. If you don't want it to spread, plant it in a confined area, such as between a sidewalk and patio.

'Gro-low' sets roots wherever its branches touch the ground. Use this shrub to help prevent soil erosion on slopes.

Add a mulch to keep the soil cool. Sumac likes moist soil, but prefers to dry out between waterings.

Experiment by cutting branches with the velvety fruit to display in dried arrangements. On the shrub, the scarlet fruit often remains on the branches through winter, standing out like bright flames against the snow.

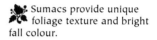

Sumacs provide unique foliage texture and bright fall colour.

Sumacs belong to an exotic family of plants. Other members include cashew, pistachio and mango, as well as poison ivy. The species of sumac listed here are non-poisonous.

Tamarisk

Tamarix ramosissima
Tamarisk

Height • 3–8 feet (91 cm–2.4 m)

Spread • 5–6 feet (1.5–1.8 m)

Flowers • feathery, pink flowerspikes in summer

Fruit • not showy

Growth Rate • fast

Lifespan • short

Zone Rating • 3

A tamarisk in full bloom looks like an explosion of fireworks. Clusters of feathery, pink flowers cover the entire shrub for at least half of summer. With its airy, light green foliage, this unusual shrub looks lovely even when it is not in bloom. Tamarisk grows as fast as most perennials, becoming a full, compact shrub even when it is cut back nearly to ground level each spring. These vigorous shrubs grow well in almost any type of soil, in windy or calm sites, and in either dry or humid conditions, but they don't like wet soil. Tamarisk is an attractive addition to any flowerbed.

GROWING

Sun.

Accent in shrub border; background in flowerbed.

Tamarisk is a beautiful, adaptable shrub that blooms for more than a month in summer.

RECOMMENDED SPECIES OR VARIETIES

'**Pink Cascade**': 3–8 feet (91 cm–2.4 m) tall and 5–6 feet (1.5–1.8 m) wide; light pink flowers.

'**Summerglow**': same height and spread as 'Pink Cascade'; dark pink flowers.

TIPS

Acidic, sandy or poor soil conditions don't deter this shrub. Tamarisk thrives even in salty soil, and it is superb for coastal gardens or for planting along driveways or roads that are salted in winter. Tamarisk is also drought resistant.

Treat tamarisk as a perennial: in spring, cut back any dead growth to about 2 inches (5.1 cm) above the ground and leave any green growth intact. Tamarisk blooms on new wood. The result of cutting back tamarisk nearly to the ground is lots of vigorous new growth that matures into a spectacular display of flowers and compact, full foliage.

If you want taller shrubs, you can leave them unpruned, but they can become rather scraggly.

TOP LEFT: Tamarisk's graceful branches wave in even the slightest breeze.
TOP RIGHT: 'Summerglow' is a pretty variety with airy, dark pink flowers.
BOTTOM: The feathery flower-spikes can be about 3 feet (91 cm) long.

Walnut

Juglans nigra
Black Walnut

Height • 50–75 feet (15–23 m)

Spread • 35–50 feet (11–15 m)

Flowers • not showy

Fruit • edible nuts in fall

Growth Rate • slow to medium

Lifespan • long

Zone Rating • 3

If you had a great big black walnut tree in your yard, it could be worth as much as $10,000 or $20,000 just for its wood. Black walnut wood is highly valuable and in great demand for veneers, gun stocks, cabinets and other furniture. Mature trees have huge, long, straight trunks that yield a tremendous amount of wood. In Ontario, when land is being cleared, stands of black walnut trees are often auctioned for timber on site while the trees are still in the ground. Unfortunately, stocks of black walnuts in the wild are rapidly being depleted. Black walnuts are marvellous shade trees, but you need lots of space to grow them—these grand trees are wide spreading as well as tall.

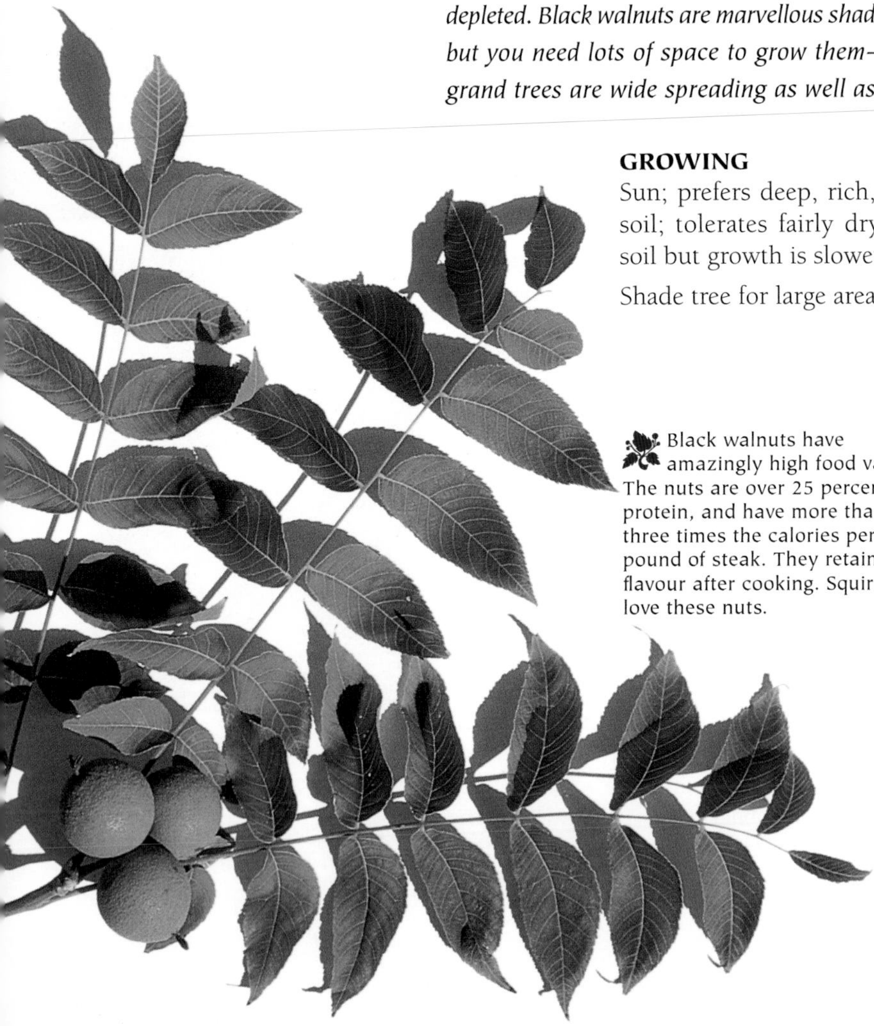

GROWING

Sun; prefers deep, rich, moist soil; tolerates fairly dry, hard soil but growth is slower.

Shade tree for large areas.

Black walnuts have amazingly high food value. The nuts are over 25 percent protein, and have more than three times the calories per pound of steak. They retain their flavour after cooking. Squirrels love these nuts.

RECOMMENDED SPECIES OR VARIETIES

Black Walnut

TOP: Black walnut is native to eastern North America. It was once common, but it has now become rare in the central and southern United States.
BOTTOM: Black walnuts are sweet and oily. The husks and fresh bark produce a yellow dye.

TIPS

The roots and leaves of black walnuts secrete a chemical called 'juglone,' which acts as a natural herbicide. The technical term for the secretion of a herbicide by a plant is 'allelopathy.' Tomatoes are particularly susceptible to juglone and should not be planted near a black walnut.

Black walnut leaves reputedly repel fleas. Try scattering them around a doghouse, or placing a few in the dog kennel or sleeping area.

Prune black walnut in late winter to early spring, before the leaves open.

The foliage sometimes, but not always, turns orange-yellow in fall.

Wayfaring Tree

Viburnum lantana
Wayfaring Tree

Height • 10–15 feet (3–4.6 m)

Spread • 10–15 feet (3–4.6 m)

Flowers • large clusters of creamy white flowers in spring

Fruit • colourful berries from late summer to early fall

Growth Rate
young plants: medium
older plants: slow

Lifespan • short to medium

Zone Rating • 3

Despite its name, the wayfaring tree is not a tree: it's a large shrub that grows as wide as it is tall. The wayfaring tree is truly spectacular when it is blooming in spring, with its large, rounded clusters of creamy white flowers. To me, however, one of its best features is the showy clusters of pea-sized berries, which turn from green to pinkish white to rose to red to purple and, finally, to black. This display lasts about a month, and the berries make wonderful jams if you can beat the birds to them. The wayfaring tree is dense, with thick branches, downy twigs and big, lustrous, dark green leaves up to 5 inches (13 cm) long and 3 inches (7.6 cm) across. It is a tough, low-maintenance shrub that makes a marvellous addition to yards and gardens.

GROWING

Sun to partial shade; moist, well-drained soil is best, but withstands dry soil.

Feature shrub, in groups in large shrub beds, for screening, foundation planting, back of shrub bed. Good for small yards.

RECOMMENDED SPECIES OR VARIETIES

'**Mohican**': 8–10 feet (2.4–3 m) tall and wide; a more compact variety; berries turn orange-red and remain coloured for about a month, longer than other varieties, before turning black; a very popular variety introduced in 1956.

'**Variegata**': 8–10 feet (2.4–3 m) tall and wide; a stunning new variety with leaves variegated dark green, light green and creamy white; every leaf has a different pattern.

TIPS

If you want lots of berries, grow more than one wayfaring tree. A solitary shrub will produce berries, but less of them. Other members of the *Viburnum* family—cranberry, arrowwood or nannyberry—will cross-pollinate with wayfaring tree, although other wayfaring trees do the best job. The flowers are wind pollinated, so greater numbers of berries are produced when the shrubs are grown fairly close to each other.

Wayfaring tree is generally a pretty tidy shrub, but when necessary, prune it after flowering to encourage denser growth or to control size.

The big leaves are covered in thick, coarse hairs, and they have woolly undersides, a defence against disease and insects.

A wayfaring tree can be trained to grow as a small tree. See *How to Train Shrubs to 'Tree' Form* on page 64.

The colourful berries are great for making jams and jellies.

Some gardeners preserve the colourful berry-clusters, to decorate wreaths or other arrangements, by immersing them in a solution of glycerine and boiling water.

TOP LEFT: Wayfaring tree has a very nice, compact, round form.
TOP RIGHT: Wayfaring tree blooms profusely in spring, with a showy display of flowers that lasts about two weeks.
BOTTOM: Wayfaring tree is one of those shrubs with inconsistent fall colour. In some years, the leaves turn purplish red, but in other years, there is little change in colour before winter arrives.

Weigela

Weigela florida
Old-fashioned Weigela

Height • 2–7 feet (61 cm–2.1 m)

Spread • 3–7 feet (91 cm–2.1 m)

Flowers • pink or red, tubular flowers in spring

Fruit • not showy

Growth Rate • medium

Lifespan • short

Zone Rating • 4 [3]

This shrub was named after a German botanist, Christian Ehrenfried Weigel (1748–1831).

If you like honeysuckle, you're sure to like weigela. Both plants have flowers that attract hummingbirds, and the two plants are, in fact, related. Weigela is an attractive shrub that blooms on and on—the show lasts about six weeks. Quite often, weigela continues to produce flowers in summer, after its initial spring show. The tubular flowers appear in large clusters along the length of the branches, and a mature shrub can bloom so profusely that its branches bow under with the weight of the flowers. Depending on the variety, the pointed leaves are green or greenish purple. This lovely shrub is easy to grow and quite resistant to bugs and disease.

GROWING

Sun.

Great for groups or mass plantings, as an informal hedge; in shrub beds.

Prune weigela annually, after flowering, to keep it full and bushy. Cut back any overly vigorous shoots and remove a few of the oldest stems. Weigela blooms mainly on old wood.

RECOMMENDED SPECIES OR VARIETIES

'**Centennial**': 5–7 feet (1.5–2.1 m) tall and wide; bright pink flowers; a very cold-hardy variety.

'**Minuet**': 2–3 feet (61–91 cm) tall and 3 feet (91 cm) wide; lots of lightly scented, ruby-red to pink flowers with yellow throats; dark green, purple-tinged foliage; cold-hardy; a dwarf, compact variety that blooms profusely.

'**Red Prince**': 5–6 feet (1.5–1.8 m) tall and wide; bright red flowers; a very showy, hardy variety.

TIPS

Weigela is rated for zone 4, but it does fine in a sheltered site in zone 3.

For the best show of flowers in spring, plant weigela in a site that is protected from winter wind. A good snowcover helps to protect the flowerbuds, which form during summer. Occasionally, after a particularly harsh winter, weigela will bloom only on branches that were beneath the snowline; extreme temperatures or late winter thaws can kill exposed flowerbuds.

After its initial main flush of flowers, weigela often blooms more modestly. To encourage more flowering, prune shrubs after the initial blooming period has finished, and give them a shot of fertilizer. Remember not to fertilize after the end of July, however, to allow the shrubs to acclimatize for winter.

For a fine display, plant weigela in mixed borders with shrubs like mockorange and with perennials, bulbs and annual flowers.

Hummingbirds prefer flowers that are long and tubular, and contain abundant nectar. These tiny birds are attracted by the colour red, and they love weigela's flowers.

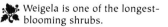

Weigela is one of the longest-blooming shrubs.

TOP LEFT: Some weigelas are not fully hardy in zone 3, although in the right spot they can thrive. This protected site in my daughter-in-law Valerie's garden is an example of an ideal location.
TOP RIGHT: Weigela's trumpet-shaped flowers are about 1½ inches (3.8 cm) long. When 'Minuet' is in full bloom, its yellow-throated flowers hide much of the foliage.
BOTTOM: 'Red Prince' is a showy variety with bright red flowers.

Willow

Salix brachycarpa
Blue Willow

Salix caprea
French Pussywillow

Salix x
Hybrid Willow

Salix integra
Japanese Willow

Salix pentandra
Laurel Leaf Willow
Bay Willow

Salix salicola
Polar Bear Willow

Salix purpurea
Purple Osier Willow

Salix alba
White Willow

Height • $1^1/_2$–50 feet (46 cm–15 m)

Spread • $1^1/_2$–40 feet (46 cm–12 m)

Flowers • catkins (pussywillows) in spring

Fruit • none

Growth Rate • slow to fast

Lifespan • short to average

Zone Rating • 2–4

Willows are among the fastest-growing trees or shrubs. They range tremendously in size and shape, from huge weeping trees to low, tidy shrubs. Depending on the variety, the foliage may be shiny green, silvery blue to white, and even variegated pink. With their diverse appearance and adaptability to various conditions, willows are extremely versatile. Grow them on slopes to reduce soil erosion, in low-lying wet areas of the yard, or in the centre of your lawn or flowerbed as magnificent showpieces.

GROWING

Sun; good in moist sites and to reduce soil erosion on banks; extremely adaptable.

RECOMMENDED SPECIES OR VARIETIES

Blue Willow

'**Blue Fox**': $1^1/_2$–2 feet (46–61 cm) tall and wide; outstanding silvery-blue foliage; dark reddish-brown bark; a small, tidy shrub; little pruning required.

TOP LEFT: 'Blue Fox' is a small shrub that grows more slowly than most willows and needs little pruning, making it a great choice for foliage accent in a shrub bed or flower garden.
BOTTOM LEFT: 'Prairie Cascade' is one of the hardiest weeping willow trees.
RIGHT: This young Weeping pussywillow planted at my son Bill's house has branches that hang to the ground, but is not very wide.

French Pussywillow

Weeping (*S. caprea* 'Pendula'): also called Kilmarnock willow; size varies according to grafted height; generally ranges from 2–6 feet (61–180 cm) tall and 4–5 feet (1.2–1.5 m) wide; occasionally available ungrafted as a sprawling mound; grafted trees have long, weeping branches that hang straight down and then trail along the ground; large, puffy, white pussywillows in early spring; a truly beautiful and unique shrub.

Hybrid Willow

'**Prairie Cascade**': 25–40 feet (7.6–12 m) tall and wide; a very hardy weeping willow with glossy, green leaves and golden bark; very adaptable; fully hardy on the Prairies; a Canadian variety from Morden, Manitoba.

TOP & BOTTOM RIGHT: Hakura Nishiki naturally grows as an exotic-looking shrub (bottom right), but it is often sold grafted to 'tree' form, resulting in a garden showpiece that is impossible to overlook (top).
BOTTOM LEFT: Few other shrubs have the outstanding leaf colour of Hakura Nishiki.

Japanese Willow

Hakura Nishiki (*S. integra* 'Alba Maculata'): also known as White Spotted Willow; 5–6 feet (1.5–1.8 m) tall and wide; an extremely attractive variety from Japan; variegated foliage is creamy white and green; new growth is pink; wine-red branches; very hardy; prune annually in winter or early spring to encourage new shoots for the next season.

Laurel Leaf Willow

35–45 feet (11–14 m) tall and 25–35 feet (7.6–11 m) wide; shiny, dark leaves shimmer even in slight breezes; an excellent, fast-growing shade tree; extremely hardy; occasionally available with a 'braided' trunk.

Polar Bear Willow

10–12 feet (3–3.7 m) tall and wide; attractive, furry, silvery-white foliage; huge pussywillows before leaves open; pussywillows almost blend into the branches, especially on new growth, because the branches are just as hairy; shrub does not spread; a Canadian introduction.

Purple Osier Willow

Dwarf Arctic (*S. purpurea* 'Nana'): 3–4 feet (91–120 cm) tall and wide; deep blue foliage stands out in a shrub bed; light grey bark; good informal hedge; a beautiful, compact shrub.

TOP: It takes 20 to 25 years for laurel leaf willow to reach mature size.
TOP RIGHT: Polar bear willow is less shade tolerant than other willows; it originates from near the Arctic Circle.
BOTTOM: Dwarf Arctic willow prefers moist or even wet conditions; a mulch helps to retain soil moisture.

LEFT: The bright stems of Golden willow are most noticeable in winter. When clothed in foliage during the growing season, the long stems form an almost perfectly enclosed round 'room'—a marvellous 'secret' play area for children.
RIGHT: Silver willow is a fast-growing tree, gaining an average of 2–3 feet (61–91 cm) each season. The silvery leaves remain on the branches well into winter.

White Willow

Golden (*S. alba* var. *vitellina*): 40–50 feet (12–15 m) tall and 35–40 feet (11–12 m) wide; a majestic tree with arching branches reaching right to the ground; beautiful, golden stems; bright green leaves.

Silver (*S. alba* 'Sericea'): 30–40 feet (9.1–12 m) tall and 25–35 feet (7.6–11 m) wide; intensely silver leaves; arching, golden branches provide a weeping effect; older bark is dark greyish brown and ridged; an excellent background tree for foliage contrast.

Willows are the source of the original aspirin. As early as 500 BC, Chinese doctors prescribed willow bark to be chewed for pain relief. Today aspirin (a synthetic derivative of salicin found in willow bark) is one of the most popular pain relievers in the world.

TIPS

Although willows prefer moist conditions, they are highly adaptable and can tolerate long periods of drought. They grow well even in poor soil.

Prune willows regularly, in winter or early spring, to maintain their size, colour and density. Rejuvenate (selectively prune) your willows every three to four years to get the best branch colour.

A hedge of Dwarf Arctic willow is attractive even in winter, when its red stems glow in the sun. If after several years your hedge becomes overgrown, cut it down almost to the ground. Bright new stems regrow quickly.

If you like, use the pruned stems for crafts. Dwarf Arctic willow is sometimes called basket willow because its pliable stems are great for weaving.

Dwarf Arctic willow can help reduce soil erosion on slopes. This shrub grows well even in windy sites.

Golden willow has the brightest colour on younger stems and branches; after two or three years, the bark becomes brownish grey rather than gold. Prune back branches to encourage new growth.

Laurel leaf willow often retains its leaves well into December, but it tends to drop small twigs throughout the year. Fortunately, the twigs are small and easy to clean up.

Weeping pussywillow should be planted in a sheltered site in zone 3 if you want showy catkins. The tree is hardy, but the flowerbuds, which produce the pussywillows, can be killed by extremely cold temperatures.

When cutting pussywillows for bouquets, keep in mind that you are, in effect, pruning the tree. Remove only the older stems to promote the development of new shoots that can be harvested for pussywillows the following year. Harvesting annually will probably keep the plant very dense and growing vigorously.

If you are wondering why your willow has no pussywillows, it may be because it's a male tree. Only females produce the showy 'flowers' commonly called pussywillows. Males produce abundant, golden catkins, which is why most plants sold today are female.

Keep cut branches of pussywillows in water only long enough for them to fully open. If you don't remove them at this point, they continue developing and become covered in pollen.

Once dried, branches of pussywillows will last for years.

Willows are found virtually everywhere on the planet—even on islands, such as Greenland, Iceland and the Canary Islands. There are approximately 4000 willow species worldwide, and a few hundred hybrid willows. Forty-eight species are native to Alberta, and 62 are native to Canada.

Yew

Taxus x media
Anglojap Yew
Taxus cuspidata
Japanese Yew
Height • $3^1/_2$–20 feet (1.1–6.1 m)
Spread • 6–20 feet (1.8–6.1 m)
Flowers • not showy
Fruit • red, berry-like
Growth Rate • slow
Lifespan • average to long
Zone Rating
Anglojap: 3
Japanese: 4 [3]

Much as olive branches symbolize 'peace,' yews symbolize 'eternity.' I don't know how the yew became the symbol of eternity, but it's not entirely surprising. One enormous English yew tree, with a spectacular girth of 45 feet (14 m), is estimated to be about 3800 years old! Unlike most needle-type evergreens, yews have bright red, berry-like fruit rather than cones. A yew's dark green, needle-like leaves aren't true needles, but rather glossy, flat leaves called 'straps.' These dense evergreens prefer moist, shady sites in the garden. They are small, beautiful and undemanding trees with an interesting history. It is said that Robin Hood made his bows from yews.

GROWING

Best in partial shade; prefers a moist, sandy loam.

In shrub borders, foundation plantings, hedges or screens; for feature shrubs and topiary. Dwarf varieties in rock gardens.

RECOMMENDED SPECIES OR VARIETIES

Anglojap Yew

'**Brandon**': 2–3 feet (61–91 cm) tall and wide; an as yet unregistered variety thought to be a variety of *Taxus x media* 'Densiformis'; very dark green foliage; extremely wind tolerant; a mature plant was found growing in Brandon, Manitoba, by a local grower.

Yews are unusual conifers in that they produce ornamental, red, berry-like fruit rather than cones.

Japanese Yew

Japanese: 10–20 feet (3–6.1 m) tall and wide; grows less than 1 foot (30 cm) a year; new growth is soft yellow-green, changing to dark green after about a month; introduced in 1853.

Golden (*T. cuspidata* 'Aurescens'): an extremely slow-growing variety that often grows less than 1 inch (2.5 cm) a year; 12–15 inches (31–38 cm) tall and 2–3 feet (61–91 cm) wide after 20 years; 3½ feet (1.1 m) tall and 4–6 feet (1.2–1.8 m) wide after 70 to 80 years; a very low-growing, compact shrub; new leaves are bright yellow, usually changing to green after several seasons.

TIPS

Yews grown in shady sites tend to have darker foliage.

Although rated as hardy to zone 4, Japanese yew can flourish in lower zones. A good site would be on the north side of a tall fence, where it would be protected from winter winds and from excessive sun. Water it well in fall and ensure it has good snowcover throughout winter. Spraying an anti-desiccant product on the foliage will help reduce moisture loss.

Yews can be pruned in late winter, early spring or mid-summer. They take well to pruning and shearing, and are commonly used for formal hedges.

Japanese yews can be trained to grow as small trees. See *How to Train Shrubs to 'Tree' Form* on page 64.

Almost all parts of a yew, including its foliage and seeds, are poisonous. The only part that isn't poisonous is the flesh of its fruit. Native Peoples, however, extracted medicines from yew bark.

Yews are rarely bothered by insects or disease.

TOP: Japanese yews are propagated by cuttings—if a cutting is taken from a vertical branch of the mother plant, it grows more or less vertically, whereas a cutting taken from the horizontal branches produces a more spreading plant.
MIDDLE: Japanese yews take well to formal pruning, and yews make great sheared hedges and topiaries.
BOTTOM: Golden yew is a dwarf variety with striking foliage.

APPENDIX

THE BEST TREES & SHRUBS FOR FALL FOLIAGE COLOUR

Why do leaves change colour in fall? It's because the shorter days and cooler temperatures trigger chlorophyll—the pigment that gives leaves their usual green colour—to break down, revealing red, orange and yellow pigments. The process takes longer with some trees. In years when we have a early heavy frost, leaves may die before colours develop.

The intensity of foliage colour is controlled by weather. A combination of warm, sunny fall days and cool fall nights below 44° F (7° C) gives the best colour. The healthier your tree is, the better its fall show is likely to be; good soil fertility and adequate moisture are needed for nice autumn colour. The best, most reliable trees for spectacular fall foliage are those listed on the opposite page.

YELLOW
Ash (some)
Aspen
Birch (some)
Crabapple
  Siberian
Double-flowering
  Plum
Elm
Ginkgo
Hazelnut
Larch
Linden
Maple
  Manitoba
Poplar

YELLOW-ORANGE
Cotoneaster
Mountain Ash
Ohio Buckeye
Rose (some)

ORANGE-RED
Azalea
Cotoneaster
Maple (most)
Plum
Serviceberry
Spirea (some)

RED
Burning Bush
Cranberry (most)
Maple
Snowball
Sumac

RED-PURPLE
Chokecherry
  'Autumn Magic'
Dogwood (some)
Nannyberry
Wayfaring Tree

PURPLE
Juniper
  Compact Andorra
  'Wiltonii'

THE BEST TREES & SHRUBS FOR SUMMER FOLIAGE COLOUR

Ninebark

Think of foliage colour as well as shape, size and flowers when planning your garden. Certain trees and shrubs have colourful foliage all season that provides a striking contrast to the usual green leaves. Some of them also produce stunning flowers, but even when they are not blooming, their foliage enhances other plants.

Trees

Birch
  'Purple Rain'
Crabapple
  'Thunderchild'
Chokecherry
  'Schubert'
Fir
  Blue
Maple
  'Crimson King'
  Silver
Mayday
  Swedish
Pine
  'French Blue Scotch'
Poplar
  Silver
Russian Olive
Spruce
  'Fat Albert'
  'Hoopsii'
  'Montgomery'
Willow
  Silver

Shrubs

Buffaloberry
Cedar
  'Golden Champion'
Daphne
  'Carol Mackie'
Dogwood
  Golden Variegated
  Yellow-leaf
Elder
  (all except
  Red-berried and
  'Adams'
Euonymus
  'Gold Prince'
Falsecypress
  'Golden Pin Cushion'
  'Sungold'
Juniper (many)
Ninebark
  'Dart's Gold'
  Golden
Pine
  'Blue Shag'
Salt Bush
Sandcherry
Sea Buckthorn
Spirea
  'Goldmound'
  'Magic Carpet'
Spruce
  Creeping Blue
Willow
  Hakura Nishiki
  Polar Bear

THE BEST TREES & SHRUBS FOR FRAGRANCE

The flowers of a few types of trees and shrubs emit enticing fragrance, sometimes powerful enough to perfume an entire yard! I can never resist snipping off a flowering branch or two to enjoy the fragrance inside my home and outside in the garden.

Crabapple
  Siberian
Daphne
Lilac
Linden
Mayday
Mockorange
Russian Olive

'Carol Mackie' Daphne

THE BEST TREES & SHRUBS FOR FRUIT DISPLAY

Fruit can be as showy as flowers, and fruit-bearing trees or shrubs often provide the added benefit of attracting wildlife to your garden. Birds don't care for the fruit or berries of some trees and shrubs (those marked with an asterisk*); the benefit is a longer-lasting display, with the fruit remaining on bare branches well into winter.

Arrowwood
Buffaloberry
Chokecherry
  'Autumn Magic'*
Coralberry*
Cotoneaster
  Cranberry
Crabapple
  Columnar
  'Red Jade'
  Siberian
Cranberry
  American Highbush
Dogwood
  'Siberian Pearls'
Elder
  'Adams'
  'Goldenlocks'
  Red-berried
Holly
  'Blue Girl'
  Oregon Grapeholly
  Winter Red*
Juniper
  Savin
  'Wiltonii'*
Maple
  Amur
Mountain Ash
Nannyberry
Rose*
Sea Buckthorn*
Wayfaring Tree

Mountain Ash

THE BEST TREES & SHRUBS FOR WINTER INTEREST

Evergreens are valued for adding colour to the winter landscape, but certain deciduous trees and shrubs also provide a decorative display after their leaves drop. One of their best features may be bark with an interesting texture or attractive colour, a showy display of fruit or the striking silhouette provided by the form of their bare branches.

Birch
- Cutleaf Weeping
  (shape, bark colour, hoar frost)
- Paper (bark colour)
- 'Purple Rain' (bark colour)
- 'Trost Dwarf' (shape)
- Young's Weeping (shape, bark colour)

Burning Bush
- regular & compact (ridged bark)

Chokecherry
- Amur (bark)

Coralberry (pink berries)

Dogwood (bark)

Harry Lauder's Walkingstick (shape)

Holly
- Winter Red (berries)

Juniper
- 'Tolleson's Weeping' (shape)

Pincherry (bark)

Sumac (seed clusters)

Dogwood

THE BEST SMALL TREES

Gardeners often ask for small trees, either because they have limited space in their yards or they want an unimposing tree for a particular area, such as near a flowerbed or deck. The following trees remain close to 20 feet (6.1 m) tall and wide when mature. Columnar crabapple is an exception; it reaches up to 35 feet (11 m) in height but never gets much more than 10 feet (3 m) wide.

- Birch
  - Young's Weeping
- Caragana
  - Fernleaf
  - 'Sutherland'
  - Weeping
- Cedar
  - 'Degroot's Spire'
  - 'Emerald Green'
  - 'Holmstrup'
  - 'Techny'
- Crabapple
  - Columnar
  - 'Kelsey'
  - 'Red Jade'
  - 'Strathmore'
- Fir
  - Compact Alpine
- Hawthorn
- Juniper
  - 'Medora'
  - 'Moonglow'
  - 'Tolleson's Weeping'
- Larch
  - Weeping
- Maple
  - Amur
  - 'Embers'
- Mountain Ash
  - Showy
- Pine
  - 'Big Tuna'
- Plum
  - Hybrid
  - 'Princess Kay'
- Serviceberry
- Spruce
  - Weeping Norway
- Sumac
  - Smooth
  - Staghorn

Weeping Caragana

THE BEST TREES & SHRUBS FOR ATTRACTING WILDLIFE

Place birdfeeders near shrubs or hang them from tree branches, where birds have shelter and easy access to perching sites.

Many people have birdfeeders in their yards in winter, but you can also grow trees and shrubs that provide food for birds year-round. To keep birds in your yard, rather than just entice them for the occasional visit, however, you need to provide shelter along with food. A mixture of trees and shrubs attracts lots of different birds and provides protective cover as well as nesting sites. In my experience, the following trees and shrubs are best loved by birds.

- Arrowwood
- Cherry
  - Nanking
- Cherry Prinsepia
- Chokecherry
  - except 'Autumn Magic'
- Cranberry
  - American Highbush
  - 'Wentworth'
- Elder
  - 'Adams'
  - Red-berried
- Mayday
  - regular
  - Swedish
- Mountain Ash
- Nannyberry
- Pincherry
- Serviceberry
  - 'Autumn Brilliance'
- Wayfaring Tree

THE BEST TREES & SHRUBS FOR CUTFLOWERS

A cedar and pine swag brightens a door at Christmas.

Don't forget that trees and shrubs can supply beautiful flowers, foliage and stems for fresh or dried bouquets. Be creative—add decorative seedheads, berries and bare branches to your arrangements.

- Alder (seedheads)
- Boxwood (foliage)
- Cedar (foliage)
- Daphne (February for flowers)
- Dogwood (stems)
- Forsythia (flowers)
- Holly (foliage, berries)
- Hydrangea (fresh or dried flowers)
- Lilac (flowers)
- Russian Almond (flowers)
- Sandcherry (flowers, foliage)

THE BEST TREES & SHRUBS FOR FORCING FLOWERS

Treat yourself to a preview of spring by 'forcing' flowers to bloom indoors. In late winter, snip off a few branches. Bring them inside, peel off the bottom couple of inches of bark, and smash the stem ends with a hammer to increase water uptake. Put stems immediately into a vase filled with warm water, and place in a sunny room. Warmth is the key to breaking dormancy. Depending on the type of stems, expect flowerbuds to open within one to four weeks.

Cherry
Double-flowering Plum
Forsythia
Lilac
Plum
Russian Almond
Sandcherry

Purpleleaf Sandcherry

THE BEST SHRUBS FOR GROUNDCOVERS

A groundcover is a massed group of a single type of plant that covers the ground with thick foliage. These plants are low growing and tough; they may provide a solution for areas where little else will grow. Many gardeners like groundcovers simply because they require little maintenance. Groundcovers spread quickly, reduce water loss and erosion on slopes, and slows the spread of weeds.

Groundcovers are attractive and useful plants; most have beautiful foliage, texture and sometimes, flowers.

Cotoneaster
Daphne
  Rose
Euonymus
  'Gold Prince'
Genista
Juniper
  'Blue Prince'
  'Calgary Carpet'
  Compact Andorra
  Effusa
    (all spreading junipers except Savin)
Larch
  Weeping
Mountain Ash
  Dwarf Chinese
Ninebark
  'Tilden Parks'
Pine
  'Hillside Creeper'
Russian Cypress
Spruce
  Weeping Norway
Sumac
  'Gro-low'
Willow
  Weeping Pussywillow

Rose Daphne

THE BEST TREES & SHRUBS FOR ROCK GARDENS

'Golden Pin Cushion' is an excellent falsecypress variety to grow in a rock garden.

Gardeners often need smaller trees and shrubs to add to rock gardens to contrast with other plants. Most of the following trees and shrubs remain less than 3 feet (91 cm) tall. Those names marked with an asterisk (*) grow slightly taller.

- Azalea
  - 'Orchid Lights'
- Birch
  - 'Trost Dwarf'*
- Bog Rosemary
- Cedar
  - 'Danica'
  - 'Little Giant'
- Cranberry
  - Dwarf European
- Daphne
  - except February
- Euonymus
  - 'Gold Prince'
- Falsecypress
  - 'Golden Pin Cushion'
- Fir
  - Dwarf Balsam*
- Juniper
  - 'Blue Star'*
  - 'Greenmound'
  - 'Mother Lode™'
  - 'Prince of Wales'
  - 'Wiltonii'
- Hemlock
  - 'Stockman's Dwarf'
- Genista
  - 'Vancouver Gold'
- Larch
  - 'Newport Beauty'
  - Weeping
- Pine
  - 'Hillside Creeper'
  - 'Mop's Mugo'
  - 'White Bud Mugo'
- Potentilla
  - 'Nuuk'
- Rhododendron
  - 'Compact' P.J.M.*
- Spirea
  - Alpina
  - 'Magic Carpet'
- Spruce
  - Creeping Blue*
  - Dwarf Alberta
  - 'Little Gem'
  - Weeping Norway
- Willow
  - Weeping Pussywillow

Bibliography

Austin, David. *English Roses*. London, England: Conran Octopus, 1993.

Baker, Margaret. *The Gardener's Folklore*. North Vancouver, BC: David Douglas & Charles, 1977.

Dirr, Michael A. *A Manual of Woody Landscape Plants: Their Identification, Ornamental Characteristics, Culture, Propagation and Uses*. Fourth edition. Champaign, IL: Stipes Publishing Company, 1990.

Facciola, Stephen. *Cornucopia*. Vista, CA: Kampong Publications, 1992.

Fiala, John L. *Lilacs: The Genus Syringa*. Portland, OR: Timber Press, 1988.

———. *Flowering Crabapples: The Genus Malus*. Portland, OR: Timber Press, 1994.

Hausenbuiller, R.L. *Soil Science: Principles and Practices*. Dubuque, IA: Wm. C. Brown Publishing, 1972.

Hosie, R.C. *Native Trees of Canada*. Eighth edition. Don Mills, ON: Fitzhenry & Whiteside, 1979.

Hillier, H.G. *Hillier's Manual of Trees & Shrubs*. New edition. Winchester, England: David & Charles (Publishers), 1977.

Johnson, Derek, Linda Kershaw, Andy MacKinnon and Jim Pojar. *Plants of the Western Boreal Forest and Aspen Parkland*. Edmonton, AB: Lone Pine Publishing, 1995.

Mastin, Collcayn O. *Canadian Trees*. Kamloops, BC: Grasshopper Books, 1994.

Neal, Bill. *Gardener's Latin: A Lexicon*. Chapel Hill, NC: Algonquin Books of Chapel Hill, 1992.

Newsholme, Christopher. *Willows: The Genus Salix*. Portland, OR: Timber Press, 1992.

Reader's Digest. *Magic and Medicine of Plants*. Pleasantville, NY: Reader's Digest Association, 1986.

Snyder, Leon C. *Trees and Shrubs for Northern Gardens*. Minneapolis, MN: University of Minnesota Press, 1980.

Stearn, W.T. *A Gardener's Dictionary of Plant Names*. London, England: Cassell Publishers, 1992.

The Guinness Book of Records. New York, NY: Bantam Books, 1994.

OTHER PUBLICATIONS

Alberta Forestry Association. Alberta Trees of Renown: *An Honour Roll of Alberta Trees*. Edmonton, AB: Alberta Forestry Association, 1986.

American National Standards Institute. *American National Standard for Tree Care Operations: Tree, Shrub and Other Woody Plant Maintenance—Standard Practices*. New York, NY: American National Standards Institute, 1995.

Arborist News. Vol 5, No. 4, August 1996. p. 53.

Pruning in Alberta. Alberta Agriculture Agdex 270/24-1.

Select Glossary

candles—the new, terminal shoots on evergreens in spring.

cultivar—a contraction of 'cultivated variety'; a named group of plants within a cultivated species (e.g., Swedish Columnar [*P. tremula* 'Erecta']; a cultivar of Swedish Aspen) that is distinguishable by one or more characteristics.

dieback—any plant part that dies; usually used to describe winter injury.

dwarf plant—a plant that is much smaller than others of its species.

graft—a shoot or bud of one plant inserted into the stem or trunk of another.

head-back—to prune the terminal portion of buds and branches to encourage denser growth.

mulch—the leaves, straw, peat moss, etc. that are spread on the ground around plants to prevent the evaporation of water from the soil and to provide insulation against the cold.

rejuvenation pruning—pruning a plant to increase its vigour.

suckers—the shoots that typically arise from the base of a tree or shrub.

tip kill—typically a less severe form of dieback involving only a few inches at the tips of branches.

'tree' form—a single-stemmed, tree-like shape into which some shrubs (normally multi-stemmed) can be trained to grow.

Index

About the Author

Lois loves to spend time outside, especially with her grandchildren and their friends.

Lois Hole and her husband Ted started selling vegetables out of their red barn more than 30 years ago; today, Hole's Greenhouses & Gardens Ltd. is one of the largest greenhouse and garden centres in Alberta. It remains a family business, owned and operated by Lois, Ted, their sons Bill and Jim, and Bill's wife Valerie.

Lois was born and raised in rural Saskatchewan, and later moved to Edmonton, Alberta. She attained a degree in Music from the Toronto Conservatory of Music.

Over the years, Lois has shared her expertise throughout Canada. She is a regular commentator on *Canadian Gardening* on CBC Television and writes a gardening column for the *Globe and Mail*. Her practical wisdom and sound advice were so much in demand that she decided to begin a series of gardening guides. The first five books in the series, *Vegetable Favorites*, *Bedding Plant Favorites*, *Perennial Favorites*, *Tomato Favorites* and *Rose Favorites*, have all been bestsellers. The Professional Plant Growers Association has recognized the series as an exceptional source of information by awarding it their Educational Media Award for 1995.